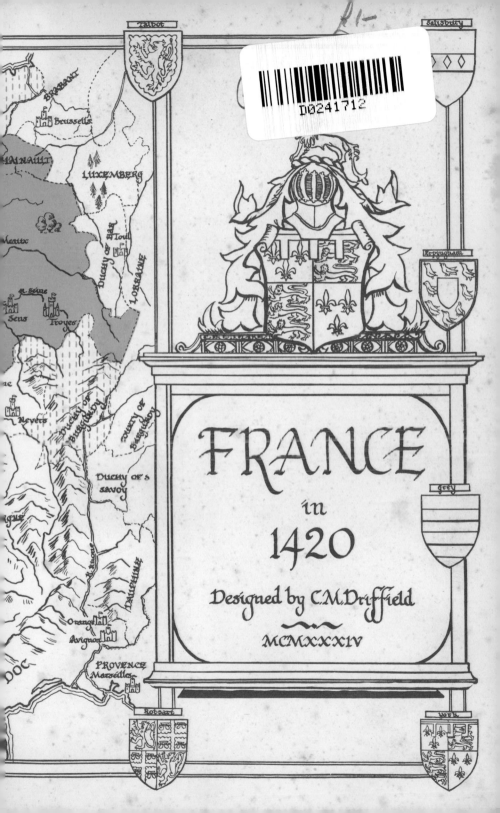

FRANCE

in

1420

Designed by C.M. Driffield

MCMXXXIV

TALBOT

SALISBURY

BRABANT

Brussells

HAINAULT

LUXEMBERG

Meaux

DUCHY OF BAR

TOUL

LORRAINE

R. SEINE

Sens

Troyes

ERPINGHAM

DUCHY OF BURGUNDY

DUCHY OF BURGUNDY

Nevers

DUCHY OF SAVOY

GREY

R. RHONE

DAUPHINÉ

Orange

Avignon

DOC

PROVENCE

Marseilles

ROBSART

YORK

HENRY V

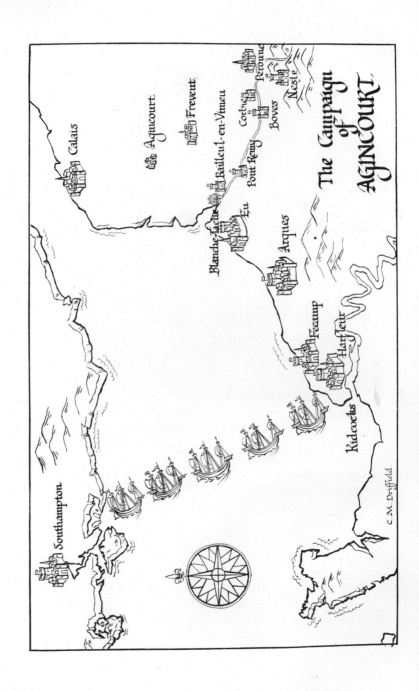

The Campaign of AGINCOURT

Calais

Agincourt.

Frevent.

Bailleul-en-Vimeu

Corbie

Péronne

Nesle

Boves

Pont Remy

Blanche-Taque

Eu

Arques

Fécamp

Harfleur

Kidcocks

Southampton

C. M. Deffield

HENRY V

BY

J. D. GRIFFITH DAVIES, M.A. (Oxon.)

AUTHOR OF
'OWEN GLYN DŴR' 'ENGLAND IN THE MIDDLE AGES'
'A NEW HISTORY OF ENGLAND' 'THE NATION AT WORK'
ETC.

LONDON
ARTHUR BARKER LTD.
21 GARRICK STREET, COVENT GARDEN

First Published 1935

PRINTED IN GREAT BRITAIN BY
MORRISON AND GIBB LTD., LONDON AND EDINBURGH

CONTENTS

EXPLANATORY AND DEDICATORY

Dear C. D.,

True hero-worship is fallen on evil days, and a *life* of a heroic figure like Henry V. is almost certain to be regarded as an anachronism by this modern generation.

I have no doubt that some of our Bright Young People will vehemently deny the truth of this assertion : they will assert that they have their heroes, and argue that they accord them the honour and glory of which they deem them to be deserving. But who are these heroes ? I may be wrong ; but as far as I can see they are crooners, dance-band leaders, sound film ' stars,' ultra-modern artists, and an occasional murderer. I confess that personally I find it impossible to regard any of these as heroes. This may be a defect—a penalty which I pay for advancing years : if so, then I have no regrets, for I was brought up to see virtue in the praise of famous men and women, and in my hero-worship to accept the criteria contained in that wonderful passage of *Ecclesiasticus*, part of which I quote without apology :

> Let us now praise famous men, and our fathers that begat us. The Lord hath wrought great glory by them through his great power from the beginning. Such as did bear rule in their kingdoms, men renowned by their power, giving counsel by their understanding, and declaring prophesies : leaders of the people by their counsels, and by their knowledge of learning meet for the people, wise and eloquent in their instructions.

In my opinion Henry V. was richly endowed with all these attributes, so cunningly named by Jesus, son of Sirach, in the above-quoted passage.

Whatever the cause, in these post-war years we have seen a great change in men's outlook on the heroic life. This may be one of the achievements of the militant pacifists, who have assiduously taught the younger generation to believe that we who fought in the war were little better than *mass-murderers*, who against our better judgment prosecuted the work of killing at the commands of unscrupulous politicians and international financiers. It is now a fact that service in the war is often concealed by those who entered that struggle from the highest motives of patriotism ; and thousands of gallant fellows, to whom a vote-hunting politician promised a country fit for heroes to live in, are to-day in want of the ordinary necessaries of life.

A people which can forget so easily and complacently the sacrifices of its manhood is hardly likely to appreciate the great works of heroes of other days. It is this forgetfulness of service which is so disquieting. It may be argued that it is a natural revulsion from the horrors of a cataclysmic war. I appreciate the *rightness* of regarding war as horrible ; but I refuse to believe that it should justify the shameful forgetfulness of which we are guilty. Shortly before these words were written died Field-Marshal von Hindenburg, the President of the German Reich, and a gallant German soldier. At the behest of the British Broadcasting Corporation we were asked to preserve silence as a tribute to his memory, and to listen to the strains of the German national anthem in the same broadcast. About the same time died Marshal Lyautey, a Christian gentleman and gallant warrior. His passing was marked by no such tribute as that which was accorded to Hindenburg. Yet he was our friend, the other was our enemy—an enemy whom we once talked of hanging ! Some of us see the irony of that situation. We are ready to admit that Hindenburg was a great German, and we may appreciate the loss which his country sustained at his passing ; but we cannot accept him as anything but a resolute and ruthless enemy ; and such an attitude of mind does not preclude us from admiration of his manhood.

It is imperative that we should face facts. True idealism can only be acquired by those who are prepared to face up to the grim realities of life. For the true idealist, like Henry V., is a man who shapes his idealism from knowledge of realism. Otherwise he is a dreamer, and his achievements are as transitory as the clouds which float over his head. In this book, therefore, I have endeavoured to present Henry V. as the true idealist—the king whose idealism never for a moment blinded him to the grim realities of life.

In this post-war age there has been developed a new form of biographical writing. The modern biographer invariably pours ridicule upon those whom mankind has hitherto accepted as worthy of veneration, or whitewashes one whom all the world used to know as a thoroughgoing rogue. He does this in a certain *slickness* of style, which charms the reader ; and he indulges in detailed analysis of motives. If, at the same time, historical veracity can be achieved, then so much the better : if not—well, the omission does not greatly worry him.

Some will maintain that this is the legacy which the late Mr Lytton Strachey bequeathed to his admirers in the world of biographical writing. You recall how we discussed Mr Strachey's sinister attack on Gordon's character : we agreed that it was brutal and unhistorical. The pity is that many believe that Gordon's greatness was a fiction of the much-abused Victorian era; and they drive their point home by smugly reminding us that Mr Strachey depicted him as a rather petty imperialist who was an addict to the b. and s.

In offering you this *life* of Henry V. I warn you that it is not a typical modern biography. It was my good fortune to read history at Oxford under Mr R. B. Mowat of *Corpus*, and Mr J. G. Edwards of *Jesus*, both of whom taught me to love historical veracity; and I have built up my story of Henry's life and work on historical data. I have refused to waste time in the analysis of motives : I had no other alternative because I don't know how to perform this task which people now find so easy. If I were a spiritualist then doubtless I could ' call up ' Henry, and ask him why he did this, that, and the other thing ; and I might then have been able to tell you and other readers many more interesting facts about his life. For example, I might have been able to discuss at greater length the incident of the killing of the French prisoners at Agincourt, for which act Henry has been unmercifully condemned by some of his biographers ; but at the back of my mind is the feeling that he had no other alternative than to kill them, and I refuse to pass judgment on him without knowing his defence.

Another characteristic of modern biography is the parading of human failings. I have not been able to escape it ; treat it as an ironic protest against this modern vogue. Thus I have mentioned that Henry's father had the pox, and I have even indulged in a short digression in order to introduce the readers to the stews or brothels of fifteenth-century London. Whether these matters improve or cheapen the narrative is something which only the reader can decide. In another particular I have followed a modernist tendency—the omission of full-note references to the sources used in the making of this biography. I offer no apology for this : I believe that footnotes have a terrifying effect on the general reader, and it is for him or her that I write. This *life* of Henry V. makes no pretence of scholarly attainment ; and I am not ashamed to say that in the making of it I have drawn freely from the works of those scholars who have made a special study of Henry's reign. At the end of the book is appended a short note on the authorities for this period ; and there I have tried to place on record the inspiration and help which I have received from so many sources. Without those works I should never have been able to write this *life* : whatever virtue, therefore, attaches to it must be shared with the authors of those works in a measure far more generous than I am entitled to receive.

You must forgive me interrupting our *causerie* to thank those who helped in the making of this book : my father, the vicar of Trelech, whose judgment and scholarship has always inspired me ; Mr F. R. Worts, with whom friendship never means false criticism [alas ! I cannot always accept his views !] ; Mr H. W. Wainwright for a careful reading of my typescript ; Miss Driffield for drawing the maps and plans. My greatest source of help always is the Leeds Public Library. Once upon a time I thought [and you agreed with me] that from the research worker's standpoint no good could come out of these public libraries, but that was a stupid notion. You could not work in a pleasanter atmosphere than that of the reference room of the Leeds Public Library ; and the courtesy and patience of Mr R. J. Gordon and his staff towards one who pesters them with endless queries is a highly treasured memory.

And why did I write this *life* of Henry V. ?

I was born within six miles of Monmouth, Henry's birthplace ; and I was at school almost within sight of the castle where his birth took place. Frankly, Monmouth does indifferent honour to the greatest of her sons and the noblest of England's mediæval kings. There is an *Agincourt Square* and a *Glendower Street* ; but these tributes to Henry's memory are completely overshadowed by a hideous statue on the façade of the Shire Hall. There, for all the world to see, is depicted a knock-kneed, stomachless Henry—the kind of person whom one might expect to meet as the mayor of some very provincial town or presiding over a country petty-sessional court ; and I felt that it was my duty as a fellow-countyman to attempt to correct so damaging an impression which the Victorian sculptor created in the minds of countless numbers of people on their journeys through that incomparable piece of Britain—the Wye Valley.

If you will accept my efforts as a piece of honest-to-goodness biography, and pass lightly over its many failings, then you will have conferred on me a great and lasting honour,

Yours sincerely,

J. D. GRIFFITH DAVIES.

LEEDS, *August* 1934.

CHAPTER ONE

The Boy

IN the sleepy county town of Monmouth, perched
high on a rock ledge above the sluggish Monnow,
will be seen a house of elegant proportions, doing
duty as headquarters of a militia regiment of
engineers ; and around it, and stretching down to
the water's edge, are the crumbling walls of an
ancient castle.   The house was built in 1673 by
Henry, 3rd Marquis of Worcester and soon to
become 1st Duke of Beaufort ; eleven years later
his daughter-in-law, a slip of a girl of sixteen and
heavy with child, was hurried painfully over the
atrociously bad stretch of road between Raglan and
Monmouth, so that she might be delivered of her
first-born

> near the Spot of Ground and the Space of Air, where our
> great Hero King Henry Fifth was born.

The house in which the happy event in the
marquis's family took place was raised from the
masonry and timbers of the once great castle of
Monmouth—in Norman and Plantagenet times a
marcher outpost against the warlike people of
Gwent, later a royal stronghold from which the
forces of the Crown could watch the movements of
turbulent marcher lords, and in the great civil war
of the seventeenth century the scene of desperate
encounters between Royalist and Roundhead.   It
is no part of this story to describe the events of those
times : sufficient is it to say that on March 30,
1647, by the order of the Roundhead governor of
the town, a certain Captain Kyrle, a gang of soldiers

and townsmen began the task of 'slighting' the castle. The outer defences were effectively breached, the towers were undermined, and the ordnance was dismantled. With one part of the fortress the wreckers dealt kindly—the central tower of the keep; for not even under the influence of a stern Puritanism were they able to obliterate the place in which had been born one of England's greatest kings—Henry V. Their generous intentions, however, came to nothing : a few months later—it was on December 22 in the same year—the great tower crashed to the ground with a terrifying roar, while townsmen and soldiery were 'at sermon.' The congregation fled madly from the church, believing that the Day of Judgment was at hand : when the panic had died down and the real cause of the commotion known, the people thronged to view the damage, and we are told that some of those present were moved to tears when they saw the masonry piled high in the hall of the keep, the room above which the victor of Agincourt was thought to have been born.

The woman who was brought to child-bed in that room was Mary de Bohun, daughter of Humphrey de Bohun, Earl of Hereford and Essex. Her's was a fierce race of warriors, men who had warred in many lands, won fortunes with their swords, and even defied the might and power of great kings ; but this Earl Humphrey had failed his ancestors in that he had not procreated male children, and at his death his vast estates, innumerable honours, and great treasure were parcelled out between his two daughters and their husbands. Mary's sister, Eleanor, was married to Edward III.'s son, Thomas of Woodstock, holder of the earldom of Buckingham and the duchy of Gloucester in his own right : after his marriage, in the right of his wife, he could style himself Earl of Essex. Eleanor de Bohun, therefore, found herself in a somewhat curious position : she was by marriage the aunt of her younger sister, for her husband was the brother of John of Gaunt, the father of Mary's husband. Truthfully, people might declare that there were no wealthier women in England than Eleanor and Mary de Bohun. It is not surprising, therefore, to find that they were allied by marriage with the sons of Edward III., who with all their faults were astute men of business, with keen perception of the advantages of position and wealth.

Mary de Bohun's husband was Henry of Bolingbroke, the eldest surviving son of John of Gaunt, Earl of Richmond, Duke of Lancaster, ' Monseigneur d'Espagne,' as he was wont to call himself after his marriage to Constance, the daughter of Pedro the Cruel of Castile: his mother was Blanche Plantagenet, younger daughter and co-heiress of Henry, Duke of Lancaster, a great grandson of Henry III. Henry of Bolingbroke, throughout his early life, was known by the title of Earl of Derby. He was, according to Froissart, a handsome young man, inheriting his good looks from his mother and paternal grandmother. Phillppa of Hainault : in 1377, when only ten years of age, old King Edward III. created him a Knight of the Garter. Far-flung though the estates of John of Gaunt were, his extravagant and lecherous living placed a great burden upon them, and nothing could be more convenient than that the wealth of the de Bohuns should be used to keep his heir in a condition of comfort, to which his birth and upbringing entitled him.

In one thing John of Gaunt had endowed his son Henry of Bolingbroke most generously : a poor constitution. A man of great charm of manner, a patron of learning, a friend of savants, John of Gaunt was notorious for his wenchings even in an age which was not unduly shocked by immorality in high places ; and his assiduous and passionate devotions at the altars of Venus placed him soon in sore need of the mercies of Mercury—mercies with which the mediæval leech and chirugeon were imperfectly acquainted ; and in consequence of irregularities of living a blood taint in his own body was transfused into the blood-stream of his children. To Henry of Bolingbroke he passed on a skin eruption, which in many histories is generally passed off as eczema ; but it was certainly of a fouler nature, and when death came to him as Henry IV., the King of England and Wales, we are told that his face was so disfigured by disease that no man dared look upon it without a sickly shudder. Nevertheless, the traditions of his caste, the knightly schooling in arms, the grim determination which was part of his character, enabled Henry of Bolingbroke to lead a full life, to adventure into far-distant lands, and to win golden opinions for his knightly bearing from his contemporaries and for his kingly virtues from posterity.

Mary de Bohun was born in 1368 or 1369 : Henry of Bolingbroke, in 1366. They were espoused in 1381, a memorable year, in which Henry came near to death at the hands of the mob, led by Wat Tyler. The palace of John of Gaunt, the Savoy, was the chief object of the rebels' displeasure : it was sacked and burnt to the ground, and when the destroyers learnt that the duke and his family were in the Tower they hurled themselves against that stronghold, and it was only by the intervention of John Ferror of Southwark that Henry's life was saved.

The espousals were carried through with ducal magnificence. Minstrels from Richard II.'s court, augmented by those of the household of the Earl of Cambridge, entertained the guests with song and music ; and they received from John of Gaunt a

payment of 20 marks for their attendance. To
his young daughter-in-law the duke gave ' a ruby '
valued at eight marks, and to his son ' 40 shillings
for as many pence put upon the book on the day of
the espousals.' [1] The bridegroom's sister, Philippa,
gave her sister-in-law a magnificent present—at least
one judges it to be so, for her father had to pay a
London goldsmith no less than £10, 18s. for it.
There was feasting and merrymaking, accompanied
by the customary gifts of largesse to the poor.

The young couple were evidently ' bedded,'
with all the grim formalities of mediæval chivalry,
soon after their wedding ; and in April 1382 Mary
was brought to bed of a son who died immediately.
But before this happened she had gone back to her
mother's house ; and that good lady was astute
enough to get from John of Gaunt an undertaking
to pay her

> the sum of one hundred marks annually, for the charge
> and cost of his daughter-in-law, Mary, Countess of Derby,
> until the said Mary shall attain the full age of fourteen
> years.

In due course—perhaps as early as 1384—the
young couple set up house on their own account ;
and it is not unlikely that they then went to Monmouth, which stood on the lands of the duchy of
Lancaster, and had been assigned by John of Gaunt
to his son as an ' establishment.' It is definitely
known, however, that they lived there in 1386, and in
September of that year a payment of three hundred
odd pounds was made for household expenses.

The everyday domestic life of a grandson of a
king of England excited little popular curiosity,
and the absence of a sensation-hunting press allowed
Henry of Bolingbroke and his wife to enjoy a decent
obscurity in their home life. His political activities
naturally provoked a certain amount of interest ;

[1] See Textual Notes at end (pp. 300–302).

2

and his future prospects, as the heir to the vast estates of the duchy of Lancaster, would assure him of an important place in the nobility. There is a tradition that Henry V. was not the first of their children to be born at Monmouth : the Countess Mary is said to have ' slipped ' a child some time in 1386 ; and it is also believed that Henry himself was born ' out of time '—a circumstance which might easily account for the subsequent fight to keep mother and child alive.

Indeed there was no great rejoicing in the castle at Monmouth on August 9, 1387. The baby was by all accounts a sickly and puny child, and in the agonies of the labour his mother's strength had been sorely tried. The women in attendance on the countess thought that mother and child would inevitably die, and their concern was intensified by reason of the fact that their lord and master was away in Windsor. Traditional evidence, picturesque if not wholly reliable, avers that Henry was born lifeless, and that the first sounds forced through his tiny lungs were caused by an old wife's remedy—a vigorous slapping of his little bottom. Moreover, it was the sound of the baby's cries which kindled the spark of survival in the breast of the countess : they were reminders that her struggles and agony had not been futile.

The happy event at Monmouth aroused no great stir in the world outside the limits of the duchy of Lancaster. The baby was merely another member of the proud feudal hierarchy of England : his future social and political position, should he survive his father, was assured by reason of the priority of his birth. It is true that in his little veins coursed the blue blood of the kings of England ; but Edward III. had been so richly endowed with sons, and they in turn had blessed him with grandsons, that there was hardly the remotest chance of a son of Henry of

Bolingbroke even coming within reach of the sceptre
—at least by fair means. The reigning monarch,
Richard of Bordeaux, the son of the people's darling,
the Black Prince, was but twenty years of age at the
time of Henry of Monmouth's birth : he had ample
time in which to procreate sons, and his love of
dalliance with ladies displayed in him no unwilling-
ness to perform his manly duties. Thus the greatest
commotion which the birth of Henry of Monmouth
occasioned was the merry ringing of the bells in the
town's churches—and a few days later, to mark
the event, his father informed the burgesses that he
would not for the space of one year take from them
the ' castle coule,' which was the eight gallons of
beer sent to the castle at the time of every town
brewing.

Henry of Bolingbroke learnt of the birth of his
son from the lips of the humble ferryman who carried
him across the Wye, near Gooderich ; and as he
leapt to his horse, to gallop to the side of his young
wife and their child, he tossed the loyal fellow a bag
well laden with coins. There is no record of the
father's reactions at the sight of the puny and ill-
natured baby ; but he quickly made arrangements
for a suitable wet nurse, his choice falling upon
Margaret, wife of John de Montacute, second son
of the Earl of Salisbury. She was a buxom, healthy
woman, and came from the family of de Monthemer
—a *parvenu* family whose social fortunes were firmly
established when one of the men folk ran away with
Edward I.'s daughter, the widow of Gilbert the Red,
Earl of Gloucester. Lady de Montacute then lived
at Courtfield, in the parish of Welsh Bicknor, not
more than half a dozen miles distant from Monmouth.

The baby thrived at her breasts, and within a
few weeks, or it may have been as long as three
months, was strong enough to travel with his parents

to their London home. He was given a new nurse :
one Joanna Waryn, and in the days of his kingship
he remembered her 'good service done to him in
former times' in the shape of an annuity worth
£20. It was in London, and within a year of Henry's
birth, that the Countess Mary was again brought
to child-bed of another son, Thomas, to be created
Duke of Clarence in 1412. He was a robust little
fellow, very unlike his elder brother ; and the
occasion was celebrated by the purchase of a 'demi-
gown' for Henry (he was being 'shortened'), and
a present of £2 to Joan, the midwife.

The family were not long in London after
Thomas's birth (the vapours from the river and the
garbage scattered in the streets made the metropolis
particularly unhealthy) before they removed to
Kenilworth. There is a pleasant little picture in
an old record of their lives at Kenilworth. The
countess's concern for her sons' welfare can be seen
in various purchases of baby clothes—kirtles and
satin and tartryn gowns of scarlet and white, and
twenty-eight pairs of russet shoes. She sang to the
guitar, and played with her dogs, with their collars
of green-and-white checked silk, and her popinjay,
a very fashionable pet in the home of a person of
quality ; and her husband 'fluted on the ricordo.'
They sometimes played chess together, on a silver
board and with silver pieces : undoubtedly the
evening's entertainment. Henry indulged in the
usual round of manly sports of that time : we read
how he lost no less than 26s. 8d. in a game of hand-
ball with two members of the Duke of York's
retinue. We also read, too, that on two occasions
he was smitten with 'the pox' : had he personally
contracted this foul disease, or was it a congenital
legacy from his lecherous parent ? Then one day
a shadow is cast over the house : the countess is
taken desperately ill, and messengers were sent post-

haste to Oxford to fetch ' Master Geoffrey Melton,' a noted physician obviously.

But the political waters of the realm had already been troubled by the factious jealousies of the king's uncles—John of Gaunt and Thomas of Woodstock —and a sycophantic court party, headed by the evil genius, Robert de Vere, Duke of Ireland and Earl of Oxford. Henry of Bolingbroke had thrown in his lot with the party of his father and uncle ; and after the defeat and flight of de Vere at Radcot Bridge on December 20, 1387—a defeat which shattered the party of the ' king's friends '—had become, with his uncle Thomas (Duke of Gloucester and, as it will be remembered, his own brother-in-law), the earls of Arundel, Nottingham, and Warwick, a member of the committee of magnates which were to manage the affairs of the realm and have passed into history by the names of the Lords Appellant. For a year they wielded sovereign power in England, achieving nothing by which they could hope to win the support of the people and making many enemies ; and when Richard in May 1389 quietly informed his council that as he was twenty-three years of age and competent to manage his own affairs the Lords Appellant retired discomfited and hastened to make their peace with the king. This peace was graciously given with no seeming show of vindictiveness ; and the very men who had opposed the king previously were admitted now to his council, and young Henry of Bolingbroke was among them.

Another son had in the meantime been born to him : this was John, who was created Duke of Bedford in 1414 and destined to become a great figure in the history of the English domination in France. It was shortly after John's birth that Henry of Bolingbroke set off to adventure in foreign lands. He crossed the Narrow Seas in the company of his king, and with him took part in a magnificent

spectacle of knightly jousting on the plain of St
Inglebert, hard by the town of Calais. The Marquis
de Saluzzo, an eye-witness of the tournament, tells
us that Henry's skill with arms and great physical
strength gladdened the hearts of the spectators,
and was in marked contrast to the feeble show which
Richard II. put up in the lists. From the plain of
St Inglebert he went with a hundred knights with
the Duc de Bourbon to fight for the doge of Genoa
against the Barbary pirates, and he was present
at the taking of their lair, Tunis. Back to Europe
he came, and next fought with the Teutonic knights
in the Baltic lands and at Dantzig ; and everywhere
men marvelled at his prowess in battle.

It was while he fought in Baltic lands that a
sailor gave him the news of the birth of yet another
son, Humphrey (1390) : he was to become Duke
of Gloucester, the stormy petrel of Henry VI.'s
minority, and a renowned patron of the humanities.
We are told that Humphrey was his mother's
favourite, and that she lavished every care upon
the baby. John, on the other hand, was the apple
of his grandfather's eye : there was something about
the boy which fascinated the ageing John of Gaunt,
and he was never happier than when he was in the
baby's company. Four boys, the eldest of whom was
only about four, necessitated a careful arrangement
of the problem of nurses. Joan Waryn had apparently devoted herself solely to the care of Henry
of Monmouth ; Thomas and John were placed in
the charge of one Joan Donnesmere ; and Humphrey's nurse was called Margaret.

The news of Humphrey's birth brought his
father back to England ; and once again the family
were reunited at their home at Kenilworth. Henry
of Monmouth would be old enough to indulge in
hero-worship of a father whose tales of far-distant
lands must have been far more exciting than the

stories which he heard from the lips of Joanna Waryn. He would see, and admire, the treasures which he had brought home with him : the highly-coloured cloths from Barbary, the cunningly wrought trinkets sold everywhere in the north Italian towns, the plumed helms of knights captured in engagements in Baltic lands. Perhaps, too, he could persuade his father to play with him—mock jousts with wooden swords : or listen to the ' flutings on the ricordo' and new songs learnt from the troubadours in his travels. It would be all very pleasant : the political storm had died down in England, old enemies were reconciled, and men were joyously amazed at the liberality of the king's good government.

The wanderlust, however, had enslaved Henry of Bolingbroke. Once again he bade his countess and their children farewell and went overseas. In the closing months of 1392 he was at Venice, waiting for the shipwrights to make ready the galley—a gift from the Duke of Austria—in which he proposed to visit the Holy Land. His disappointment must have been intense when he was forced to turn back within sight of Jerusalem : he had set his heart upon visiting the Holy Sepulchre, but the infidels held that treasure in their impious grasp, and it would have been suicidal to attempt to wrest it from them. The memory of that journey remained within his heart for the remainder of his life : he was, even when King of England, always eager to lead a crusade to Palestine.

On his return home he found that there had been another addition to his family : this time, a girl, with the Plantagenet name of Blanche, born near Peterborough soon after he had left for Venice in 1392. A mother's joy had found expression in the splendour of the baby girl's baptism, and the font was decorated with a profusion of fine linen from Flanders and Champagne.

Again the children's delight would know no bounds at the sight of this hero-father. Henry was older now, a lanky little fellow of six ; and Thomas and John would clamber round and listen to tales of adventure and derring-do. One gift the father bequeathed to his eldest son—a burning zeal for ridding the Holy Land of the infidel ; and had the fates given him a longer life Henry V. would undoubtedly have led an army eastwards—and, who knows, he might have repeated the feat of Agincourt, and brought back under Christian rule the most precious spot of earth to Christians in the whole world.

The happiness of the children's home life was suddenly shattered. In July 1394 Mary de Bohun was brought to bed of another child, Philippa : within a few hours she was dead. Mary de Bohun had done her duty nobly to her husband and her country. She had brought forth six children, two of whom—Henry and Philippa—were destined to wear the purple ; and Blanche became the wife of an emperor's heir. For when Henry of Bolingbroke became King of England he married Philippa to Eric, King of Denmark, Norway and Sweden, and Blanche to Duke Louis, son of Rupert of Bohemia. The boys were a brilliant quartette. Henry was the greatest soldier of his age—perhaps of the Middle Ages ; Thomas of Clarence and John of Bedford, by no means mediocrities in the art of leading men, were capable administrators ; and even Humphrey of Gloucester, despite his tantalising and erratic outbursts, was a man of more than ordinary brilliance. As brothers they stood together, models of love and loyalty, while the peace of other families was rudely broken by fraternal differences and hatreds ; and the work of Thomas and John in particular was a generous contribution to the achievements of their eldest brother—achievements for which posterity has accounted him great.

Shortly before her death Mary de Bohun placed the four boys in the charge of a governess, Mary Hervey. On her now devolved the mother's duties. The children lived their lives on their father's estates at Kenilworth and Tutbury ; and we get a glimpse of the pleasures which were provided for them—the singing of the St Nicholas clerks, doubtless wildly excited at the prospect of the fun which always came with the annual election of boy bishops ; and the minstrelsy of Wilkin Walkin and other mounted minstrels. Then one day in March 1395, when the little family was staying at Leicester, the bustle of the household was stilled : young Henry was taken alarmingly ill, and a certain Thomas Pye—probably a physician—was hastened with all speed from London to attend to him. The two girls had gone on their mother's death with their nurse to Bytham Castle in Lincolnshire. Their father, occupied with the business of managing his estates and probably taking a hand in party politics, was not altogether neglectful of his fatherly duties. We read how in 1395 a messenger from Bytham went to London to buy clothes ' to smarten up ' Blanche and Philippa against the coming of their father to see them ; and on that occasion he took them back with him to London, to spend Christmas in his London house, very probably with their young brothers.

The calls of adventure still dinned in Henry of Bolingbroke's ears. In 1396 he again sailed overseas, and in September fought at the head of ' 1000 English lances ' in the battle of Nicopolis. It was a desperate encounter, in which the Turks drove back the forces of Sigismund, King of Hungary, and then indulged in an orgy of slaughter and destruction. Henry of Bolingbroke, so we are told, barely escaped with his life : he boarded a galley, and with Sigismund, fled up the Danube. Nothing daunted by

this experience, he cast about him for further oppor-
tunities of warlike activity.   The Count of Ooster-
vant was seeking the services of lances to fight for
him in Friesland : the Frenchman, Marshal Boucicaut, was collecting a force to march to the succour
of the emperor at Byzantium, hotly pressed by the
relentless forces of the infidel Turk.   Both expeditions offered splendid opportunites for fighting—
and plunder, the reward for such service.   But in
the end, Henry of Bolingbroke marched with
neither expedition : persuaded by friends, he returned to his native land, doubtless in the
knowledge that his cousin, Richard II., needed
his services to counteract the factious influence
of Thomas of Woodstock, Henry's uncle and
brother-in-law.

Even as early as 1394 there were signs of trouble
in England's political life.   The Earl of Arundel had
roundly accused John of Gaunt of exerting ' undue
influence ' over the king, and of browbeating the
council with ' rough and bitter words ' in order to
carry through his selfish policies in Spain.   The earl
was compelled to eat his words and apologise to the
duke ; and for the moment the trouble was at an
end.   But Arundel renewed his attack in 1395, and
he did so in a way which left no doubt as to his
contempt for the king : he appeared at the funeral
of Anne, Richard's queen, when the service was half
over.   Maddened by grief at the loss of a woman
whom he loved sincerely and passionately, the king
struck Arundel to the ground, and had him haled
off to prison—to relent of his action with his release
in a week's time.   Once again there was a patched-
up reconciliation, but it must have been obvious
to all that there was in the country a powerful
opposition to the king's government.   Richard's
reckless life, after the death of Anne, was the talk of
the realm : he would sit up all night drinking, the

nods of middle-aged courtesans were better heeded
than the counsel of his barons, pageantry was carried
on with shameless waste of money. Loyal subjects
advised him to mend his ways : his enemies saw in
his weakness their opportunity. There was talk
about the waste of the people's money and the
influence of evil counsellors ; and every one knew
that behind the criticism lurked three of the five
Lords Appellants of 1388—Thomas, Duke of Gloucester, the Earl of Arundel, and the Earl of Warwick.
Richard's resolve to marry Isabella, the infant
daughter of Charles VI. of France, was used by this
opposition as a proof of his lack of concern for the
honour of his realm : it was said that the price
of this alliance was a dissipation of the conquests
of Edward III., and Englishmen were justly proud
of their victories over the French.

But Thomas of Woodstock and the two earls
had underestimated the real strength of the king :
he was the son of the Black Prince, the glamour of
whose military exploits made him the idol of the
nation ; and he had the wholehearted support of
his uncles, John of Gaunt and Edmund of Langley,
Dukes of Lancaster and York respectively. Thomas
of Woodstock took as his text the statement that
' the kingdom is being brought to ruin by our King
Richard ' ; and he tried to persuade some of the
notables to join him in a plot to imprison Richard
and his uncles of Lancaster and York. Arundel,
as might be expected, accepted the invitation to
join the conspiracy ; but Henry of Bolingbroke and
the Earl of Nottingham refused to do so, and it was
divulged to the king. Richard was now resolved
to strike down his enemies. By none too honourable
means he got the three ringleaders into his power ;
they were put on their trial, and found guilty of
treason. Arundel, proudly insolent and unrepentant
to the very end, met his death on Tower Hill ;

Thomas of Woodstock died mysteriously while he was in the custody of the Earl of Nottingham ; and Warwick, ' like a wretched old woman . . . wailing and weeping and whining,' made a full confession, and for his craven behaviour was rewarded with a life sentence.

Richard at last was a free man, no longer going in dread of opposition to his rule ; and he knew that he had gained this boon largely through the unqualified support given to him by John of Gaunt and his son, Henry of Bolingbroke. Their good services were generously rewarded. The new Duchess of Lancaster (the notorious Katherine Swynford, whom John of Gaunt, after having kept her as his mistress for many years and had children by her, married in 1396) was received at court—a gentle reminder to the great ladies of the land that their ostracism of the duchess was no longer desired or deserved ; and the children of the union were legitimatised by royal letters patent, the eldest son, John Beaufort, being created Earl of Somerset. Henry of Bolingbroke's reward was the right to style himself Duke of Hereford.

Henry of Monmouth was now in his tenth year ; and a boy of ten in those days was much nearer manhood than he is to-day. The sum of four shillings paid in 1396 ' for seven books of Grammar contained in one volume and bought at London for the young Lord Henry ' shows that he was kept hard at his lessons. A year later harpstrings ' for the harp of the young Lord Henry ' were purchased : this is the first indication that we have of his love of music, to be commented upon by more than one chronicler in later times. Manly exercises, too, were indulged in—horsemanship, fencing, wrestling ; and there are records of payments of ' 12d. to Stephen Furbour for a new scabbard of a sword,' and ' 1s. 6d. for three-fourths of an ounce of black silk bought

at London of Margaret Stranson for a sword of young
Lord Henry.'

On March 18, 1397, the young Henry was
present at a tournament at Pleshy : it was prob-
baly his *first* tournament.   We know that on that
occasion a special horse was sent from Tutbury
for his use, as well as black silken stuff for his spurs
and black housings for his saddle.   That would have
been a great treat for the boy, and he must have
been awestruck at the splendour everywhere around
him ; for Richard II. was an enthusiastic patron of
the tournament, and in his reign the joustings were
most magnificently staged.   No doubt his father
took part :   he was a great performer in the feats
of chivalry ;   and Henry would watch eagerly and
acquisitively the finer points of his fighting.

But the young boy's life was not wholly given
over to these pleasurable pursuits :   there were
lessons to be learnt.   Thus about this time he
appears to have been placed in the charge of his
father's half-brother, Henry Beaufort, later to be
honoured with a cardinal's hat.   Beaufort was still a
young man —not more than twenty two years of
age ; and the brilliance of his scholarly attainments
was equalled only by the wildness of his life.   Henry
Beaufort had entered Queen's College at Oxford in
1391, and seven years later he was raised to the
dignity of chancellor of the university.   He would
be the ideal person to supervise the education of the
young Henry, and by virtue of his exalted position
in the university he could see that he received
the best possible education.   Unfortunately there
is no written record of the future Henry V.'s connection with Oxford, but tradition has stoutly
maintained that he was a member of Queen's
College ;   and Thomas Fuller, the Elizabethan
divine and ecclesiastical historian, stated that his
friend, Thomas Barlow, informed him that ' his

(Henry's) picture remayneth there to this day in brass.' [2]

Henry of Monmouth's career, however, was cut short by the quarrel between his father and the Duke of Norfolk (whom we have previously met as Earl of Nottingham). It is extremely difficult to get to the bottom of this quarrel, and a lengthy discussion of the points at issue is not needed in this place. Apparently Norfolk believed that Richard II. meant to destroy him and Henry of Bolingbroke, the only survivors of the Lords Appellant ; and he told his friend of his fears. Henry laughed them to scorn, and told his father of the talk which he had had with Norfolk. Whether John of Gaunt passed the story on to the king or advised his son himself to do so is not a matter of great importance : sufficient is it to remark that as soon as Richard heard of the business he ordered the arrest of the two dukes, pending a thorough examination by a commission of the story. Complications set in when Henry of Bolingbroke accused Norfolk of having deliberately made away with Thomas of Woodstock, and in vain did Richard (who probably had something to hide) try to hush up this part of the quarrel. When the commission failed to reach a verdict the king ordered the two dukes to decide their differences by single combat ; and for this purpose a great tournament was arranged to be held at Coventry on September 18.

Popular excitement knew no bounds, and the world and his wife thronged to Coventry for the occasion. No doubt the young Henry of Monmouth was there, and perhaps his brothers : they would have their seats in the great pavilion which was set up for John of Gaunt and his retinue. The boy Henry would admire the splendid suit of armour which his father had asked his friend, the

Duke of Milan, to send him for the combat. It was finely made, the work of the armourers of the northern Italian towns, then accounted past masters of their craft ; and it had cost a great deal of money. His father was mounted on a white charger, ' barbed with blue and green velvet, sumptuously embroidered with swans and antelopes of goldsmith's work,' and armed after the fashion of the period. The Duke of Norfolk was not less richly arrayed : he rode a charger ' barbed with crimson velvet embroidered with mulberry trees and lions of silver.' Richard was attended by the peers of the realm, and sat in a magnificent pavilion, bedecked with flags and pennons ; and ten thousand royal retainers—men of Cheshire in the livery of the white hart—stood around to prevent disturbances. The sun had not long risen when the two dukes advanced to the barriers of the lists, to await the royal signal to begin combat. The heralds came out and made the usual proclamation that valour would decide the right ; and the combatants gripped their lances, placed them firmly in their rests, and made ready for the charge. All of a sudden there was a commotion in the royal pavilion : Richard had thrown down his warder—a signal that the fight must not begin, and orders were sent to the dukes to dismount and come into the presence of their king. To the amazement of the crowd Richard himself pronounced sentence : Henry of Bolingbroke was to be banished from the realm for a period of ten years, Norfolk for ever ; and the latter was also to be deprived of his estates, though in his lifetime he would be paid an income of a thousand pounds a year.

The folly of Richard's act was apparent to all : though he had shown clearly that he thought Norfolk culpable he had meted out a savage punish-

ment to his adversary ; and in doing so had given
proof that Norfolk's fears were not altogether un-
founded—that the king meant to rid himself of
all the Lords Appellant. Few would have questioned the justice of his punishment of Norfolk :
the popular feeling was that the duke had received
no more than his just deserts for his part in Thomas
of Woodstock's mysterious death. The sympathy
of the crowd, however, went out to Henry of Bolingbroke : he had apparently done no wrong, and when
a little later he set out on his exile the Londoners
flocked round him, and many accompanied him as
far as Dover.

In the interval between the passing of the
sentence and his departure for France, Henry of
Bolingbroke made arrangements for the care of his
young family. The two girls and Humphrey were
placed in the care of Hugh Waterton of Eaton
Tregoes, near Ross, in Herefordshire ; and instructions were given that they were to attend
daily Mass for the repose of their mother's soul.
We cannot be certain what happened to Thomas
and John : probably they went to their grandfather's household, for, it will be remembered, the
latter was a great favourite of old John of Gaunt.
As to the future of the young Henry his father had
no say : Richard had announced that he must
remain with him at his court. From the king's
point of view this was a wise move : the young
Henry at liberty would easily become a rallying-
point for those friends who saw in the father's exile
signs of royal tyranny. Father and son said good-
bye to each other at Eltham, whither Henry of
Bolingbroke had come to pay his respects to his
king ; and it was on that occasion that Richard,
perhaps relenting of his action, reduced the period
of exile from ten to six years.

At the court the young Henry had as a com-

panion the son of the murdered Thomas of Woodstock : his movements called for careful watching,
and although he was only a youth his name and
paternal connections were powerful enough to constitute a menace to Richard. Together the two
boys probably took part in the festivities of Christmas at the court : festivities carried out on such a
magnificent scale that men held up their hands in
horror at the extravagance of the king and the riot
of the life at the court. Adam Usk was merely
retailing popular gossip when he wrote :

> He (Richard) continued with such wordly pomp as ear hath
> not heard, neither hath entered into the heart of men.

It is from the same chronicler that we get a
pathetic picture of the plight of the realm in these
last months of Richard's reign :

> The king meanwhile, ever hastening to his fall, among
> other burdens that he heaped upon his kingdom, kept in
> his following four hundred unruly men of the county of
> Chester, very evil ; and in all places they oppressed his
> subjects unpunished, and beat and robbed them. These
> men, whithersoever the king went, night and day, as if
> at war, kept watch in arms around him ; everywhere
> committing adulteries, murders, and other evils without
> end. And to such a pass did the king cherish them that
> he would not deign to listen to any one who had complaint
> against them ; nay, rather he would disdain him as an
> enemy.

There was one restraint upon the king. Lecherous living might have sapped the vitality of John of
Gaunt, but he was to his generation ' time-honoured
Lancaster,' the son of a great warrior king ; and
even Richard in his most reckless moments feared
the old man's power. But in February 1399—
actually on the morrow of St Blaise (February 4)—
John of Gaunt died : they carried his body for burial
in ' Paul's Church,' laying it in a tomb near to the
high altar. By the law of primogeniture and the
custom of the realm the dukedom of Lancaster,

3

with all the honours and dignities attached to it, passed to his son, the exiled Henry of Bolingbroke. By a solemn pledge Richard had promised the exile his patrimony, and it was a staggering blow not only to the friends of Henry of Bolingbroke, but also to the honour of the Crown when in March the vast Lancastrian estates were declared forfeit to the king. There is only one explanation for this act of injustice—the royal determination to crush the ancient nobility and to rule through the agency of favourites, new men owning no hereditary allegiance to the great families of the kingdom and looking solely to the king for advancement.

But Henry of Bolingbroke was not to be disposed of so easily. We are told by Froissart that the people of England, and especially the Londoners, ' spoke much and loudly of Derby's return ' after the death of John of Gaunt. Moreover, he had the sympathy of the French, ' for he was an agreeable knight, well-bred, courteous, and gentle to every one,' and (a point which Froissart missed) French-men would not hesitate to embarrass a king whose realm was virtually at war with their country, though for the moment a truce had put an end to actual fighting.

Despite the kindness of the French, Henry of Bolingbroke suffered fits of intense depression during his stay in Paris. His thoughts fled back to Eng-land, where his four boys and two ' lovely ' daughters were at the mercy of a man whose acts proved that he was bent upon the extermination of the Lancas-trian connection : at any moment messengers might come to him with the news that they had been done away with. And as an Englishman he could not remain unmoved by the tales which he heard of the plight of his native land—the acts of tyranny done in the king's name, and probably with his connivance, the forced loans exacted from honest citizens, the vice in which the court was steeped, the hopelessness of the future. He was in a receptive mood, therefore, to listen to Thomas Arundel, Archbishop of Canterbury and like himself an exile from his native land, who came to him in Paris with the invitation to set up his standard and win back the realm from the ' redeless ' king. Henry listened, but he was not persuaded easily to act the traitor's part : victory meant perhaps the crown, defeat the destruction of those whom he loved. In the end, after Arundel had brought friends to help to press home his arguments, he resolved to invade the kingdom of England. He left Paris, and at a Breton port embarked on his perilous undertaking, having with him only a handful of friends.

Trouble in Ireland called for Richard's personal attention, and he had been in that country more than a month when his cousin landed at Ravenspur on the Yorkshire coast. With Richard were the young Henry of Monmouth and Humphrey, son of the Duke of Gloucester. The two lads had not had much fighting since they came to Ireland, for the Irish preferred ambushes to open battles, finding them the better way to disconcert their hated English enemies ; and they must have seen much of the glamour shorn from war in the futile marchings and counter-marchings through a desolated territory. The young Henry was now a royal pensioner to the tune of £500 a year ; and by all account he enjoyed the complete confidence and favour of his kind. It was during the Irish campaign that Richard conferred upon him the honour of knighthood, and as he raised him to his feet he said :

> Fair cousin, henceforth be gallant and bold, for unless you conquer you will have little name for valour.

Little can Richard have realised that the future would reveal in generous measure the truth of that advice.

The royal army had scarcely put into quarters at Dublin when messengers from England arrived with the news of Henry of Bolingbroke's landing and, worse still, of the joyous reception which he had received from the people of England. The chronicler, Thomas Otterbourne, records how Richard upbraided the young Henry for his father's treason :

> Henry, my child, see what your father hath done to me. He has actually invaded my realm as an enemy, and, as if in regular warfare, has taken captive and put to death my liege subjects without mercy or pity. For you I am sorry ; because of this unhappy proceeding of your father you must perhaps suffer loss of your inheritance.

Henry replied with boyish sincerity :

> In truth, my gracious king and lord, I am grieved by these tidings ; and, as I hope, you are fully assured of my innocence in this proceeding of my father.

The royal wrath was stayed, and Richard accepted the young lad's protestation in a generous outburst :

> I know, my child, that the crime which your father has perpetrated does not attach at all to you ; and therefore I hold you excused of it absolutely.

But what was Richard to do ? Some of his friends urged him to proceed to England to challenge in battle Henry of Bolingbroke's invasion ; others suggested that he would be safer in Dublin. Richard, who was by no means a coward, preferred the latter plan ; but he sent John de Montacute, Earl of Salisbury, over to England with orders to protect his interests and rally to the royal cause the men of north Wales and Cheshire ; and he promised to follow with the main body of his army within a week. Three weeks were to elapse before that promise was carried out ; and in the meantime the king had taken steps to hold the young Henry of Monmouth and Humphrey of Gloucester in the castle of Trim.

Well might Richard be apprehensive of the reception which he would receive on his return to England. North of the Humber the country was whole-heartedly with Henry of Bolingbroke, in whose army now marched men of the Percies of Northumberland and the Nevils of Westmoreland ; and while at Doncaster the invader had sworn that he had returned solely with the object of regaining his patrimony he had been at pains to observe that Richard *should be allowed* to reign until the end of his life. At best he would be a king on sufferance : perhaps he might never be king again.

During Richard's absence in Ireland the regent was Edmund, Duke of York, an amiable person, but the last man in the world to meet an emergency with spirit and determination. He did his best and made some show of resistance at Berkeley ; but his troops deserted or changed sides, and in hopeless disgust he himself rode into Henry of Bolingbroke's camp. Nor did the citizens of Bristol show more enthusiasm for the king's cause : they opened their gates to the invader, and handed over to him the three ' evil counsellors ' — Bushy, Green, and Scrope ; and doubtless witnessed with delight their summary executions. Northwards, through the border counties, Henry of Bolingbroke advanced, being acclaimed on all sides as the saviour of the realm ; and without any serious difficulty he forced the Earl of Salisbury to leave Chester and made it the rebel headquarters.

Richard made the southerly crossing of the Irish Sea, and landed at Milford Haven with an army of considerable size. But the game was up, and before he had time to array his men for an advance on Chester the majority of them had deserted, and disguised as a friar he himself travelled across Wales to join the Earl of Salisbury in Conway Castle. Hopeless despondency reigned in Conway :

yet the king sent forward to Chester the Dukes of
Surrey and Exeter to ask Henry of Bolingbroke his
intentions. When he heard that the two dukes
were forbidden to leave Chester (probably both
welcomed the duress placed upon them) Richard
and a handful of companions wandered about
north Wales, trying first one castle and then another
in the hope of finding a secure place of refuge ;
and then in a fever of indecision and disgusted with
the roughness of the quarters in strongholds like
Caernarvon and Beaumaris, he returned to Conway
to await his fate. And while he waited he cursed
that fate, boasting that once he had Henry of
Bolingbroke in his clutches he would mete out to
him a punishment ' which should be spoken of
long enough even in Turkey.'

It was Henry Percy, Earl of Northumberland,
who came into the royal presence as Henry of
Bolingbroke's emissary. He spoke to the hapless
man fair words, promising him the consideration
which kingship commands : that Richard should
proceed amicably with Henry of Bolingbroke to
London, where a parliament should meet to try
and punish those individuals who had caused the
king to rule harshly. The sincerity of the promise
was emphasised by an oath upon the sacred Host ;
and Richard and Northumberland were by no
means disturbed by the knowledge that each meant
to repudiate that solemn pledge on the first occasion. So Richard went forth with Northumberland :
they dined that day at Rhuddlan and put up for
the night in the castle at Flint. Next morning
Richard attended Mass in the castle's tiny chapel,
and as he walked back to his chamber the noise
of an advancing army fell upon his ears. There
was no need to tell him what that noise meant :
he cannot fail to have realised that the ring of his
enemies was closing inevitably around his helpless

person. During the morning Archbishop Arundel
came to him from Henry of Bolingbroke : he, too,
assured the king that no hurt would come to him.
And in the afternoon, in the great hall of the castle,
the two cousins came face to face.

Richard went down to meet his cousin, and
addressed him in these words :

> My fair cousin of Lancaster, you be right welcome.

To which the duke, observing all the ceremony of
a royal audience, replied :

> My Lord King, I am come sooner than you sent for
> me, the reason whereof I will tell you. The common
> report of your people is that you have for the space of
> twenty years and more governed them very badly and
> very rigorously ; and they are not well contented there-
> with ; but if it pleaseth you, my Lord King, I will help
> you to govern them better.

There was only one answer, and Richard gave it :

> Fair cousin, since it pleaseth you, it pleaseth me well.

The sceptre was quickly slipping out of Richard's
hands.

But Henry of Bolingbroke did not allow the
king to remain long in suspense. As they made
ready for the progress to London he ordered the
king to be mounted on a miserable palfrey ; and
little was done to save him from the abuse of an
infuriated people. Richard must have welcomed
the solitude of his unasked-for quarters in the
Tower, whither he was hurried after the cavalcade
reached London. Adam Usk reports on the fatal
resignation of the monarch as he lay in the Tower
waiting for the official announcement of a fate
which was already determined by his enemies.

> A wondrous and fickle land is this, for it hath exiled,
> slain, destroyed, and ruined so many kings, rulers, and
> great men, and is ever tainted and toileth with strife,
> variance, and envy.

It was in the depths of degradation that Richard

achieved the greatness of soul which endeared him
to an Elizabethan play-going public and gave him
loyal friends among the men whose business in
later times it was to write the record of his futile
reign.

Henry of Bolingbroke was resolved to act
cautiously and spectacularly. On arrival in London
he had gone to ' Paul's church ' to offer up a
thanksgiving for the success of his venture ; and
a grief-stricken pause by the tombs of his father
and mother won him the admiration of an admiring
crowd. He stayed for a short space—not more
than a week—in the palace of the Bishop of London ;
and from there he went to the priory of the knights
hospitaller—the Hospital of St John without
Smithfield. Finally he took up his residence at
one of his mansions—Hertford ; ostensibly detached from the affairs of State but keeping a
strong hand upon them, and eagerly awaiting the
meeting of the parliament, summoned ironically
enough by Richard himself, in which he would
put forward his claim to the throne of England.

On September 30, 1399, the parliament-men
crowded into the Great Hall at Westminster, not
long since rebuilt at Richard's orders by Henry
Yevele, his ' chief mason,' and Henry Herland,
' the king's carpenter.' The first sight which met
their eyes was the empty throne, richly draped
with cloth of gold ; and they knew that although
they had come to this assembly in response to
Richard's writs they would not see him seated upon
that throne. When silence had fallen upon the
assembly Richard Scrope, Archbishop of York
and brother of one of the victims of the popular
wrath against the misgovernance of Richard, stood
up, and from a document in his hands read to the
members the deed of abdication signed by the
imprisoned king—whether as a result of persuasion

or by threats of violence no man will ever know. With a mighty shout the parliament-men accepted the king's decision ; and then, as if to emphasise the rightness of their action, they asked that the articles of accusation against the late king might be read to them. It was a lengthy business, for the indictment contained thirty-two articles or sections ; and there was repetition, couched in dull legal phraseology. The late king had governed ill : he had violated the laws and customs of the realm by his arbitrary acts, he had squandered the people's hard-earned money in profligate living, he had not kept his word. The nobles and commonalty were thereupon asked to determine whether the king's crimes did not demand a formal pronouncement of deposition ; and again with a mighty shout they signified their assent. Eight members were constituted into a committee to carry out the members' will : solemnly they came before the empty throne and in the name of the Parliament of England declared that it was vacant and that no man ought to render allegiance or obedience to him whom they had only a few moments before deprived of his right to sit upon it. No sooner had this been done than Henry of Bolingbroke [3] rose in his place, and signing himself with the cross on forehead and breast, said in his native tongue :

> In the name of God, I, Henry of Lancastre, challenge this roiaume, this the corone, with alle the membris and appurtenaunce therto, save the ryght blood comyng of the Kyng Henry, and thorghe that ryght that Gode of hys grace hath sent me, with the help of my kyn and of my frendes to recovere it ; the whiche roiaume was in poynt to ben undon for defaute of governaunce and undoyng of the lawes.

The assembly at once proclaimed that Henry should be their king, and the hall rang with their shouting as Thomas Arundel, Archbishop of Canterbury, led his friend to the vacant throne. The

archbishop's moment had come, and when the
tumult had died down he preached a short sermon
from the text 1 Samuel ix. 17. A speech from the
throne followed the archbishop's sermon ; and in
simple language the new king declared his
intentions :

> Syres, I thank you espiritelx and temporelx, and alle
> the estates of the lond, and I do yow to wyte that it ys
> nought my wil that no man think that by wey of conquest
> y wolde desherte any man of hys heritage, fraunchis, or
> other ryghtes that hem ought to have, ne put hym out of
> that he hath and hath had in the godes lawes of this
> reiaume except hem that han ben ageyn the gode purpos
> and the commune profyte of the reiaume.

The sanctity of private property, so dear to men
of property, had been enunciated as a rule of law :
many in that Great Hall — the men who had
coquetted with both sides in this struggle for a
sceptre—must have heaved a pleasurable sigh of
relief when they listened to the new king's words.
The work of parliament was done. It was thereupon dissolved, but proclamation was made that
a new parliament would assemble on October 6,
and the coronation was fixed for the 13th of the
same month.

Where was Henry of Monmouth when these
stirring events were taking place ? It is difficult
accurately to follow his movements in the interval
between the departure from Ireland of Richard II.
and the meeting of his father's first parliament.
There is little ground for suggesting that the boy
was present at the meeting of the parliament which
elected his father king of England. No doubt
as soon as the news reached Ireland that Henry of
Bolingbroke's venture had been brought to a
successful conclusion the men acting as gaolers of
Henry of Monmouth and his cousin, Humphrey of
Gloucester, at Trim, would deem it expedient to
release the young boys ; and we know that a certain

Henry Dryhurst of West Chester was sent across
the Irish Sea to bring them to England. But it is
almost impossible to fix the date of their return,
though there is some evidence for suggesting that
it took place early in August. Tradition has consistently maintained that the young Humphrey of
Gloucester died during the crossing, and a pathetic
allusion in his mother's will, dated August 9, to
' the mischances and uncertainties of this change-
able and transitory world ' may be taken to mean
that the grief-stricken duchess, now a nun, was
mourning the loss of her only son.

Why, then, if this argument is sound chronologi-
cally, was not the young Henry at his father's side ?
We are treading on the dancing shadows of historical
mystery. Shakespeare, too good a dramatist to
bother himself about accurate chronology or even
just evaluation of character, makes the newly-
elected Henry IV. say :

> Can no man tell me of my unthrifty son ?
> 'Tis full three months since I did see him last.
> If any plague hang over us, 'tis he.
> I would to God, my lords, he might be found.

We must later pause to reflect upon the so-called
wildness of young Henry's youth and the relation-
ship which existed between him and his father ;
and consequently it is necessary here only to say
that for some reason or other, either of his own
volition or at his father's command, the boy was
kept well in the background of the drama of Richard's
downfall and his father's usurpation of the Crown.

But the young Henry was present with his
brother Thomas at the parliament—actually the
first parliament of his father's reign, for the previous
one had been summoned by Richard—which met
in the Great Hall at Westminster on St Faith's day
(October 6), and in the right of his position as the
king's eldest son he took pride of place among the

temporal peers, while Thomas bore the wand of his
new office of Steward of England.   The proceedings
were short : Archbishop Arundel, speaking on the
king's behalf, apologised for the haste with which
the parliament had been summoned, and announced
that it was the royal intention solemnly to respect
the laws of the kingdom and to govern with the
advice of parliament.   But the king did not wish
to proceed with any formal parliamentary business
until his election had been hallowed by the act of
coronation on the 13th, and ' the faithful commons '
were thereupon commanded to elect their speaker
and the whole assembly to appoint a committee to
deal with petitions.   With that the parliament was
adjourned.

Henry IV. inherited some of the late king's
love of pageantry, and the coronation ceremony was
planned on a magnificent scale.   On the night of
the 11th he made his headquarters in the Tower,
and in the presence of the hapless Richard founded
a new knightly order, ' the Knights Companions of
the Bath '—so-called from the mediæval custom of
bathing the body on the eve of great religious
festivals and ceremonies.   Sunday came, and after
hearing early Mass, Henry, bareheaded, clothed in
a richly-woven tunic of cloth of gold, and mounted
on a snow-white charger, rode through the streets
of the city to receive the huzzas of the Londoners.
In his cavalcade were the young Henry, six dukes,
six earls, and eighteen barons ; and they were
escorted by some six thousand mounted men.   The
city of London had prepared a right royal entertainment for the new king, and we are told that in
Cheapside no less than nine fountains flowed with
white and red wine.   On Sunday night Henry
slept in Westminster Palace, and on the following morning, being the feast of St Edward
Confessor, he was solemnly crowned in the abbey

church. It was the anniversary of his banishment by Richard.

On the 14th Sir John Cheyne came to the king as the Commons' choice of speaker. He was a renegade clergyman, suspected of dabbling in Lollardy, and hated by the bishops and clergy. Henry, acting constitutionally, accepted Cheyne as the Commons' leader ; but next day he resigned—on grounds of ill-health, but actually because pressure had been brought to bear upon him ; and a new speaker was found in the person of John Doreward, one of the members for the county of Essex. Parliament was now ready to do business. The king was given the usual grants of money and the right to levy taxes and tolls according to the custom of the time ; and steps were immediately taken to right the wrong done in the late king's reign by a formal annulment of the measures passed in the parliaments of 1387–88 and 1397–98. There was a murmur of enthusiastic delight when Henry personally announced that the statute of 1351 should alone be the law of treason ; and the assembly ' most humbly thanked him ' for sweeping aside the additional legislation of 1397 which extended the law of treason to dangerous limits.

It was on the same day—Wednesday, October 14—that Archbishop Arundel informed the parliament that Henry IV. proposed to create his eldest son, Prince of Wales, Duke of Cornwall, and Earl of Chester ; and he asked the members to declare him the lawful heir to the throne. When this was settled the assembled parliament was treated to the spectacle of the solemn investiture of the young prince, who throughout the proceedings was sponsored by his great-uncle, Edmund of Langley, Duke of York. A few days later the king conferred on the boy the additional honours of Duke of Lancaster and Duke of Aquitaine—honours borne by his grandfather, John of Gaunt; and generous provision was made for the younger sons, John and Humphrey, in grants of lands in various parts of the realm. [It will be remembered that the second son, Thomas, had already been suitably provided for with a high office of State.]

The victorious party could not afford to ignore the existence of the wretched Richard in the capital. For the moment he was safely guarded by one of Henry's staunchest friends, Sir Thomas Rempston ; but men were fickle in their loyalties in feudal England ; and there was always a danger that determined friends might effect his rescue. The faithful Commons, on October 21, went so far as to pray Henry to put Richard on his trial for the evil which he and his advisers had done ; but the king hesitated to stain his hands with blood ; and the matter was referred to a committee of spiritual and temporal peers. They eventually decided that Richard ought to be placed in secret confinement somewhere away from London, and this decision was communicated to parliament on the 27th. On the following day Richard, disguised as a forester, was hastened away from the Tower at midnight. He was taken to Gravesend, and from there moved to Leeds Castle, in Kent ; and finally taken to an unknown place.

It was about this time that the faithful Commons petitioned Henry about the safety of the young prince :

> forasmuch as the prince is of tender age that he may not pass forth from this realm.

There were rumours that the Scots and Irish were about to make a military diversion against the realm of England, and it was very necessary from their point of view that the Lancastrian succession should not be jeopardised, for a restored Richard would show them no mercy. But parliament's

concern about the safety of the prince's person must
not be taken as evidence of their admiration of a
young man who had already given evidence of a love
of manly sports ; and a little while after the presentation of this petition these same faithful Commons were brutally discussing his ' marriageable
value ' in negotiations with the king of France.
It was thought that the young Henry's marriage
to one of the French king's daughters might lessen
French wrath at the deposition of the husband of
a French princess—and incidentally obviate the
repayment of Queen Isabella's dowry, which would
have to be done now that she had lost her status
of queen. This project came to nought, and on
November 19 the first parliament of Henry's reign
was dissolved.

Henry and his four sons kept Christmas at
Windsor. A mysterious sickness took hold of the
young Prince Henry and some of the household, and
it was whispered that enemies had attempted to
poison their food. The king himself, his strength
severely taxed by the events which had happened
since his landing at Ravenspur, was out of sorts ;
and more than once he querulously said that he
wished Richard was out of the way. Some of his
intimate friends suggested that this step ought to
be taken, but Henry drew back from a deed which
he inevitably realised to be detrimental to his own
interests, although he went so far as to announce
that a popular rising in Richard's favour would
mean his instant death. Was this threat meant to
frighten the desperate spirits who about this time
were plotting to overthrow the Lancastrian dynasty ?
It is by no means certain that Henry as yet knew of
the solemn pledges made by the Earls of Huntindgon,
Kent, Rutland, Salisbury, and their friends to restore
the imprisoned king or die in the attempt. Unfortunately for the conspirators they had taken too

many people into their confidence, and at last the
scheme to attack Windsor and capture Henry and
his sons came to the king's knowledge.   Henry
acted swiftly : he abandoned the castle at Windsor
barely twelve hours before the traitors descended
upon it, and threw himself upon the loyalty of the
Londoners.   To the mayor of the city he entrusted
his four sons, with stern injunctions that he was to
guard them well ; and he himself took charge of the
preparations for the crushing of the rising.   The
militia from a number of shires was mobilised, and
a sharp look-out was kept in the Channel for ships
bearing French help for the four earls and their
satellites.   The wildest rumours circulated throughout the country—Richard had been liberated, the
Royalist forces had been scattered, the Lancastrian
dynasty was overthrown ; and in such an atmosphere of uncertainty the bonds of allegiance were
strained to breaking-point.   Rumour lied.   From
the outset Henry's position was not seriously
threatened, and although in one or two places
Richard had been proclaimed the lawful king there
was no popular enthusiasm for his cause ; and eventually the plot came tumbling about the conspirators'
ears when one, John Cosyn, the bailiff of Cirencester,
surprised the leaders and held them prisoners for the
king in the priory of the Austin Canons in his town.
But the Cirencester mob was out of hand, and
thinking that a fire in one of the houses in the town
was started by friends of the prisoners they dashed
into the priory, seized the Earls of Kent and Salisbury,
and put them to death.   Rutland (incidentally the
son of Edmund of Langley, Duke of York) had taken
no active part in the rising : either by accident
or design (many said that it was he who betrayed
the plot to the king) he was in his father's household
when the attack had been made on Windsor, and
he apparently deemed it wiser to remain there.   But

Huntingdon was handed over to Joan, the aged
Countess of Hereford, Henry's mother-in-law ; and
she had no qualms of conscience or pity when the
men of Essex came before her castle of Pleshy and
asked her to hand the prisoner over to them for vengeance.   Had he not been among those who brought
to death her son-in-law, Thomas of Woodstock, and
did not popular report aver that it was his friend,
the Lord de Spenser, who had poisoned her grandson,
Humphrey of Gloucester, as he journeyed back with
the prince Henry to England ?

There was great rejoicing when the king returned
to London on January 15, 1400 : in ten days he had
crushed a dangerous conspiracy.   The city made
holiday.   The king was welcomed by Archbishop
Arundel and 'a long file of bishops and abbots,'
by his sons and the mayor of the city ; and the
company went to ' Paul's Church ' to sing a solemn
Te Deum, and the archbishop asked that all would
offer up a special prayer of thanksgiving to the
Blessed Virgin for her intervention on Henry's
behalf.   On the following day the king and his sons
gave the citizens of London an opportunity of
participating in the royal triumph by means of a
spectacular progress through the streets of the city ;
and wherever they went they were met with wild
shouts of

> God preserve our Lord King Henry and our Lord the
> Prince !

or

> God guard our King Henry, and God bless my Lord the
> Prince ! Now we will wage war with all the world—except
> the Flemings.

Neither Henry IV. nor his son looked in vain for
loyalty among the Londoners during their reigns :
the citizens of England's greatest city were the
king's men heart and soul, and they were ready to
fight in defence of his right.

4

What of the hapless Richard, the centre around which the treason of the four earls had revolved ? He now lay in a dungeon in one of Henry's castles —Pontefract, being in the custody of Robert Waterton and Sir Thomas Swynford. By the end of January 1400 the news went round the kingdom that he was dead, but no man knew by what means he had died. So the gossips invented a form of death for him. Some said that he starved himself to death ; some, that he was starved to death by the king's orders ; and others, that he was murdered, after putting up a stern fight, by Sir Peter Exton, acting on Henry's orders. Be this as it may, Richard was assuredly dead, and Henry was thereby the more secure on his throne. The secrecy which surrounded the death was in itself a danger ; impostors would come upon the scene and claim that they were the dead king, and many would accept their claims without question. The council, therefore, advised Henry to show Richard's body

> to the people in order that they might have certain knowledge of his death.

The corpse was brought in great state from Pontefract to

> the church of Saint Paul in London, the face not covered but shown openly to all.

Henry himself (and no doubt he insisted that the young prince should also be present) carried the pall at the solemn requiem said on the morning following the arrival of the body in the city. It was then handed over to the Dominican Friars of Langley (Chiltern Langley), in Hertfordshire, and was privately buried in their conventual church. The irony of the burial struck one contemporary most forcibly : wrote Adam Usk in his *Chronicle* :

> My God ! how many thousand marks he (Richard) spent on burial places of vain-glory for himself and his wives,

among the kings at Westminster ! But Fortune ordered it otherwise.

And in March 1400, perhaps as a salve for a troubled conscience, the king consented to the payment of £16, 13s. 4d. for a thousand Masses for the repose of Richard's soul.

CHAPTER TWO

APPRENTICE TO ARMS

FIGHTING in Wales was often the military apprenticeship of the great leaders of England's mediæval armies. The gaunt mountains, riven with narrow valleys, the bogs, seemingly so simple to negotiate but treacherously impassable, the swiftly-moving streams, quickly put in spate by the heavy rains, called forth a generous display of military genius in the men who carried through successful campaigns in Wales; and the experiences won in these Welsh wars were often turned to good account elsewhere—in Scotland and France. England's mediæval kings, with the one exception of the great Edward I., grossly under-estimated the military power of the people of the Principality. They believed that a spectacular progress through their land at the head of a great army was sufficient to strike terror into the hearts of Welshmen; and this opinion seemed to them to be justified when they found that the Welsh forces would not give them battle. Experience quickly taught the people of Wales that not only does he who fights and runs away live to fight another day, but the English aggressor would eventually defeat himself by (dare a Welshman say it?) his own stupidity.

Mediæval warrior kings were seldom concerned with a vital problem of modern warfare—the defence of lines of communication. Mediæval armies lived on the country in which they operated, and they fought their way in and then fought their way out. An inevitable desolation came to the invaded country : it was effected either by the natives themselves, grimly resolved to make it impossible for the men of the invading armies to fill their bellies, or by the ravages of the invading foraging parties. This happened to Wales, not once but scores of times, with the result that a naturally poor country became notoriously poverty-stricken.

The Welshman is not a cautious fellow : his warm Celtic blood fires him with impetuosity which can sometimes become no better than a reckless insanity. In the Welsh wars of the mediæval kings of England, therefore, the Welsh indulged their love of fighting—a love intensified by the fiercest hatreds—in skilfully planned ambushes and lightning attacks upon a straggling rearguard. Reconnoitring parties were exterminated by the deadly shooting of the archers of Gwent, Brycheiniog, and Morgannwg : stragglers and sutlers fell victims to the shower of spears hurled by the men of Eryri, Eifionydd, and Lleyn. No quarter was asked for in these engagements : men fought to kill.

Edward I., astute and able soldier that he was, quickly realised that the conquest of Wales was not to be carried out by a succession of royal military progresses through the Principality of Wales ; and his campaigns against the Welsh were well planned and protracted over long periods, his captains relentlessly hunting down and annihilating the marauding bands which preyed upon the English forces and not ceasing their military activities until hostile resistance had been crushed. And in the end, after two Welsh wars, he could call himself the conqueror of Wales and compel the Welsh to accept his eldest son as their prince. But if Edward I. extinguished the tribal nationalism of mediæval Wales he had learnt to admire the sterling military qualities of Welsh archers and spearmen, and by employing them in

his armies campaigning in Scotland he evolved a
new method of warfare. The disaster of Bannockburn was caused by a reversal of Edward I.'s
military tactics : the archers were kept in reserve
and the knights charged in the vanguard of the
battles—to fall into confusion in the pits dug by the
Scots. In the Hundred Years' War Edward III.
and his son, Edward, the Black Prince, used the
archers of Gwent, Brycheiniog, and Morgannwg to
such deadly advantage that their name was feared
throughout the possessions of the king of France ;
and at Agincourt Henry V.'s use of them won for
them immortality in the annals of mediæval
warfare.

The Edwardian conquest did not result in the
annexation of Wales by England. What was
known as ' shire ' land—the counties of Anglesey,
Caermarthen, Caernarvon, Cardigan, and Merioneth
—were placed under the immediate authority of
the English Crown : the remainder of Wales was
parcelled into a number of marcher lordships. In
the former the king's writ ran, the common and
statute law being administered by specially
appointed justices in the county courts ; but in
the latter the ' custom of the march ' placed serious
limits upon the royal authority ; and it would be
hard to find more typical examples of the mediæval
idea of an *imperium in imperio* than the marcher
lordship and its relation to the Crown.

The Welsh had grievances typical of those of
any conquered people. They were conscious, even
in the ' shire land,' that they were looked down upon
as inferior to the English ; they sent no representatives to the parliament at Westminster ; they
could not forget the glorious traditions of their race
and the independence which their ancestors had
enjoyed. In the marcher lordships the line of
demarcation between English and Welsh was more

clearly marked. The inhabitants were divided into the *Englishry* and the *Welshry* ; and although in the latter they were able to retain many of their peculiar customs and laws they were definitely a people apart from their English neighbours. The process of anglicisation had been carried to inconvenient extremes among the clergy : in both ' shire land ' and marcher lordship the control of many advowsons was in the hands of Englishmen, and they appointed to benefices in Wales men who were not only unable to converse with their parishioners in their mother tongue, but were also childishly indifferent to their nationalist aspirations. By reason of these glaring differences and not owing to the harshness of English rule the weight of the conqueror's heel upon the necks of the Welsh people seemed at times unbearable ; and all that was needed to produce a great national uprising was the man to take advantage of the irritation which was bound to arise because of the lack of sympathy between the two races. That man appeared on the scene in 1400 : he was Owen ap Gruffydd Fychan, better known to Englishmen as Owen Glendower and to Welshmen as Owen Glyn Dŵr, a cultured gentleman, who was lord of Glyndyfrdwy and Cynllaith Owen.

The rebellion of Owen Glyn Dŵr was a thorn in the flesh of the English during the greater part of Henry IV.'s troubled reign. The actual cause of the outbreak is none too clear : it is generally thought to have originated in a dispute over the possession of ' a piece of commons ' called Croesau, which lay between the lands of the lord of Ruthin and those of the lord of Glyndyfrdwy, and was claimed by both. That Reginald, Lord Grey of Ruthin, was not a particularly friendly neighbour seems certain : he was the worst type of English marcher, overbearing and rapacious, and he de-

lighted in showing his hatred and contempt for the
'Welch doggis.'   Before he had provoked Owen to
rise in arms in defence of his rights this Lord Grey
had involved himself in a quarrel with a somewhat disreputable gentleman of North Wales, one
Gruffydd ap Dafydd ap Gruffydd, who has passed
into history by the name which Grey gave him—
'the strengest thiefe of Wales,' and deserves
immortality by reason of the daring impudence of
his letter writing.[4]   As a result there was considerable ' riot ' in North Wales, and we find Grey
urgently requesting the council in London ' to . . .
giffe me a moore pleyner commyssioun ' in order
to quell the disturbance.

Owen already had good reason for participating
in these attacks upon the lord of Ruthin.   In his
capacity as chief marcher of North Wales it was
part of Grey's business to summon those who held
lands directly from the Crown to serve in the royal
expeditions ; but when Henry early in 1400 decided
to invade Scotland and called for an expeditionary
force Grey deliberately withheld Owen's summons
until it was too late for him either to appear in
person in the royal array or to send an explanation
of his absence.   This had happened before the
' affaire ' of Gruffydd ap Dafydd ap Gruffydd ; and
yet Owen did not raise a finger to help his fellow-
countryman.   The reason for this forebearance is
perhaps his belief that the king would understand
his position, and pardon his seeming disloyalty.
But Henry, undoubtedly advised by Grey, who was
a fast friend, soon made it clear that he regarded
Owen's non-appearance in the royal expeditionary
force as evidence of treason.

By September 1400 Owen had decided to
renounce his allegiance ; and a conspiracy was
made in his mansion at Carrog on the banks of the
Dee in his Glyndyfrdwy lordship.   Among the con-

spirators were his wife's two brothers, Gruffydd
and Philip Hanmer, sons of Sir David Hanmer of
Hanmer in Maelor Saesnig, and in Richard's reign
a judge of the King's Bench, Hywel ap Madog
Kyffin, Dean of St Asaph, and Robert Puleston,
who had married Owen's sister, Lowri. It was not
a deep-laid plot ; for in a letter which Owen sub-
sequently sent to Henry Don, a South Wales friend
and later one of his captains, he apologises for not
inviting his help with the excuse that ' it behoved
us to rise without fore-warnings.'

Why this sudden move ? Obviously Owen had
heard that Henry IV., unable to bring the Scots to
battle and aware that he could not support his
army any longer in a desolated country, was
marching southwards ; and he was anxious to
strike the first blow, knowing that attack is always
the best defence. Perhaps, too, news had reached
him that an excellent opportunity presented itself
for a raid upon his adversary's stronghold at
Ruthin. Be this as it may, about September 21 he
dashed his men into Ruthin when the little town
was *en fête* for the great event of the year—the St
Matthew's Fair ; and so unexpected was the assault
that his men carried all before them. True, they
failed to take the great red castle, but they had
the satisfaction of having twisted the lion's tail
by burning and pillaging the town, and they
had doubtless made the undertaking profitable by
acquisition of loot.

The success of this raid on Ruthin filled Owen
and his men with warlike enthusiasm : they
advanced through the vale of Clwyd and attacked
Flint, Hawarden, and Holt. The news of the
rising spread like wildfire through the hill country
of North Wales, and men flocked to serve under
Owen's banner ; and within a couple of days of
the sack of Ruthin the rebel force was repeating its

terrible depredations at Oswestry.   Next, the town
around the castle of ' Pole,' now called Welshpool,
was pillaged and burnt ; and it was only the prompt
action of Hugh Burnell, Sheriff of Salop, which
saved Shrewsbury from a similar fate ;   for he
hastily mustered the levies of his shire and checked
the rebels in a sharp engagement fought on the
banks of the Severn, or possibly the Fyrnwy.

About the time when Owen and his men were
wreaking their vengeance in Ruthin, Henry IV.
had ordered the mobilisation of the local levies of
some ten midland shires.   The sheriffs were told
to march their men to meet the king without delay,
and the objective was the subjugation of ' our
rebels of Wales.'   The urgency of the matter had
been repeatedly impressed upon the king as he
came southwards :   the distracted people of the
English shires bordering Wales knew that they
would receive no quarter from the wild men of
Wales, and they had bombarded their king with
appeals for his personal assistance in the defence
of their homes and families.   On September 26
Henry and the bulk of the expeditionary force
marched into Shrewsbury, where he was joined by
his son, Henry of Monmouth, then a lad in his
fourteenth year.

Father and son had no time to waste in Shrewsbury, but before leaving the town they sat in judgment on one of Owen's friends, a certain Gronw ap
Tudur, whom they condemned to death, ordering his
' quarters ' to be sent for exhibition on the main
gates of Bristol, Chester, Hereford, and Ludlow.
During the first week in October the royal army
advanced through North Wales, vainly looking for
Owen and his bands, and cursing the hopeless
poverty of the countryside ; and only once—somewhere near Beaumaris—did the royal soldiers come
to grips with the rebels, and then they suffered from,

rather than benefited by, the occasion. The young
Henry must have been a witness of the savage
destruction of the Franciscan house at Llanfaes,
done at his father's express orders ; but probably
he shared the popular sentiment that

> shall nevir cece this clamour of kyng Richard til thise
> Freris be destroid.

The expeditionary force, returning by way of
' Mouche ' (Mawddwy), marched into Shrewsbury
on October 13. Henry had achieved little : Owen
was still at large. But he considered that he could
be generously disposed towards the rebels, who
were offered a full pardon provided that they laid
down their arms and made a profession of allegiance
before the royal commissioners. Owen Glyn Dŵr,
Gruffydd and Philip Hanmer, and Robert Puleston
were excepted from this pardon : they were out-
lawed, and their estates were confiscated. On
November 9 Henry granted to his half-brother,
John Beaufort, Earl of Somerset, all Owen's lands
in Wales : he little knew that the earl would not
be able to enjoy his gift for many years to
come.

The young Henry probably returned to London
with his father, and was present in the parliament
which met in January 1401 when the Welsh
' affaire ' was discussed. Did he share the opinions
of many of the members from the border shires
that the so-called pacification was the prelude of
greater disasters ? He could not fail to be aware
by the bitterness with which the penal laws against
the Welshmen were moved : they formed a brutal
code of hate which must inevitably aggravate the
relationships of the two peoples.

In March 1401, however, the prince was at
Chester, for in that month he issued an offer of
pardon to the people of Anglesey, Caernarvon, and
Merioneth, provided that they would abandon the

cause of the brothers, Rhys and Gwilym ap Tudur, of Penmynydd, kinsmen of Owen Glyn Dŵr and ancestors of the English Tudor dynasty. Precisely what they had been doing we cannot say, though Rhys—better known as Rhys Ddu of Erddreiniog —had commanded the force which at Beaumaris had skirmished so successfully with the royal army in October in the previous year. The prince's efforts at pacification, however, were not successful : failure was due to the fact that he had excluded from his offer of pardon Rhys and Gwilym ap Tudur. On All Fools' Day these intrepid warriors were in control of the great castle at Conway. They had taken it by a ruse while John Massy of Puddington and the garrison were attending the Good Friday service of *Tenebræ* in the town church. Gwilym was within the fortress : his brother, ' the Black ' Rhys, hung about the neighbourhood with a formidable force, waiting to pounce down upon and harass the relieving force.

The directing force behind the English government in North Wales was Sir Henry Percy, son of the Earl of Northumberland. He was a man of nearly forty years of age, and was rich in experience of marcher affairs, having been associated with his father in the defence of the Anglo-Scottish border for sixteen years before he was rewarded for his help in the struggle which culminated in the usurpation of Henry IV. by the office of Justiciar of North Wales. No better tutor for a young prince could be found than this ' Harry Hotspur,' as his contemporaries called him. He was recklessly daring in action and opinions ; he had a name for generosity towards his enemies ; and his manly figure, tempered by a life of war and adventure, gave him that valuable asset—*presence*. His wealth of experience forced him into the forefront of the prince's council, and by his handling of the Conway Castle incident

he was to demonstrate real ability in the management of a disaffected province.

The prince and Hotspur were at Denbigh, taking
part in the great festival of Easter, when messengers
brought the news of the capture of Conway Castle.
With as little delay as possible they marched to the
scene of the disaster, attacked the rebels within the
castle, but were repulsed. Hotspur quickly saw that
surrender could only be effected by means of a
properly organised siege. The castle was ' ringed '
by men-at-arms and archers, and there was nothing
to do but to await ' the sweet reasonableness ' which
starvation, ultimately brought to a beleagured garrison. Hotspur, in the meantime, went on with his
normal duties : he would return in due season to
Conway. He was due to preside over the sessions at
Caernarvon, and with the prince he journeyed towards that town, making their progress the occasion
to display leniency to the people of the districts
through which they passed. The wisdom of this
policy, so different from that to which the people
of Wales had been accustomed to receive from the
hands of the English overlords, was demonstrated
in the public submission of the ' commons ' of the
counties of Caernarvon and Merioneth.

On May 3, therefore, the king was duly informed
of the success of their work : the incident at Conway
was explained as a flash in the pan and not the centre
of a nationalist rising. This optimism was justified.
In the middle of April Gwilym ap Tudur had notified
Hotspur that he was willing to surrender provided
that he was guaranteed a full pardon for himself
and his brother, Rhys, and complete immunity
from any legal actions which the people of Conway
might bring against them in the courts for damage
done during their occupancy of the castle. Hotspur
readily accepted the first condition, but not the
second ; and the negotiations broke down, though

it must have been obvious to the men on the spot
that the rebel resistance was weakening.   On his
return to Conway from Caernarvon discussions again
took place, and eventually a basis—a shamefully
dishonourable one [5]—for surrender was reached.
Conway Castle was duly surrendered, and peace
returned to the district.

Henry IV. was not impressed by terms of the
settlement which had been reached by Hotspur and
his son.   He considered it

> not at all honourable to us, but a matter of most evil
> precedent ;

and he frankly suggested that they should have
punished the

> said rebels . . . according to their deserts.

He faithfully honoured the pledges which had been
given to Gwilym and Rhys ap Tudur ; but there is
no doubt that he did so with a very bad grace.

As far as can be ascertained Owen Glyn Dŵr
took no part in the Conway Castle incident, although
the brothers from Penmynydd were his cousins ; and
it is hard to find a reason for his inactivity.   It has
been suggested that he was away in South Wales
trying to persuade his fellow-countrymen in that
part of the principality to join in his rebellion against
the English king ; and this very well may have been
the case.   About the time when Gwilym ap Tudur
was handing back Conway Castle to its rightful
owners bands of rebels were causing some commotion in the neighbourhood of Dolgelley, and Hotspur
—almost certainly accompanied by the prince—
fought an indecisive engagement with them near
Cader Idris.   But he lost no time in extricating
himself from a country which was ideally suited for
ambuscades, and did not follow up whatever advantage he may have had.

It is quite possible, however, that Hotspur withdrew from these operations for another reason. The greater part of the cost of defending the royal interests in North Wales had come out of his own pocket. On May 17 he wrote to Henry IV. saying that he needed money in order to pay his troops, and warning the king that unless financial help was sent he would find it almost impossible to carry on. There is no record to show that Hotspur's need was met : on the contrary, it would appear to have been ignored, for on July 3 he not only repeated his request for funds, but also hinted that his services were not being appreciated.

In this wrangle over money we detect the first clash between Henry IV. and the Percies. That great noble family had thrown the weight of its influence and power into the scales on Henry's side from the moment when he landed at Ravenspur, and it was patent to all that Percy's support had made the usurpation successful. Those who violate the law are peculiarly sensitive to ingratitude, and it is also proverbial that there is little honour among thieves. The Percies had received from Henry IV. very little : indeed, the king owed both father and son vast sums of money, and he showed little inclination to make restitution. Is it not possible that the non-payment of his debts to these Percies was part of a policy which aimed at their ultimate reduction to impotence ? Henry IV. was a shrewd, far-seeing, unscrupulous monarch ; and he was not above an action of that kind.

We must leave the matter for the moment. Either in July or August 1401 Hotspur left North Wales and returned to his native north of England. His loss to the royal cause in Wales must have been acutely felt by the young prince ; and it is significant that there was considerable rebel activity in these summer months. Owen Glyn

Dŵr had again put himself at the head of his
fellow-countrymen, and he was carrying fire and
sword through those parts of central Wales which
were favourably disposed towards the English;
and had struck terror into the people of the border
counties by the threat to slay all who spoke English.
A resolute stand by John Charlton, lord of Powys,
had the effect of stemming for the moment the
advancing tide of rebellion; but by September
1401 Owen found himself master of the situation in
his native land, and his successes at last forced
Henry IV. to take action.

On September 18 writs were issued to the
sheriffs of a number of counties, ordering them to
muster their forces and to march them to meet the
king at Worcester. A great expeditionary force
marched out of Worcester, led by Henry IV. in
person, early in October. The young prince was
with his father. On the 9th a halt was called at
Llandovery, where father and son sat in judgment on Llywelyn ap Gruffydd Fychan—quaintly
described by Adam Usk as 'a man of gentle birth
and bountiful who used yearly sixteen tuns of wine
in his household'—for leading the royal force on
a wild goose chase through the hills with a promise
of taking Owen's headquarters. His was a fine
piece of treachery, which to all Welshmen must
remain a glorious act of patriotism. From Llandovery the army was moved up the vale of Teifi
to Ystrad-fflur or Strata Florida, where orders were
given for the desolation of the great Cistercian
church, the burial-place of a score of Wales's
princes; and terrible punishments were meted out
to the people in the surrounding districts.

> The English . . . left them a desert, not even sparing
> children or churches.

Such was the story which Adam Usk told.

It was almost certainly during this campaign that the young prince Henry suffered a personal loss at Owen's hands. The rebel leader swooped down from the hills and seized

> the arms, horses, and tents of the king's eldest son, the prince of Wales, and other lords, which he bore away for his own behoof to the mountain fastnesses of Snowdon.

That apparently was the most stirring thing which took place. Lack of supplies, intensified by a ruined countryside, caused the English soldiery to murmur ; and a retreat was ordered. On October 15, Henry IV. and his son led a despondent army back to Shrewsbury : the second expedition against Owen had failed in its purpose.

Henry remained long enough on the Welsh border to make some sort of arrangements for the protection of English interests in Wales. Thomas Percy, Earl of Worcester, was made Lieutenant of South Wales, and Guy de Mona, Bishop of St David's, was ordered to see that the castles in the south-west of the Principality were kept well victualled and in a good state of defence. In the centre of Wales the bulwarks of the English power were Edward Charlton (he succeeded his brother as lord of Powys) and Hugh Burnell ; and John Oldcastle and Dafydd Gam kept watch along the middle reaches of the Wye.

We come now to a strange interlude in this story of the greatest of all the Welsh rebellions. There is evidence that Owen himself was inclined to ' return ' to his allegiance about this time, provided that the terms were generous. Unfortunately the incident is blurred and shadowy, and the element of the mysterious is introduced by the person of Sir Edmund Mortimer, uncle of the imprisoned boy Earl of March, the rightful heir to Richard's throne. Mortimer's sister, Elizabeth,

5

was the wife of Hotspur ; and apparently he acted
as intermediary in the negotiations which his
brother-in-law was carrying on with Owen. We
know that shortly after Hotspur left Wales it was
reported

> that Jankyn Tyby of the north countrei bring the lettres
> owte of the northe cuntri to Owein, as their demed from
> Henr. son Perci.

It is not improbable that Henry IV. knew of these
negotiations, and allowed them to proceed because
he wanted peace in Wales ; but it has been suggested that they were a blind for more treasonable
business ; and, in the light of subsequent events,
it has been argued that the three were already
resolved to upset the Lancastrian dynasty. It
would be as ungenerous as it is difficult to read into
these negotiations such a sinister purpose ; and in
the absence of evidence we must give Hotspur,
Owen, and Mortimer the benefit of the doubt. It is
incontrovertible, however, that the question of
Owen's pardon was discussed by the council in
London at the end of 1401 ; but opinions were
sharply divided as to the nature of the conditions
under which a pardon was to be offered. Some
urged that the matter be fought out to the bitter
end, and some cunningly suggested that a full
pardon be offered in order to get Owen into the
king's power for punishment ; a minority wisely
favoured a full pardon, realising that it would
quickly bring peace to the Principality.

The year 1402 was a black one for the English
in Wales. On January 2, Owen dashed in on
Ruthin, burnt the town, slew the inhabitants, and
harried the adjacent lands ; and a few days later
he unexpectedly returned to seize Reginald, Lord
Grey, the cause of ' the greet debaat ' in Wales.
Grey was hurried into the rocky heart of Snowdonia,

and immured in Dolbadarn, a strong fortress over-
looking Llyn Peris ; and Owen gave out that his
ransom would cost the fabulous sum of 10,000
marks.[6] This was more than a personal humilia-
tion of a tiresome neighbour : it was a direct
blow at Henry IV., for Grey was looked upon as
one of his staunchest friends and favourites. The
month of March brought ' a blasing starre ' into the
heavens, and the sight of it filled the people of
England with dismay, for rumour declared that it
foretold a ' great effusion of blood . . . about the
parts of Wales and Northumberland.' Terrifying
thunderstorns came in the early summer months :
they did much material damage to growing crops
and property, and with the superstitious they were
inevitably the forerunners of greater disasters.

Owen in Wales had things very much his own
way ; and at the end of May and in the beginning
of June rebel bands began a systematic harrying of
parts of the counties of Hereford and Radnor. The
lands of the Mortimers suffered in this raid, and at
last Sir Edmund Mortimer marched out of Ludlow
to give the rebels battle. At Pilleth, in the valley
of the Teme, he fell in with Rhys Gethin, called by
contemporaries ' the Fierce,' and a terrible battle
ensued. The Mortimer tenants from their Welsh
lands in Maelienydd turned their arrows against
their friends in Mortimer's force, thus confounding
the confusion which prevailed ; and among the
many gallant gentlemen of England who fell that
day was Thomas Clanvow, the author of *The Cuckoo
and the Nightingale.* For centuries afterwards tales
were told of horrible mutilations performed on the
dead bodies of the English by the women of Wales.
But the real significance of the rebel victory was
the capture of Sir Edmund Mortimer. It was said,
almost as soon as the news went round, that he was
not an unwilling captive.

Either about this time or perhaps a little earlier steps had been taken to provide the young Prince Henry with ' a tutor or guardian ' during his service in the field in Wales, and four names were suggested for that position—the Earl of Worcester, Lord Say, Lord Lovel, and Mr Thomas Erpyngham. The choice fell upon the Earl of Worcester, and until the great battle at Shrewsbury he was constantly at the prince's side.

In the meantime the prince had again been made a pawn in the game of royal marriages, and shortly before the fight at Pilleth had signified his willingness to marry Katharine, daughter of Eric, King of Denmark, Norway, and Sweden. But the contract was never completed, and the alliance which Henry IV. meant to secure by the wedding was later formed when his daughter married Eric's son.

In the summer of 1402 Henry IV.'s position was desperate. French sailors raided the ports of southern England, the Scots harried the northern border, the Irish were everywhere in open revolt, and in Wales the royal authority was completely effaced by the rebel Owen. In addition, grave suspicion attached to the Percies ; and Mortimer was a captive in a Welsh prison. The king was a man of resolution. He knew that in the north the Scots would be held in check by the Percies not because they were his loyal subjects, but because they would have to defend their patrimony ; he hoped that the vigilance of the English sailors in the Channel would prevent a French invasion ; and Ireland was far enough removed to be left for the moment to her own devices. He must strike down his enemies one at a time ; and the first must be Owen, now styling himself Prince of Wales.

In July 1402, therefore, Henry IV. took up his headquarters on the Welsh border, preparatory to another invasion of the Principality. He first of all placed the defence of the border from Chepstow to Wigmore under the Earl of Stafford, and from Wigmore to Holt under the Earl of Arundel ; and a number of important castles were strengthened. By the beginning of August the muster rolls of the levies for service in Wales were complete ; and Henry decided to advance in three columns into the heart of the rebel Principality. The southern column was commanded by the Earls of Arundel, Stafford, and Warwick ; and its base was Hereford. The centre column, under Henry IV. himself, was to move from Shrewsbury. The command of the northern column was given to the young Prince Henry : his headquarters were at Chester.

Once again Henry IV.'s luck was out. Just as the columns were ready to begin their advance at the end of August news came of Scottish activity in the north of England ; and men destined for service in Wales were rushed to reinforce the royal forces in those districts. Moreover, when the advance actually took place the elements fought against the English ; and there is good history in the words which Shakespeare made Owen utter in *King Henry the Fourth :*

> Three times hath Henry Bolingbroke made head
> Against my power ; thrice from the banks of Wye
> And sandy-bottom's Severn have I sent him
> Bootless home and weather-beaten back.

The English soldiers believed that Owen was a magician, and men do not fight well against the unknown ; and once again a grand army came pathetically back to English soil, having failed to bring to battle scattered bands of poorly-armed rebels. Henry IV., however, must have derived some consolation from the news which he received either on his return to Shrewsbury or shortly afterwards that the Percies had defeated the Scots in a fight at Humbledon Hill (September 14). He could not know that this victory would add to his own difficulties. The Percies had captured many of the chief notables of Scotland—the Earl of Douglas and Lord Murdoch, son of the Duke of Albany, being the two principal prisoners ; and they were resolved to retain for their own use the money by which these men would buy their liberty. Henry lost no time in making it clear that he must receive the ransoms. We are not surprised, therefore, to learn that the Percies solemnly bound themselves to resist this demand, made incidentally by one who owed them vast sums of money. A month later came the news that Sir Edmund Mortimer had married Owen's daughter, Catharine ; and finally in December Henry received a copy of a missive which Mortimer had addressed to certain of his tenants in Maelienydd. There was no longer reason to doubt his intentions : they were plainly set forth in his letter.

> . . . the object is, if king Richard be living, to restore him to the crown ; and if not that my honoured nephew, who is the right heir of the said crown, shall be king of England, and that the said Owyn will assert his right in Wales.

The shadow which must always fall across the usurper's path was slowly changing into a substance of dangerous proportions.

The young Prince Henry was now virtually a man. He was sixteen years old, he had had service in the field in Ireland and Wales, he had shown himself to be serious of purpose and skilful in the use of arms, and it was time that he was given a more definite position in the affairs of Wales. On March 7, 1403, therefore, the king and his council formally appointed the prince to be the ' king's lieutenant in the Marches of Wales ' ; and he was empowered to use as a permanent force levies from the counties of Gloucester, Hereford, Salop, and Worcester. The wisdom of this move was made abundantly clear two months later when Henry of Monmouth pushed boldly into the enemy country and ravaged Owen's estates at Glyn Dyfrdwy and Cynllaith Owen. The details of this raid are preserved in a letter which he sent to his father on May 15 :

Very dear and entirely well-beloved, we greet you much from our whole heart, thanking you very sincerely for the kind attention you have given to our wants during our absence ; and we pray of you very earnestly the continuance of your good and friendly services, as our trust in you. As to news from these parts, if you wish to hear of what has taken place, we were lately informed that Oweyn de Glyndourdy had assembled his forces, and those of other rebels, his adherents in great numbers, purposing to commit inroads ; and, in case of any resistance to his plans on the part of the English, to come to battle with them : and so he boasted to his own people. Wherefore we took our men, and went to a place of the said Oweyn, well built, which was his chief mansion, called Saghern,[7] where we thought we should have found him, if he had wished to fight, as he said. And on our arrival there we found no person. So we caused the whole place to be set on fire, and many other houses around it, belonging to his tenants. And then we went straight to his other place of Glyndourdy, to seek for him there. There we burnt a fine lodge in his park, and the whole country round. And we remained there all that night. And certain of our people sallied forth and took a gentleman of high degree of that country, who was one of the said Owyn's chieftains. This person offered five hundred pounds for his ransom to save his life, and to pay that sum within two weeks. Nevertheless, that was not accepted, and he was put to death ; and several of his companions, who were taken the same day, met with a like fate. We then proceeded to the commote of Edirnyon in Merionethshire, and there laid waste a fine and populous country ; and thence we went to Powys, and, there being in Wales a want of provender for horses, we made our people carry oats with them, and we tarried there for . . . days. And to give you fuller information of this expedition, and all other news from these parts at present, we send

to you our well-beloved esquire, John de Waterton, to
whom you will be pleased to give entire faith and credence
in what he shall report to you on our part with regard to
the above-mentioned affair.

This is the dispatch of a serious-minded student
of the art of war. Young in years he had learnt
a lesson too many old generals forget—the military
advantage of the *moral attack*. Owen's boast that
he would fight the English was meant to imply
throughout Wales and the marches that the English
were afraid to fight him ; and the main object of
Prince Henry's raid was to make the Welsh leader
prove his words. When Owen, true to the military
traditions of the greatest of the Welsh strategists,
refused to be drawn into a pitched battle, the
English prince boldly struck a blow at his adversary's
prestige by raiding his lands and destroying his
mansions at Cynllaith Owen and Glyndyfrdwy.
That such a disaster had a distressing effect upon
the spirits of Owen's adherents we may be certain :
the mansions at Sycharth and Carrog were famed
throughout the Principality for the magnificence
of their hospitality and the generosity of their
sanctuary. Second, the Prince Henry had realised
the weakness of the English practice of sending an
army into Wales and believing that it could live
on the country ; and when he turned aside to attack
Powys, normally one of the more fertile districts of
Wales, he took his stores with him.

The military effect of this raid must not be
exaggerated. Owen was still at large, and un-
defeated. Lack of funds forced the prince back to
Shrewsbury, at the head of a force which found it
difficult to regard the success of the raid as a recom-
pense for arrears of wages. Henry IV. was a
poverty-stricken king, and his council and parliament were parentally parsimonious in providing him
with money for the undertakings of State. ' The

unquiet times ' of Henry's reign, a fact which called forth comment from contemporary chroniclers, laid heavy financial burdens upon his shoulders, and neither council nor parliament showed a readiness to give the king the support to which he was justly entitled. The war in Wales was a constant drain upon the royal resources ; and the lack of funds not only hampered the work of pacification, but allowed the revolt to drag on for years.

On May 30 the young prince sent to his father and the council a pathetic appeal for financial help :

> . . . And because that our soldiers desired to know if they will be paid for the third month of the present quarter, and tell us that they will not wait here unless they are soon paid their wages according to their indentures, we pray you very dearly that you will order our payment for the said month, or otherwise let us know, and to take order promptly for the safety of these marches, for the rebels hear every day if we are paid, and they know well that without payment we cannot continue ; and they strive to raise all the forces of North Wales and of South Wales to over-ride and destroy the march and the counties adjoining thereto ; and there is no resistance here, so that they can well accomplish their malice ; and when our men shall have retreated from us, it is necessary that we should by all means retreat into England, there to be disgraced for ever. For every one must know that without troops we can do no more than another man of inferior rank. And at present we have very great expenses and have made all the pawning of our little jewels to defray them, for two of our castles, Hardelagh (Harlech) and Lampadern (Aberystwyth) are besieged and have been for a long time, and we must rescue and provision them within ten days ; and besides defend the march around us with the third body against the entry of the rebels.

A postscript was added—it was meant to emphasise the urgency of the situation :

> And be pleased to be well advised that we have well and fully shown you the peril which may happen whatsoever thing may come hereafter if remedy be not sent in time.

In the face of this warning something had to be done to assist the prince. On June 16 the sheriffs of the counties of Gloucester, Hereford, Salop, and Worcester were ordered to muster

> all knights and esquires who have lands to the value of 100s. and all yeomen and other lieges whatsoever who have lands to the value of 40s.

These were to be marched to the prince for his use in the protection of the border ; for, as the writs to the sheriffs had it,

> Owen Glyndourdy and other rebels are purposing to come suddenly to the marches to seek victuals and waste those parts and to destroy the king's lieges.

Within a fortnight, however, the whole of the South Wales march was panic-stricken. Owen had descended into the country, and was everywhere received with wild enthusiasm. The outposts of the English power were relentlessly attacked, and the men who held them trembled for their safety. In the first week of July 1403 the prince was bombarded with letters from his officers in the disaffected district ; and each had a dismal tale to tell. John Skidmore, holding for the king the castle of Cerrig Cennen, sent messengers post-haste to warn John Faireford, canon of St David's and Receiver of Brecon, that the rebels were in control of the greater part of the county of Caermarthen ; the same tale was told by Jankyn Havard, warden of Dinefwr, who emphasised the seriousness of the position with the intelligence that the rebels were resolved to ' march to the town of Brechon for the destruction of the same ' ; and Ralph Monnington held on like grim death in his castle at Llandovery. Rhys ap Gruffydd handed over to Owen the castle of Dryslwyn, and Jenkyn ap Llywelyn of Newcastle Emlyn followed his example, the both men joining the rebel cause. On July 8, Richard Kyngeston, archdeacon of Hereford and 'general administrator' of the marches of South Wales, placed the facts before the king in language which allowed of no misinterpretation.

> From day to day letters are arriving from Wales, by which you may learn that the whole country is lost unless you go there as quick as possible. Be pleased to set forth all your power, and march as well by night as by day, for the salvation of those parts.

Throughout this trying time the Prince Henry was labouring manfully to strengthen the defences on the border : it seemed impossible that a rebel attack could be long delayed.

In July 1403 a Damoclean sword hung perilously over the house of Lancaster. In Wales the royal authority was trampled under foot, and a native-born Welshman styled himself Prince of Wales. There was still danger from the sides of France, Scotland, and Ireland ; and to crown these misfortunes came the treason of the Percies.

The king's refusal to meet his debts to the Percies was bound to lead to trouble between them. The amount of these debts was £20,000, and yet Henry IV. not only refused to meet them, but continued to look to the Percies for the defence of the northern parts of his realm against the Scots. There was another cause of distrust between the king and these powerful subjects. In the previous summer Hotspur had gone into the royal presence with the object of begging the king to assist in securing Sir Edmund Mortimer's release, but he had been met with the taunt that his brother-in-law was a willing prisoner in Owen's hands, and was dismissed with a blow in his face from the royal hand. Men of spirit do not easily forget treatment of this kind, and although the Percies were willing to call themselves 'the king's loyal lieges' one of

them at least nursed a grievance, which could only
be satisfied by the sword.

Despite the news from Wales, Henry IV.—
perhaps because he feared the loyalty of these
Percies and intended to meet it on the spot—
deemed it wiser to march against the Scots who
were threatening an attack on the north of England.
On July 11 he had halted at Lichfield, and it was
there that he learnt that at last the Percies were
in open rebellion against his government. That
dread news had travelled slowly. Hotspur two
days previously had lodged in Chester, having
behind him a considerable force of gentry from the
counties of Lancashire and Cheshire ; and daily
friends were coming in from the troubled parts of
North Wales. With him, too, were the captured
Scottish notables, the chief being the Earl of
Douglas—the prisoners taken at Humbledon over
whose ransoms the king and Percies had wrangled.
There was no subterfuge about Hotspur's action.
He marched, not as a disgruntled subject, but as a
true-born patriot bent upon ridding his country of
a tyrant ; and he catalogued the acts of oppression
and tyranny of which Henry, not now called by
him ' the fourth,' but ' of Lancaster,' was adjudged
to be guilty. He proclaimed that by right the
throne belonged to the boy Edmund Mortimer,
Earl of March ; and that by the sword of the
Percies he would receive his inheritance.

There were many highly-placed men in the
kingdom who were willing to accept Hotspur at
this valuation—powerful influences like Richard
Scrope, Archbishop of York, and even Edward
Plantagenet, Duke of York, who lurked suspiciously
in the background of the treason ; and it was
common knowledge that the rebels marched to
join forces with the forces of Owen Glyn Dŵr of
Wales. From Shrewsbury quietly slipped away

Thomas Percy, Earl of Worcester, in whose charge the Prince Henry had been ; and he quickly made his way to his nephew's camp. The king himself was momentarily paralysed by the misfortune which had overtaken him. He lay at Burton-on-Trent, and did not know whether to go forward against the rebels or retire upon London, the centre of Lancastrian sympathies. The Scottish Earl of March, who was with him, urged him to turn and fight ; and on July 16 writs went out to the sheriffs of eleven counties ordering them to bring their forces to him ' wherever he might be.' On the following day he requested the members of the council (with the exception of the Treasurer) to join him in the field : it was essential that these men should be immediately under his eye in the event of a temporary check to his arms, for they had it in their power to threaten the permanency of the Lancastrian settlement. The council obeyed loyally, and before leaving London had summoned the men of the city, and the counties of Essex, Hertford, and Middlesex to go to Henry's succour.

On July 19 or 20 Hotspur and his men were outside the town of Shrewsbury. Within was the Prince Henry and a small force. The rebels demanded admittance : Henry refused their request. Hotspur thereupon lay about the town, with the purpose of taking it ; but so careless a watch did they keep that the king and his army slipped by their outposts and entered Shrewsbury. The rebel force was then withdrawn about two miles to the north-west of the town, and was arrayed in battle order in front of the hamlet of Berwick. It is difficult accurately to state the strength of the two forces : the Percies may have had with them about 20,000 men, and Henry probably had about the same number, or even less. The news had gone forth that Hotspur meant to give battle on the

23rd. Henry IV. knew that he dare not delay so long, for at any moment in his rear might appear the wild men of Wales, marching pell-mell to aid their north-country friends. For weal or woe he must fight at once.

Early on the eve of St Mary Magdalene's Feast (July 21) he arrayed his men into three battles. The Earl of Stafford commanded the leading battle, Henry IV. the centre, and his son, the Prince Henry, the rear. The king, however, hoped to avoid bloodshed, and sent forward Thomas Prestbury, Abbot of Shrewsbury, to offer terms to Hotspur provided that he and his friends would disperse in peace. In response to these overtures came into the royal camp Thomas Percy, Earl of Worcester, whom the chroniclers make the villain of the drama, which was to be enacted that day.

Resentment and anger stifled in the breast of the earl that ' sweet reasonableness ' so essential in the composure of a bitter quarrel. Straight at the king's head he hurled the taunt : " You are not the rightful heir " ; and he met the royal attempt at conciliation with the brutal observation : " We cannot trust you." Reluctantly Henry ended the audience, saying :

> Then on you must rest the blood shed this day, and not on me.

The earl returned to his friends, and shortly after midday the order was given for battle to commence.

> Then suddenlie blew the trumpets, the kings part crieng St. George vpon them, the aduersaries cried Esperance Persie, and so the two armies furiouslie ioined.

Harvest-time was at hand. The corn stood in the fields yellow and uncut : patches of vetches were scattered over the front. A terrible hail of arrows from the bows of the archers of Cheshire and Flint staggered the onrush of the royal soldiery, and for a moment the royal army was thrown into confusion. The men rallied, stood their ground, and ' the battell began more fierce than ever.'

It was Prince Henry's first real battle. He acquitted himself like a soldier and a man. Early in the fight he was wounded in the face by an arrow, but

> he refused to leave the field lest his departure from amongst his men might happilie haue striken some feare into their harts.

Thomas Elmham, the chronicler, gave a more detailed account of this incident. To the repeated suggestions that he ought to withdraw from the fighting the prince gave reply :

> My lords, far be from me such disgrace, as that, like a poltroon, I should stain my novitiate in arms by flight. If the prince flies, who will wait to end the battle ? Believe it, to be carried back before victory would be to me a perpetual death ! Lead me, I implore you, to the very face of the foe. I would not say to my friends, " Go ye on first to the fight." Be it mine to say, " Follow me, my friends."

How far this is a record of fact or a fiction of the imagination we cannot determine. That Henry was badly wounded is certain ; and his later career shows that he was generously endowed with personal courage.

Hotspur and Douglas flung themselves into the thickest of the fight, resolved to hack their way to the place where stood Henry IV. Time after time they were thrust back, and the lanes through which they had carved their way closed to meet the next onslaught. Hotspur fell, ' and no man wist of whom.' Douglas was taken prisoner : so were the Earl of Worcester and Sir Richard Vernon. When the cry went up that ' Henry Percy is dead ! ' the rebel resistance cracked, and the great battle was over. Chief among the casualties on the royal side was the Earl of Stafford ; but many knights of lesser name fell that day ; and countless scores of simple folks. Contemporaries were agreed that it was one of the bloodiest of battles.

> One of the wyrste bataylys that ever came to Inglende, and unkyndyst.

So wrote one of them : another described it as a day

> rather to be celebrated with teares than triumphs.

The dead, which are said to have numbered about 1600, were huddled for burial into a great trench ; and their memorial is the present Battlefield church, to be founded by Henry IV. a few years later. When the king saw the corpse of Hotspur he wept : it was the reminder that a great friendship was ended, tragically for blame attached to both sides. Tenderly John Talbot, Lord Furnival, bore it away for burial in the church at Whitchurch ; but political expediency made it impossible for the body of Hotspur to rest in such a peaceful spot. A few days later, at the royal command, it was dug up, brought in a common country cart to Shrewsbury, where after being rubbed in salt it was set up between two upright stones in the common pillory. The head was cut off and sent as an adornment for the gate at York, through which men passed on their way northwards to the Percy country. Two days after the battle the Earl of Worcester, Sir Richard Vernon, and a number of other prisoners were summarily executed at Shrewsbury ; and their heads went to grace that gruesome exhibition which mediæval rulers maintained on London Bridge.

The Battle of Shrewsbury had been fought and won ; and Owen Glyn Dŵr had failed to make it a victory for the king's enemies. Where was he? Here we come to one of history's many mysteries. Tradition long maintained that his force was in the locality and that Owen himself watched the fortunes of the fight from a vantage-point, refusing to engage his men. This story can probably be dismissed as thoroughly unreliable ; but it is still difficult to exonerate him from the charge of wilfully failing to come to the assistance of his friends. He was master of the greater part of Wales, and actually at the time of the battle was within reasonable distance of Shrewsbury. It is more than likely that the Welsh tradition of avoiding pitched battles lost for him and his cause an opportunity which was never to occur again.

Prince Henry lay at Shrewsbury recovering from his wound : his father pushed northwards to deal with the factious Earl of Northumberland. Not many days after he had left with the main body of the army, Owen's men appeared in the district north of Shrewsbury, where they did their usual toll of damage ; and in August they were actively engaged in despoiling the southern part of the county of Hereford and the northern districts of Gwent. On the 23rd of that month William Beauchamp, Lord of Abergavenny, wrote a piteous appeal for help ; and eleven days later the record of the rebel successes is taken up by Richard Kyngeston :

> Four hundred of the rebels of Owyn . . . have robbed and captured within your county of Hereforde many men and beasts in great number, our truce notwithstanding.

The mention of the ' truce ' is interesting : it proves that so ineffective was the prince's resistance at this time that the ' commons ' of Hereford had been compelled to make terms with the rebels. Kyngeston followed this letter up with another, dated

6

September 3.   He urged the king to send without delay

> one hundred lances and six hundred archers, until your
> most gracious arrival to the salvation of us all, for other-
> wise . . . in good faith I hold all our country to be
> destroyed, since the hearts of all your faithful lieges in our
> county, with the commons, are utterly lost.

A week later Henry IV. marched into Hereford. He had broken up the Percy rebellion in the north. Beneath the eyeless skeleton of Hotspur king and earl composed their differences—for the moment ; and the former hurried back to deal with the re-bellion in Wales, and the latter to defend his patri-mony against the turbulent Scots.

But experience had taught Henry IV. nothing in the matter of warring against the Welsh.   A week after reaching Hereford, he began another armed progress, passing by way of Hay, Talgarth, Brecon, Dyfynnog, into the vale of Tywi ; and when he halted outside Caermarthen his men had scarcely seen a rebel, although it was known that Owen himself and his captains lurked in the locality. Henry IV. put his half-brother, John Beaufort, Earl of Somerset, in charge of the castle at Caer-marthen, and gave him strict injunctions to repair the town defences, seriously damaged by recent rebel raids.   Then he marched back to Hereford, his men grumbling from lack of food and oppor-tunities of plunder.   No sooner was the royal army out of sight than the rebels were again active ; and John Beaufort quickly decided that he would not remain in Caermarthen ' for anything in the world.'

On the very day on which the royal army entered Hereford (October 3) the constable of Kidwelly penned an urgent dispatch to the king that ' men from France and Bretagne ' had landed to assist Owen.   They were the first-fruits of the negotiations which were being carried on between the Welsh

rebels and Charles VI. of France. The stubborn
loyalty of the Flemings of Pembroke gave the invading army an uncomfortable time ; and they
withdrew by sea to North Wales to assist Owen in
his attack on the great castle of Caernarvon. But
William of Tranmere, the castellan, and a handful
of men beat off every attack, and eventually Owen
and his French friends went off to ravage Lleyn
and Eifionydd. The defences of Criccieth castle
were razed to the ground, and Harlech was hotly
beset.

From the English point of view it looked as
though their doom in Wales was sealed ; and when
parliament met in January 1404 the gloomiest view
of the situation was taken. Obviously they had
little confidence in the king's military methods
against the Welsh rebels : he had marched into
Wales so many times without registering a tangible
success. The time had come to place the direction
of the campaign in other—and more competent—
hands ; and it is significant that such was their
confidence in the ability of the young prince that
they selected him for the task of bringing Owen to
book. He was to be assisted by Thomas, Earl of
Arundel, and Edward, Duke of York. Then with
the usual indifference which parliament-men have
towards the conduct of military affairs they neglected
to vote him the money without which successful
campaigning in Wales was impossible.

So serious was the position in June that Richard
Kyngeston was compelled to write ' in haste ' to
Henry IV. :

> The Welsh rebels in great numbers have entered
> Archenfield, and they have burnt houses, killed the
> inhabitants, taken prisoners, and ravaged the country
> to the great dishonour of our king and the unsupportable
> damage of the country.

He went on to say that Owen's men were ' resolved

to make an attack ' within the next eight days ;
and he concluded with a pathetic appeal for a loyal
subject :

> And for God His sake remember that honourable and
> valiant man, the Lord of Bergavenny, who is on the point
> of destruction if he be not rescued.

The prince had moved his headquarters to
Worcester. Until the government supplied him
with adequate funds for the conduct of a campaign
he could do nothing. To his father he wrote on
June 26, with exemplary forbearance :

> I will do all I possibly can to resist the rebels and save
> the English country, to the utmost of my little power . . .
> ever trusting in your High Majesty to remember my poor
> estate, and that I have not the means of continuing here
> without the adoption of some other measures for my main-
> tenance, and that the expenses are unsupportable for me.
> And may you thus make an ordinance for me with speed,
> that I may do good service, to your honour and the pre-
> servation of my humble state.

To the council, however, his appeal was more
direct :

> . . . unless you make provision for us, we shall be com-
> pelled to depart with disgrace and mischief, and the
> country will be utterly destroyed, which God forbid.
> And now since we have shown you the perils and mischiefs,
> for God His sake make your ordinance in time, for the
> salvation of the honour of our sovereign lord the King our
> father, of ourselves, and of the whole realm. And may
> Our Lord protect you, and give you grace to do right.

Nor did he let matters rest at that : within a couple
of days he sent another urgent message to the
council, emphasising the impossibility of holding
out unless they gave him the support he asked for.

The prince faced the situation squarely. Richard
Beauchamp, Earl of Warwick, was sent into south
Herefordshire to check the rebel ravages. He
forced them to fight at ' vynydd Kamstwm ' (Camp-

stone hill) in the neighbourhood of Grosmont, and inflicted on them a sharp reverse ; but for some reason or other (the information about the engagement is tantalisingly scanty) he did—or could—not follow up whatever advantage he had ; and Owen fell back on the Mortimer lands at Usk, Trelech, and Caerleon. There is a tradition that Prince Henry then took up his headquarters in his birthplace, and fought a drawn battle with Owen at Craig-y-dorth, two miles south of Monmouth. That a battle was fought there is certain, but there is no evidence that Henry was engaged, and it is more probable that the royal troops were led by Beauchamp. Drawn, the battle might be ; but Owen quickly removed from that neighbourhood, and in August was ravaging as far afield as Salop, where the ' poor commons ' were praying the council to allow them to make a truce with the rebels.

On July 14 a formal treaty of alliance was concluded between Charles VI. and ' the illustrious and most dreaded Owen, prince of the Welsh,' in the house of Arnaud of Corbie, the chancellor of France. The contracting parties bound themselves to make common cause against ' Henry of Lancaster,' and definite promises of French help were given. The success of Owen's arms and diplomacy had the effect of drawing many to his side : in the latter part of 1404 he received the allegiance of one who had been a loyal friend of Henry IV., namely, John Trefor, Bishop of St Asaph ; and also of a competent ecclesiastical lawyer, Lewis Byford, whom he made Bishop of Bangor. The fall of the castle of Aberystwyth—the great de Clare stronghold which had withstood so many desperate assaults—gave Owen an official and dignified headquarters for his government ; and already Harlech acted as his domestic residence.

The council had done little to meet the prince's demands. It is true that in August they had voted him a limited supply of money, and had a few weeks later provided him with a fairly competent force of men-at-arms and archers ; but these measures were quite inadequate to the needs of the situation. In November 1404 news came that Sir Laurence Berkerolles was desperately held in his castle of Coety in Morgannwg, and the sheriffs of four counties were commanded to take each a force of

> twenty men-at-arms and two hundred archers . . . to Henry, prince of Wales, and Thomas, the king's sons, at Hereford.

The expedition was successful : Coety was relieved.

Henry undoubtedly spent the greater part of the winter months on the border, watching the situation. In January 1405 he learnt that a great rebel force was being mustered in order to invade England ; and once again he urged the council to give him the means to prevent such a calamity. Apparently this request did not fall upon deaf ears : reinforcements were sent to him at Hereford, and a royal force was posted at Monmouth. The leader of the Welsh attacking force was Rhys Gethin ' the Fierce,' as capable a soldier as Owen had in his army, though reckless in battle. He ploughed his way through Morgannwg and entered Gwent. A terrible harrying of the lordship of Wentllwch took place, but whether he took the castles of Newport, Caerleon, and Usk or detached small bodies of men to mask the movements of their garrisons is not known. He certainly avoided the Beauchamp lordship of Bergavenny (Abergavenny), and hurled his entire force on Grosmont, a Lancastrian castle, then held by Prince Henry himself and a handful of men. Of the fight that took place on that March day no better account could be given than that which Prince Henry penned to his royal father the night after the battle.

My most redoubted and most sovereign lord and father, I commend myself to your majesty, requesting your gracious blessing. My most redoubtable and most sovereign lord and father, I verily pray that God may show you His miraculous power in all parts. Praised be He in all His works : for on Wednesday, the 11th day of March, your rebels of the parts of Glamorgan, Morgannwg, Usk, Netherwent, and Overwent, were assembled to the number of 8000 people, by their own account, and went the same Wednesday in the morning and burnt part of your town at Grosmouth within your lordship of Monmouth. And I at once sent off my very dear cousin the lord Talbot, and the small body of mine own household, and with them the valiant and faithful knights, William Neuport and Johan Greindre, who were but a small force in all ; but it is well to be seen that the victory is not in the multitude of people, and this was well shown there, but in the power of God and in the aid of the blessed Trinity, your people held the field and conquered the said rebels, and killed of them according to fair account in the field to the time of their return from the pursuit, some say eight hundred, some say a thousand, being questioned upon pain of death. Whether it be the one or the other I will not contend. And in order to inform you fully of all that is done, I send you one worthy of credit, my loyal servant and the bearer of these (dispatches) who was at the engagement, and did his duty most faithfully as he has done on all occasions. And such amend has God granted to you for the burning of your houses in the above-mentioned town. And of prisoners there was taken only one, and he was lately a great chieftain among them, and whom I would have sent but that he is not yet able to ride at his ease. And concerning the government which I propose to effect after these (events), may it please your highness to vouchsafe full credit to the bearer of these dispatches in that he will show to your same highness on my part. And I pray to God that he may preserve you always in joy and honour, and grant to me that I may (be able to) solace you speedily with other good news.

Written at Hereford, the said Wednesday in the night.
Your most humble and obedient son,
HENRY.

The prince did not miss his opportunities : a small force hung upon the retreating rebel army, and brought it to battle near the town of Usk. Tradition has long maintained that in this engagement Tudur, Owen's brother, was slain ; but it is not easy to prove this. On the other hand, among the prisoners was Gruffydd, Owen's son ; and it is known that the entire rebel force was driven helter-skelter out of the district. These two reverses did irreparable damage to Owen's cause in the south-eastern districts of Wales, where many of the inhabitants now returned to their allegiance.

Two complications, however, arose in the summer. First, in order to create a diversion in Owen's favour, the old Earl of Northumberland again rebelled ; but Henry IV. scotched the movement before it had gathered strength ; and the earl and his principal supporters were compelled to seek sanctuary in Scotland. Second, in July a great French force, commanded by such notable captains as Jean de Hangest, the Sire of Hugueville, and Robert de la Heuze, nicknamed la Borgne (One-eyed), was landed at Milford Haven. After a considerable amount of skirmishing in south-west Wales this force, now considerably strengthened by the advent of Owen himself and some 10,000 men, marched towards the border ; and about the middle of August took up position within ten miles of Worcester. But there was no great battle, and after eyeing the English force opposite them for some days, Owen and his French friends withdrew. Nor did this superior force show any inclination to fight when Henry IV. marched in September to relieve Coety, again besieged by the rebels ; though it is true that on its return either through or across the Rhondda valley the royal army suffered considerable inconvenience from a Welsh chieftain, who had the picturesque name of Cadwgan-of-the-battle-axe.

But the power of the rebel resistance was weakening. The details of the engagements which were fought in the autumn of 1405 have not survived the passing of time ; but it is known that they went against Owen. Gruffydd Yonge, his ' chancellor,' his brother-in-law, John Hanmer, and his secretary, Owen ap Gruffydd ap Rhisiart, were taken prisoners, and ' many Welshmen were killed.' The French found Wales a poor country to campaign in, and after differences with the Welsh withdrew the greater part of their force.

Nevertheless the people of the centre and north of Wales were unwaveringly loyal to Owen's cause ; and he could count upon the friendship of the old Earl of Northumberland. It was some time early in 1406 that the earl, Owen, and Sir Edmund Mortimer made the agreement which is known as the *Tripartite Indenture*. The realm was to be parcelled into three principalities : Owen was to rule in Wales, Northumberland in the north, and Mortimer in the south of England. It was a brave reply to the quiet but efficient methods which the young Henry was employing for the pacification of Wales. We are only vaguely aware of the nature of the prince's activities, but they were striking enough to cause the ' faithful commons ' on April 3 to pray their king to convey their thanks for the services which his son had rendered the State in repressing the rebels in Wales. The thanks of these ' faithful commons ' were more spectacularly given on June 7 by the Speaker himself, addressing the king ' seated on his royal throne.' The record relates that

He (the Speaker) made a commendation of the many excellencies and virtues which habitually dwelt in the honourable person of the prince, and especially of the humility and obedience which he bears towards our sovereign lord the king, his father, so that there can be no person, of any degree whatever, who entertains or shows more honour and reverence of humbleness and obedience to his father than he shows in his honourable person. Secondly, how God hath granted to him, and endowed him with a good heart and courage, as much as was ever needed in any such prince in the world. And, thirdly, (he spoke) of the great virtue which God hath granted to him in especial manner, that howsoever much he hath set his mind upon any important undertaking to the best of his own judgment, yet for the great confidence which he placed in his council, and in their loyalty, judgment, and discretion, he would kindly and graciously be influenced, and conform himself to his council and their ordinances, according to what seemed best to them, setting aside entirely his own will and pleasure ; from which it is probable that, by the grace of God, very great comfort and honour and advantage will flow hereafter. For this the said Commons humbly thank our Lord Jesus Christ, and they pray for its good continuance.

After such a fulsome testimony of the prince's virtues could any assembly refuse to recognise him as the legal heir to the throne occupied by his father ? Or could any father refuse his son that right, after listening to the Speaker's petition ?

That item of business transacted, the Commons humbly begged the king to send his son into Wales without delay, for the air was filled with rumours that the Earl of Northumberland and Owen were concocting a great military movement. Nothing, however, came to it ; though the prince was busily engaged in Wales for the greater part of the remainder of the year ; and we get a glimpse of his methods in the record of a special commission which sat at Beaumaris on November 10 to deal with some two thousand applications for pardon from inhabitants of Anglesey. It was inconceivable to the mediæval mind that a pardon should be granted without due and proper payment of a fine : at Beaumaris, however, the prince's financial demands were surprisingly modest.

In the summer of 1407 Prince Henry made a bold
bid to wrest from Owen the castle of Aberystwyth.
Doubtless the English had heard the tale which
circulated freely among their Welsh enemies—that
with the fall of the de Clare fortress the cause of
Owen would be hopelessly lost.   Nothing therefore
was to be left to chance ; and men, guns, and stores
were concentrated on the Welsh border against the
opening of the campaign.   A number of ' gonnes '
were sent to the front by sea from Bristol ; others
made the journey overland.   *The Kinge's Gonne*, a
magnificent cannon weighing four and a half tons,
went by road to Aberystwyth, and had in its am-
munition train 538 lb. of powder, 971 lb. of saltpetre,
and 303 lb. of sulphur.   But artillery in a fifteenth-
century campaign had its disadvantages : we learn,
for example, that one cannon ' burst ' when Anthony
Gunner was ' proving it ' at Worcester prior to the
march into Wales ; and two other ' gonnes'—*The
Kinge's Daughter* and *The Messenger*—blew out
their breeches during the operations before Aberystwyth.

It had been arranged that Henry IV. himself
should lead the army into Wales, but falling a victim
to the ' seasonal pestilence ' the command devolved
upon the prince.   He had with him the most
competent military captains of the day—Edward,
Duke of York, Richard, Earl of Warwick, Sir John
Oldcastle, stout defender of the royal interests along
the middle reaches of the Wye, Sir Francis Court,
leader of the Flemish attacks on Owen in Pembroke,
Sir John Greyndor, John Touchet, Lord Audley,
Ralph Monnington, Thomas, Lord Carew, and many
knights of lesser fame ; and the ' general commander
and enginer in the timber works ' was Thomas,
Lord Berkeley, a leader equally at home on land and
sea.

The castle at Aberystwyth was held for Owen

by one of the most daring of his captains—Rhys
ap Gruffydd ap Llywelyn ab Ieuan Fychan of
Cardigan, commonly called Rhys the Black. Attack
after attack was beaten off, and it was only when
supplies were running short and Owen showed no
inclination to relieve the garrison that Rhys the
Black entertained the suggestion for a parley. That
parley, arranged by Richard ap Gruffyd, Abbot of
Ystrad-fflur, ' for the saving of human blood,' took
place on September 12. Besiegers and besieged
met before the altar and received from the hands
of Richard Courtenay, a brilliant young man who
had not long before been appointed chancellor of
the university of Oxford, ' the Body of our Lord,'
upon which they swore solemnly to obey the conditions of the indentures for capitulation. The
Welsh promised to hand over to the prince the castle
unless they were relieved by Owen

> between the 24th October next coming at sun-rising and
> the Feast of All Saints next to come (November 1).

This typical mediæval arrangement allowed the
prince to leave Aberystwyth, though it was of course
understood that he would return in time to try
conclusions with the Welsh in the prescribed week.
A small English force of 120 men-at-arms and 360
archers went to Ystrad-fflur to await events. Rhys
the Black at once went in search of Owen in order
to acquaint him with the terms of the capitulation.
He found him in North Wales, and was promptly
told that unless he repudiated his pledges and
admitted Owen and his men to the castle at once he
would lose his head.

A terrible winter followed : no man could
remember its like. Snow lay deep on the ground
from December until the end of March, and the
greater part of Europe was for weeks in the icy
grip of frost. At the end of January that tiresome

old rebel, the Earl of Northumberland, staked his last throw in his attempt to overthrow Henry IV., but the quick action of a sheriff of Yorkshire forced him to fight a losing battle at Bramham Moor, and in the fighting he was killed. No longer had Henry IV. any need to fear the power of the Percies.

In the summer of 1408 Prince Henry renewed his efforts to take Aberystwyth. This time he meant effectively to tie Owen's hands ; for while he himself conducted operations against Rhys the Black his two captains, Gilbert, Lord Talbot, and John, Lord Furnival, were besieging Harlech, the fortress which was Owen's domestic headquarters. It was in this summer that the prince pacified the vale of Tywi, which had been wholly in sympathy with the rebel cause ; and there is evidence that even in Caernarvon and Anglesey the people were showing a disposition to lose interest in Owen's fortunes. Rhys the Black was starved into surrender in the late summer, and he was allowed by the prince to march out with the honours of war. Harlech fell some time before January 1409, and with its capture Prince Henry gained some notable prisoners — Owen's wife, two daughters, and the three Mortimer grandchildren. Sir Edmund Mortimer had died during the siege.

The end of the greatest rebellion in the history of the people of Wales was in sight. Owen's sons, with the exception of Maredudd, were slain or captives ; and his wife and two daughters languished in the Tower. Here and there resolute men stood loyally by their allegiance to him. In a raid on the Salop border in 1410 three of his staunchest friends fell into the hands of Edward Charlton, Lord of Powys—Rhys the Black, Philpot Skidmore of Troy, and Rhys ap Tudur of Penmynydd—and the inevitable fate of death was meted out to them, their heads adorning the gates of Shrewsbury and

Chester, and London Bridge. Owen himself slid
quietly away into an obscurity from which historians
cannot drag him, and it has been left to the weavers
of tales to relate of his later years. To the bitter
end he was unconquerable, for he spurned even the
generous offers of pardon which the prince, by that
time elevated to the throne of England, offered
him.

After 1409 Prince Henry was not actively
engaged in Welsh affairs. The ill-health of his
father, assuming now the somewhat alarming form
of epileptic seizures, caused the council to advise
that he should remain in attendance on the king.
He had now come to manhood ; and strong men
were needed to direct the nation's affairs. For the
greater part of the preceding nine years he had
been at war in Wales, and that experience had
taught him the minutiæ of war-craft, which were to
stand him in such good stead in the dominions of
the king of France. Not once but many times he
had seen demonstrated the terrific missile power of the
Welsh archers, and the deadly cunning of the Welsh
knifemen ; and it is significant that he used both
types of soldiery in his French campaigns. But
it was not Prince Henry alone who benefited by the
experiences of the war against Owen Glyn Dŵr.
The captains who fought with him in Wales were
the captains who won such high renown for English
leadership overseas.

CHAPTER THREE

Father and Son

As early as 1407 the council urged that Prince
Henry ought to remain in attendance upon his
father. The king's health was failing. He had
been attacked by strange fits of fainting, and the
chief men of the realm, too deeply committed to
the Lancastrian usurpation to entertain any thought
of a change of dynasty, were alarmed lest death
should provoke civil strife in a land already much
troubled by foes. The seriousness of Henry IV.'s
illness was carefully hidden from the majority of
his subjects : the fact that no parliament was
summoned between December 1407 and January
1409 suggests that indisposition prevented Henry
from transacting the normal business of the State ;
and it is known that two Italian physicians—David
di Nigarelli and Pietro di Alcobasse—were brought
to England to check the ravages of a disease which
apparently had completely baffled the royal doctor,
Master Malvern. Whether the suggestion that the
prince should attend upon his father came from
Henry IV. himself or was pressed upon him by the
members of his council is not known ; but the
advice was duly heeded, and it was in this period
that Prince Henry began to participate in the
political affairs of the nation.

Unfortunately the record of the next four or
five years of the prince's life is blurred by tales of
reckless living and unfilial conduct ; and so realistic
are the details, and so widely believed, that we
are often at a loss to know where truth begins and

legend ends. On the one hand, there is a picture of a prince loyally playing his part in the affairs of State, and in the intervals of his father's indisposition presiding over the meetings of council. Here is the serious-minded youth, eager to learn the tricks of statecraft, and to prepare himself for the duties of kingship which would devolve upon him at his father's death. On the other hand, are tales of loose-living and madcap pranks, done in the company of the lowest and most disreputable comrades ; and instead of being the strong arm upon which an invalid father could lean he is the petulant opponent of his policy—so much so that he cannot even escape from the charge of wanting to thrust himself into his father's throne.

While the tales of this misspent youth were not created by Shakespeare it was that prince of Elizabethan dramatists who popularised them ; and it has been frequently observed that many people are content to learn their history from the historical plays of Shakespeare. Thus, it has been taken for granted that in his youth the prince was an *enfant terrible*, the darling of the prostitutes in the London stews, the terror of the watch, and the best customer of Lewis John, the Welshman who owned one of the ' bright spots ' of fifteenth-century London in the Vintry. Mankind's morbid interest in human frailty makes it impossible for these stories to perish. And indeed why should they perish, when in all probability they contain germs of historical truth ?

Ever since the sixteenth century Englishmen have taken infinite delight in these stories ; and the secret of this pleasure surely lies in the fact that the prince's youthful indiscretions were proof of his manliness. It was no namby-pamby prince who frequented the lowest taverns in East Cheap, made companions of Falstaff and Bardolph, used the coarsest oaths, played the cutpurse, and wined and wenched like a hardened reprobate : it was a young man wallowing in the restless energies of manhood.

Shakespeare was more concerned with dramatic possibilities than accurate history. He wished to present to the London playgoers a picture of hero-kingship ; and in order to make the details of that picture stand out in bolder relief he used the powerful contrast of the ever-popular theme—a rake's progress to virtue. The ' gods ' in the Elizabethan playhouse howled with merriment at the antics of the rake-prince and his companions. To the London journeymen and apprentices that fooling humanised the victor of Agincourt : it revealed him in what they believed was his true character—a man and not a plaster-saint ; and as a result they were the better able to understand and appreciate the glorious achievements of Henry V. and his subjects on the battlefields of France and Normandy. Shakespeare made Henry V. the living embodiment of that Elysium to which an ageing mankind inevitably turns—' the good old days.' The wonderful record of his kingship helped men to forget the senseless caste struggles of the wars of the Roses, and to inspire boundless confidence in the future. The deeds of Englishmen in Henry V.'s time had set the whole of Europe talking ; and the Elizabethan Englishman meant Europe again to stand in awe of his native country. When Shakespeare's plays were being produced the eyes of the people of England were turned towards the High Seas and the lands across them. English pride was wounded when the subjects of His Most Catholic Majesty, the king of Spain, claimed the right to those seas and lands ; and their breasts were filled with patriotic emotion when news came—as it frequently did—that some

7

daring English sailor had challenged the Spaniards
to prove that right by arms. The audience who
watched a performance of *King Henry the Fifth* saw
a great similarity between the odds against which
Henry fought at Agincourt and those which faced,
say, Sir Richard Grenville ' at Flores in the Azores,'
Henry V.'s military genius had given Englishmen
a place in the sun ; and for this magnificent gift a
later generation was willing to pardon his youthful
indiscretions and to think nothing of his opposition
to his father. Did not the Elizabethan Englishman regard Henry IV. as a cold, calculating
monarch, a usurper, probably a murderer, and
certainly the instigator of death by burning as
the punishment for defiance of catholic doctrines ?
The facts that Henry V. was also a usurper and the
scourge of the Lollards were passed over—or, more
accurately, obliterated by the glories of his reign.

How far, then, do these stories represent true
facts of history ? This is a question which every
biographer of Henry V. must attempt to answer ;
and at the outset it must be admitted that the
solution will be more or less unsatisfactory, since it
cannot always be presented with the accompanying
proofs.

Was Henry V. a dissolute young man ? Two
chroniclers, who lived near enough his times to be
classed as contemporaries, state definitely that he
was fond of women.

> He fervently followed the service of Venus as well
> as of Mars, as a young man might he burned with her
> torches, and other insolences accompanied the years of
> his untamed youth.

Elmham's verdict is endorsed by the evidence of
the Italian Titus Livius, who wrote :

> He exercised meanly the feats of Venus and Mars and
> other pastimes of his youth for so long as the king his
> father lived.

It would be difficult to impugn the veracity of this evidence. Indeed, is it necessary to attempt to do so ? Healthy youth is notorious for its moral recklessness ; and society only despises young men for sowing wild oats if the harvest is conspicuously discreditable. Life on the Welsh front, burdened as it was for the prince by endless worries connected with the campaign against Owen Glyn Dŵr, demanded relaxations ; and men returning from the wars, as many will recall from their experiences in the Great War of 1914–18, are not particularly discriminating in their entertainments.

Fifteenth-century London was by no means a dull place to live in. It had an amazing wealth of taverns, whose cellars were well stocked with Gascon and other wines ; and the cookshops were capable of producing delicacies which are unknown to us to-day. No rigid licensing laws compelled revellers to go to their beds before their thirst was assuaged ; and although the watch in the various wards of the city were supposed to prevent disturbances in the streets no one cared very much about them or their authority, and evidence suggests that they generally had the facility of a Victorian policeman for avoiding trouble. On the river side, near the Church of St. Mary Overy, were the stews—the brothels and houses of assignation : here men and women met in delicious abandon to ' exercise the feats of Venus '; and though the fifteenth-century husband certainly possessed great authority over his wife he could not prevent her, if she was so minded, from entertaining a lover in the solar when perhaps he was attending a ' mornspeech ' or ' drinking ' at the local gild-house.

It is quite conceivable, and by no means unnatural, therefore, that Prince Henry celebrated his return to London from the Welsh border by an ' evening out.' As the eldest son of the king of

England he could not expect to escape recognition, and the gossips would assuredly see to it that the most innocent of pranks were magnified into heinous moral lapses.   Men who are fond of the companion-ship of women inevitably run the risk of being paraded before society as adulterers and fornicators by the less charitable—but in their own estimation eminently respectable—members of the community ; and it is quite conceivable that Prince Henry suffered considerably from such people.   It can be argued that it is to his credit that his moral behaviour is stigmatised only by a general statement ;   for mediæval chroniclers had as great an appreciation of the sensational as the modern news editor, and nothing would have given them greater pleasure than to give the public details of the prince's *affaires*.   There was no virtue in concealing his immorality in an age which took a very tolerant view of a great man's amours.   Did not the prince's grandfather, old John of Gaunt, live for more than twenty years with his mistress, Katherine Swynford ? No one thought the worse of him for that : indeed the age had witnessed the spectacle of a legitimisa-tion of the children born out of wedlock, and even Holy Church had given her blessing to the arrange-ment.

The evidence of Elmham and Livius, therefore, suggests that in his youth Prince Henry was guilty of certain moral indiscretions ; but it does not bring against him the charge—not infrequently made in a later age—of indiscriminate wenching in some of the most ' doubtful ' districts of London.   If he ever went to the stews, then he was merely doing what half the youth of the nobility did at that time ; and habits have not greatly changed though the location of the houses of assignation has altered from genera-tion to generation in London.

Turning next to the subject of the prince's

pranks in and about the taverns of East Cheap, it is
not difficult to prove that Shakespeare's dramatic
tale is without any stable foundation in history.
First, let us attempt to place the prince's inseparable
companions in that tale—Sir John Falstaff and
Bardolph. In *King Henry the Fourth* the former
is portrayed as a most disreputable person ; and
even a dissolute prince can tell him to his face that
he is

> fat-witted with drinking old sack, and unbuttoning thee
> after supper, and sleeping upon benches after noon.

He is ' a whoreson round man,' whose grey hairs
should have taught him greater discretion. Bardolph is the despicable coward, who would run away
even though he had fire and sword on his side ; and
in *King Henry the Fifth* Shakespeare even makes
the boy show his contempt for him.

> For Bardolph, he is white-livered and red-faced ; by
> the means whereof, 'a faces it out, but fights not.

In this play Bardolph is hanged by Henry's orders
for looting a church on the march towards Agincourt.

Now it happens, as Professor Mowat has pointed
out, that living contemporaneously with Henry V.
were men bearing names similar to those of Shakespeare's characters—Falstaff and Bardolph ; but
they were more or less respectable members of
society, and from the record of their lives it is inconceivable to think that they should ever do the
things which Falstaff and Bardolph did.

At Caister, in Norfolk, lived a certain Sir John
Fastolf. He was about ten years older than Henry
V. ; he fought at Agincourt as an esquire ; and in
Henry V.'s reign was entrusted with an adminis-
trative post in the conquered French territory. In
the following reign this man won fame and obloquy :

he won the 'battle of the Herrings,' but lost the
fight at Patay ; and as a result of the latter was
accused—quite groundlessly—of cowardice. He
died in 1459, leaving behind him a reputation for
integrity in public life, a miserly management of
his own estates, and an interest in education ; for
not only did he subscribe handsomely towards the
endowment of the school of philosophy at Cambridge, but he left in his will money for the founding
of a college at Caister. [This legacy was diverted
to the use of Magdalen College in the university of
Oxford.]

Furthermore, there lived at the same time
another knight of the same name, but described as
' of Nacton,' wherever that might be ; and a record
of 1403 supplies the information that this Sir John
Fastolf was committed to prison for contempt of
court. To endeavour to argue that a committal
for contempt of court is proof of a lawless nature
would be dangerously stupid.

Nor is it easier to place Shakespeare's Bardolph.
Two men in the period bore this name. They were
Thomas, fifth Baron Bardolph, and his brother, Sir
William Bardolph. The former was deeply implicated in the rebellion of the Percies, and died of
wounds which he received at Bramham Moor when
Sir Thomas Rokeby, sheriff of Yorkshire, dealt the
Percy insurrection its death-blow. In *King Henry
the Fourth* Shakespeare correctly describes this man
as ' Lord Bardolph.' Sir William Bardolph, as far
as can be ascertained, never swerved from his
allegiance. He was entrusted by Henry IV. with
the work of conducting delicate negotiations in
France, and later held the important office of
captain of the castle of Calais : in short, a man of
the highest character.

It is obvious, therefore, that these men were not
the originals of Shakespeare's characters ; and we

are driven to the conclusion that Falstaff and
Bardolph are creations of his dramatic genius, and
were used by him as high-lights in his characterisa-
tion of Prince Henry as the rake. In this guise
they have served their purpose well—so well that
their unsavoury habits and evil ways have done
much to create an entirely unhistorical picture of
the prince's character.

In one particular history is on Shakespeare's
side : it cannot be denied that Prince Henry had
an intimate connection with that part of London
called East Cheap. On March 18 his father gave
him as a private residence the ' stately hostel ' of
Coldharbour in East Cheap. This mansion had
been in the possession of the De Bohun family, and
came to Henry IV. on the death of his first wife,
Mary de Bohun ; and there Prince Henry resided,
when in London, until he came to the throne in
1413. It is to be expected that his London residence
should be the headquarters of his party (for as we
shall see he had a party) ; and there is no doubt
that from time to time were entertained within its
walls some of the young men with whom Henry
had made friends during his active service in Wales.
In the wildness of youth they might even decide
upon a tour of the local taverns, and on such an
expedition a good deal of horse-play might be
indulged in. Prince Henry certainly was always
accessible to his subjects, and except on State
occasions he progressed through London in a free-
and-easy way, more like an ordinary citizen than
the heir-apparent to the throne. Thus, it is quite
likely that he was known to the Londoners as a
hale-fellow-well-met—a prince who could drink his
pot with the next, cosset a pretty serving-wench,
and perhaps go home tipsy.

It was in 1410 that an incident occurred which
caused considerable excitement in London, chiefly

because it involved the king's sons. It was recorded
by John Stow, the sixteenth-century historiographer
of London :

> In the year 1410, upon the eve of St. John the Baptist
> (June 23) the king's sons, Thomas and John, being in
> East-cheap at supper, or rather breakfast (for it was after
> the watch was broken up, betwixt two and three of the
> clock after midnight), a great debate happened between
> their men and other of the court, which lasted an hour,
> even until the mayor and sheriffs, with other citizens
> appeased the same : for the which afterwards the said
> mayor, aldermen, and sheriffs were sent for to answer
> before the king ; his sons and divers lords being highly
> moved against the city. At which time William Gascoigne,
> chief justice, required the mayor and aldermen, for the
> citizens, to put them in the king's grace. Whereunto they
> answered that they had not offended, but according to the
> law had done their best in stinting debate and maintaining
> of the peace : upon which answer the king remitted all
> his ire, and dismissed them.

No mention is made by Stow of Prince Henry
in this record, and we are bound to exclude him
altogether from the incident, unless, of course, the
words ' other of the court ' refer to members of the
prince's household at *Coldharbour.* That Thomas
and John—and even Humphrey—were wild youths
we know ; but even their wildness was not of a
very terrible kind. They may on this occasion
have been entertained by their elder brother at his
London home ; but even this is doubtful, and in
the absence of more positive evidence the only
possible explanation is that the affray in East
Cheap was the natural outcome of a quarrel between
the liveried retainers of two rival factions—a
common enough experience in fifteenth-century
England.

According to Stow's account William Gascoigne,
chief justice, plays a somewhat sycophantic part
in the proceedings which were ultimately brought
against the authorities of London. As a good judge

he should have been the first to recognise that they had done nothing more than their duty in dispersing the brawlers : instead he is found advising the mayor and aldermen to put themselves in the king's mercy—in other words, to plead guilty. It is to their credit that they spurned that advice, and behaving like men, defended their action. Yet by the sixteenth century this same Gascoigne is metamorphosised into the fearless judge, who in his administration of equal justice to the king's subjects was not afraid to commit to prison the Prince of Wales for contempt of court. This legend has been dramatised, and in countless popular history books clothed with the robes of historical veracity. In point of fact it first appeared in *The Boke named the Gouvernour*, written by Sir Thomas Elyot in the reign of Henry VIII.

The moste renomed prince, Kynge Henry the fifte, late kynge of Englande, during the life of his father was noted to be fierie and of wanton courage. It hapned that one of his servantes whom he well favoured, for felony by hym committed, was arrayned at the kynges benche ; whereof he being advertised, and incensed by light persones, aboute hym, in furious rage came hastily to the barre, where his servant stode as a prisoner, and commaunded him to be ungyved and sette at libertie, where at alle men were abasshed, reserved the chief justice, who humbly exhorted the prince to be contented that his servant might be ordred accordyng to the auncient lawes of this realme ; or, if he wolde have him saved from the rigour of the lawes he sholde obtain, if he myghte, from the kynge his father his gracious pardon, whereby no law or justice should be derogate. With which answere the prince nothynge appeased, but rather more inflamed, endevored hym self to take away his servant. The juge consideringe the perilous example and inconvenience that might thereby ensue, with a valiant spirit and courage commaunded the prince upon his alegeance to leve the prisoner and depart his way. With which commandment the prince, being set in all fury, all chafed and in a terrible maner, came up to the place of jugment, men thinkyng that he wolde have slayne the juge, or have done hym some damage. But the juge,

> sitting styll, without moving, declarying the majestie of
> the kynges place of jugement, and with an assured and
> bolde countenance, hadde to the prince these words
> folowyng : Sir, remembre yourself : I kepe here the place
> of the king, your soveraigne lorde and father, to whom
> you owe double obedience . . . And now for your con-
> tempt and disobedience, go you to the prisone of the
> kynges benche, where unto I commit you. . . . With
> which wordes being abasshed, and also wondering at the
> marvailous gravitie of the worshipful Justice, the noble
> prince, laying his weapon aparte, doinge reverence, de-
> parted and went to the kynges benche as he was com-
> manded.

Shakespeare could not resist such a story : not only
did he identify the servant as Bardolph, but he
emphasised the nobility of Henry's character by
making him, after his accession, confirm Gascoigne
in his office as Chief Justice.

As many writers have pointed out, such an
incident could not hope to escape notice by contemporary chroniclers. A king's son—and such a
popular young man—committed to prison : what
a titbit in their narratives ! There is no record
that Prince Henry was ever committed to prison :
as a matter of fact, the story is older than his times,
being told about Edward I.'s punishment of his
son, Edward, on the occasion when he insulted one
of the royal ministers. Shakespeare's historical
' howler ' of the reappointment of Gascoigne as
Chief Justice is at once nailed down by the fact
Henry gave that office to William Hankeford
when the time came to distribute portfolios and
offices.

Another popular story is that the prince delighted in playing the part of cutpurse in London's
streets. Here again Stow's record must supply
the details :

> . . . while his father lived, being accompanied by some
> of his young lords and gentlemen, he would wait in dis-

guised array for his own receivers and distress them of
their money, and sometimes at such enterprises both he
and his companions were surely beaten, and when his
receivers made to him their complaints how they were
robbed in their coming to him, he would give them their
discharge of so much money as they had lost, besides that
they should not depart from him without great rewards
for their trouble and vexation, especially they should be
rewarded that best had resisted him and his company
and of whom he had received the greatest and most
strokes.

This, too, must be dismissed as a piece of delightful
fiction, the only foundation for which is the general
historical truth that the prince was not a plaster-
saint in his youth.

Let us now look at the other picture—that
which reveals Prince Henry as an active member
of the government.

In 1409 he was appointed Warden of the Cinque
Ports and Constable of Dover—offices which carried
with them a salary of £300 a year, and involved
considerable responsibilities. The Cinque Ports were
the depots of the mediæval English navy : their
charters stipulated that they must provide the king
with so many ships, properly manned and equipped
for fighting ; and it must not be forgotten that
throughout the mediæval period there was never
peace in the Narrow Seas. The official truces made
by English and French governments were ignored
by the bands of corsairs—from both countries
incidentally—which preyed upon merchant shipping
to their hearts' content ; and depredatory raids on
seaport towns on either side of the Channel were
common occurrences. Moreover, on the same day
as Henry IV. gave his eldest son the residence of
Coldharbour—March 18, 1410—the council confirmed his appointment as the Captain of Calais, in
succession to John, Earl of Somerset, his half-uncle,
who had died a few days previously. This post

was even more important than that of Warden of
the Cinque Ports, for Calais was the most important
base held by the English in France, and only men
of tried experience and undoubted integrity were
entrusted with the delicate and difficult task of
governing the town of Calais.

Prince Henry had been a member of the council
for some years, and when illness made it impossible
for his father to attend meetings the prince presided. His presidency was naturally limited by
the duration of the king's indisposition : when
Henry IV. was well enough to attend the meetings
of the council the prince vacated the chair in his
father's favour. Less than a week after Prince
Henry's appointment as Captain of Calais the
Commons, through the mouth of Thomas Chaucer,
son of Geoffrey Chaucer the poet, begged the king
to constitute a new council ; and on the following
May 2 they asked for the names of the members
to be submitted to them. It is here that we begin
to scent a political crisis. Henry IV. told the
Commons that a number of people had asked to be
excused from service on the council, and then
announced that he had nominated his son, Prince
Henry, the bishops of Bath, Durham, and Worcester,
the Earls of Arundel and Westmoreland, and Lord
Burnell. Thereupon the prince, speaking on behalf
of himself and his colleagues, said that they would
only accept office on condition that they were
provided with sufficient money to conduct the
business of government, and they would accept no
responsibility for any financial obligations incurred
by them in the proper exercise of their duty.
Apparently the prince was not sworn as a member
of the council : one biographer—Tyler—states that
this omission was due solely to the fact that the
Commons had such great respect for ' the high
dignity of his honourable person ' that they did not

deem it necessary for him to take the ordinary oath.
The other members named by Henry IV. were duly
sworn in. When parliament was dissolved a week
or so later the matter appeared to be settled to
every one's satisfaction, and the council took up
their duties ; but at the end of the parliamentary
session of 1411 an echo of this crisis was heard when
the king, in response to the wish of the Commons
that their thanks should be conveyed to the prince
and his colleagues for their work, tartly reminded
the Commons that

> they (the council) would have done more had they had
> more ample means, as my lord the prince declared when
> they were appointed.

It is impossible to say how often the prince
visited Calais ; but his first visit there seems to
have been paid in April and May of 1410. On his
return to England he applied himself to his
duties as president of the council : he presided
over meetings held on June 18 and 19, and July
11, 22, 29, and 30. Here emerges an interesting point : the affray in East Cheap took place on
June 23, according to Stow—five days after the
prince had presided over a meeting of the council
held in the London house of the Bishop of Hereford.
It is well-nigh impossible to believe that he had a
hand in this affray, for he was virtually at that
time head of the government ; and he would be
more concerned with dispersing than supporting
rioters.

The state of Henry IV.'s health accentuated
party differences ; and there is no doubt that by
1410 two definite parties existed in the realm. One
was headed by Henry Beaufort, who, after a distinguished academic, ecclesiastical, and political
career, had been preferred to the bishopric of
Winchester in 1404 : at the head of the other party

was Thomas Arundel, Archbishop of Canterbury,
then a man in the late fifties. The former party
was the *progressive* party. It was made up of young
men who wished to move with the times, and
youthful enthusiasms already made them dream of
the time when the leopards of England would float
serenely above the great French fortresses on the
Seine and Loire. They had unbounded confidence
in the abilities of Prince Henry, and they believed
that he could bring these things to pass—if he was
allowed to do so. Archbishop Arundel, on the
other hand, was the champion of the *status quo*.
No man had done more than he to set the House
of Lancaster upon the throne of England, and he
had no desire to see his work endangered or un-
done by the recklessness of youth. An old man's
caution took the edge off the appetite for drastic
change ; and his greatest political asset was the
complete confidence which Henry IV. reposed in
him.

But for two years—January 1410 to December
1411—the conservative party was in the wilderness, and the political power was wielded by the
progressives. At the chancery, the archbishop was
replaced by Sir Thomas Beaufort, later to be
created first Earl of Dorset and then Duke of
Exeter ; and at the treasury John Tiptot made
room for another Beaufort protégé—Henry, third
Baron Scrope of Masham. The office of chamberlain was held by John, Earl of Somerset, until his
death in March 1410 ; and that of marshal by
another friend of the prince—Ralph Nevil, Earl of
Westmoreland. Of all the chief ministers in the
previous administration only John Prophet, Keeper
of the Privy Seal, kept his place : apparently his
conscience allowed him to trim his sails to suit
the changed political winds.

History is discreetly silent as to whether

Henry IV. favoured or frowned upon these changes in the administration. Perhaps his illness made it impossible for him to bother about them : or if hostile he may have been quite unable to counteract the influence of the progressives. It might even be argued that it was this new government which placed Prince Henry in the august position of deputy for his father : this would at least explain how it came about that he was given so prominent a place in the political sun. History is silent on the behaviour of Archbishop Arundel and his party during the time that they were in opposition : they had the decency at least not to follow the usual mediæval practice of showing their disappointment at the loss of office by the use of force.

Where did the king's other sons stand in this matter ? The question is a pertinent one. Thomas, only a year younger than Prince Henry, had seen service against pirates in the Channel, and had held high administrative office in Ireland. His record of service was excellent, even though his diversions were accompanied by youthful wildness. John held titular offices on the Anglo-Scottish march ; but as yet he had taken no great part in the political affairs of the realm. Humphrey was probably up at Balliol College, Oxford. On the death of John, Earl of Somerset, Henry IV. cast covetous eyes on his young widow, Margaret Holland, as a suitable bride for Thomas. The widow's portion would provide him with a decent heritage in lands, which would make him more or less independent of his father — and financial considerations weighed heavily with the impoverished Henry IV. The Beauforts, however, were opposed to the marriage at first ; then when it was settled they haggled over Margaret's dowry, and a good deal of bad blood was stirred up. Prince Henry seems to have supported the Beauforts (could he afford to do

otherwise when the leader of his party was Henry
Beaufort ?) ; and an estrangement took place
between the two brothers. Labouring under a
sense of grievance, Thomas would naturally turn
for consolation towards the party of Archbishop
Arundel ; and it is significant that as soon as the
conservatives returned to power in 1412 the king
bestowed upon Thomas the dukedom of Clarence.
In the instrument by which this dignity was
assured to him the name of Prince Henry does not
appear among the list of witnesses.

Now is it possible to connect the affray in East
Cheap in June 1410 with this quarrel between
Thomas and the Beauforts ? Stow mentions that
the men of Thomas and John fought with ' other
of the court ' ; and it would not be unreasonable
to suggest that the court there referred to is the
court of Prince Henry at *Coldharbour*. The Beauforts would always be sure of a welcome at the
prince's London house, and it may well be that on
that eve of St. John Baptist, 1410, the retainers
of both parties came to blows. The fact that one
party were the supporters of the prince would lead
people to suppose that his own retainers took part
in the riot ; and this would explain the view that he
was a party to it. This, however, is nothing more
than a historical reconstruction ; and since there is
no contemporary evidence to support it, it must be
used with the greatest caution.

There is another popular belief which demands
examination. For centuries historians have told
how king and prince were at loggerheads during
the latter part of Henry IV.'s reign ; and it has been
openly suggested that the prince made no secret of
his intention to force his father to abdicate in his
favour. This story has considerable colour lent to
it by the quarrel between Thomas and the Beauforts over Margaret Holland's dowry : as we have

seen, Thomas looked to his father for support, the Beauforts to the prince. Moreover, Henry Beaufort at least advocated the abdication of Henry IV., and he did so in open parliament ; and as his suggestion came to nothing, and was soon followed by the retirement of Prince Henry from active participation in the affairs of State, the conclusion is that Henry IV. literally broke with his eldest son.

At first sight the action of Henry Beaufort has the impression of political factiousness ; but, as Professor Mowat has shown, the loyalty of the Beauforts to the House of Lancaster—a loyalty extending over three-quarters of a century—was never in question. That was only natural : they owed their very position and wealth to the House of Lancaster ; and since they intended to keep both they would hardly embark upon a policy which would jeopardise their own position. The suggestion that Henry should abdicate in favour of the prince, therefore, can be regarded as a sincere desire on the part of Henry Beaufort to do the best thing for the realm : the king was desperately ill, and the times demanded that the helm of government should be in the hands of a strong and vigorous prince. He had reckoned without Archbishop Arundel : on November 30, 1411, the rule of the progressives virtually came to an end.

As the following record shows, the dismissal was done with dignity and without recriminations.

> The Speaker, in the name of the commons prayed the king to thank my lord the prince, the bishops of Winchester, of Durham (Thomas Langley), and others who were assigned by the king to be of his council . . . for their great labour and diligence. For as it appears to the said commons, my lord the prince and the other lords, have well and loyally done their duty according to their promise.

8

And upon that my lord prince, kneeling, with the other lords declared by the mouth of my lord the prince how they had taken pains and diligence and labours, according to their promise, and the charge given them in parliament, to their skill and knowledge. This the king remembered well, and thanked them most graciously. And he said besides, that " he was well assured, if they had possessed larger means than they had, in the manner it had been spoken by the mouth of my lord the prince at the time the king charged them to be of his council in the said parliament, they would have done their duty to effect more good than was done, in divers parts, for the defence, honour, good, and profit of him and his kingdom." And our lord the king also said, that he felt very contented with their good and loyal diligence, counsel, and duty, for the time they had been of the council.

The parliamentary session dragged on until December 19. On that day Archbishop Arundel again took office as chancellor : on the morrow his friend, John Pelham, went to the treasury. The old statesman had watched carefully for an opportunity to strike at his political opponents, and he had not mistimed the attack.

The real explanation of the change of administration is to be found in the late government's handling of the Anglo-French situation. They had taken a line of action of which Henry IV.—now sufficiently recovered from his illness to put himself at the head of affairs of State—did not approve ; and since Prince Henry was responsible for that line of action, and undoubtedly regarded it as better than his father's, it was no longer possible for father and son to work together. There is nothing in the records of the period to suggest that this political disagreement (it was nothing more) was accompanied by personal animosity, though, as will presently be seen, the prince found retirement somewhat irksome, and showed his discontent in an unmistakable manner. But a digression is necessary in order that the reader can grasp in general form the march of events on the other side of the English Channel.

Charles VI. of France was subject to periodical fits of madness—or, as a contemporary put it, was ' smit with the wrath of heaven.' The madness had made its first appearance in 1392, and while it lasted the poor king was quite unable to take any hand in the government of his country. In a kingdom where the ' overmighty subject ' was always a force to be reckoned with, it was inevitable that a regency should always provoke rivalries. The control of the mad king, therefore, was bitterly disputed by two rival parties : the one was headed by the king's brother, Louis, Duke of Orléans ; the other, by Philip *le Hardi*, Duke of Burgundy, his uncle. Each made good his claim to the title of regent by displays of armed force ; and while the mad king frothed at the mouth, wolfed his food like an animal, and was forcibly washed and undressed by a score of attendants, the streets of Paris echoed with the sound of marching feet. A return to sanity more than once postponed civil war ; and in fairness to the reputation of Philip *le Hardi* it must be said that during his lifetime he kept a firm hand on feudal factiousness, and did little to provoke his opponent to anger, though this statement must not be taken to mean that he was actuated by high motives of public-spiritedness. In April 1404 he was stricken down with the marsh fever, so prevalent in Flanders in the Middle Ages ; and on the 27th of the month he died at the hostel of the Stag in Hal, not far from Brussels. On his death-bed he had counselled his sons to keep the peace, and to do nothing which would distract the realm of France.

His eldest son, known to his contemporaries as Jean *Sans Peur*, had no intention of respecting his dead father's wishes to the detriment of the dignity of his duchy and the advancement of the hated Duke of Orléans, and the struggle for power was continued. Duke John shrewdly consolidated his position by effecting the betrothal of his eldest daughter, Margaret, to the dauphin, Louis, then a boy of nine ; and thanks to the good offices of the University of Paris and the friars the people of the capital were won over to his side. They regarded him as the champion of the poor and oppressed against the high and mighty—a disinterested hero trying only to bring order out of chaos in a distracted realm. That illusion was worth much to Burgundy.

But his adversary, the Duke of Orléans, was not so easily thwarted : with the help of the queen (and everywhere men said that she was one of his mistresses) he endeavoured to undermine the Burgundian influence at court, and during the latter part of 1405, when the rivals' armies faced each other for weeks in the neighbourhood of Paris, civil war seemed unavoidable. But wiser counsels prevailed, and in October the two dukes were reconciled. Paris, that city of changing moods and tempers, accepted the reconciliation in good part, and applauded wildly when the queen entered her capital in triumph, and the two dukes sat side by side and drank from the same goblet at the banquet which followed. Burgundy was a cunning young fox : in November he secured the formal appointment of the dauphin as regent during the insanity of his father. As the boy's father-in-law-to-be, he anticipated that he would be virtually in control of the government.

Until 1407 the two parties behaved more or less discreetly in their enmities. The king was in better health, and disorders in Paris were less frequent, though the people still murmured at the rapacity of the tax-gatherers and the extravagance of the court. Then the world toppled about the ears of the people of France : the kingdom was in future to be sharply divided into two camps, and feudal self-interest was to indulge itself in acts of the basest treason. On the night of November 23 the Duke of Orléans was enticed from the caresses of the queen by a message which purported to come from the king, asking for his immediate attendance at court. The duke accepted the message as genuine, and he had hardly gone a hundred yards from the house in the Rue Barbette when seven or eight armed men sprang out of the shadows and cut him down. At first it was thought that the murder had been done by a jealous husband, and suspicion fell upon Aubert le Flamenc, Lord of Cany, whose wife Orléans had seduced and debauched ; and in view of the murdered man's notorious lecheries no one was greatly surprised at the turn of events. Then came the news that the death of the duke was no jealous husband's revenge for the fouling of his marriage couch, but a political murder of the utmost importance, done by a Norman esquire named Raoul d'Anctoville ; and despite the fact that John of Burgundy was grief-stricken when they laid the corpse of his adversary to rest in the church of the Celestin monks near the Porte St. Antoine, it was openly said that the assassination had been carried through by his orders. His flight to his duchy was followed by his public confession that he had rid France of a troublesome pest ; and when he learnt that the Parisian mob applauded his act, he returned to the city and received a royal reception (early 1408). Holy Church, speaking through the mouth of a distinguished Franciscan friar named Master Jean Petit, converted the murder into an act of divine vengeance which justified any trickery or cunning accompanying it, and in due course the king gave Burgundy a free pardon.

If Burgundy had triumphed, the dead man's widow, the Duchess Valentine, cried to the heavens for vengeance ; and to confirm her steadfastly in her purpose she had Doucet, the duke's pet dog, constantly in her company. But she died in December 1408, before she had time to strike ; and not long afterwards her son, Charles, and the Duke of Burgundy were reconciled before the high altar in the cathedral church of Chartres. *Une paix fourrée :* such was the verdict of a court fool, and for once wisdom outshone his wit.

The Duchess Valentine's implacable hatred was revived in 1410. Charles of Orléans, whose love of poetry blunted the sharp edge of senseless vindictiveness, married in that year Bonne, daughter of Bernard VII., Comte d'Armagnac. Bernard was a man of great ability ; he was a capable leader of men ; and his ambition compelled him to marshal the Orléanist forces for the overthrow of the Duke John of Burgundy. The Orléanist party were now known as the Armagnacs.

The two rival parties were so nicely balanced that neither could hope to triumph without outside help. But where was that help to come from ? The idea first struck John of Burgundy that the English king might furnish it—upon terms. Early in 1411, therefore, Burgundian envoys arrived in England to negotiate a treaty of alliance. They announced that the duke was ready to surrender to the English the four towns of Dixmude, Dunkirk, Gravelines, and Sluys ; and to assist in the reconquest of the duchy of Normandy. As an earnest of friendship it was further suggested that the duke's fifth daughter, Anne, might be married to the Prince Henry.[8] The project was discussed at great length, and in September 1411 an embassy consisting of Bishop Chichele, the Earl of Arundel, Sir Francis Court, Hugh Mortimer, and John

Caterick proceeded to Arras to deal with certain outstanding details. There is evidence that Henry IV. himself took the satisfactory settlement of the treaty for granted : ships were ordered to stand by in the Channel ports ready to carry him and his army over to France, and men were mustered and ordnance collected. But all of a sudden Henry IV. changed his policy and abandoned the idea of an alliance with Burgundy.

Nevertheless in October there appeared in Arras a competent English force of 600 men-at-arms and 2000 archers, commanded by the Earl of Arundel ; and in the earl's train were Sir William Bardolph, Sir Francis Court, Sir Robert Umfraville, Sir Gilbert Umfraville, Sir John Grey, and Sir John Oldcastle. In due course they marched with the Burgundians and entered Paris by the Porte St. Jacques. The Parisians gave a grand reception to the Duke and his people ; but they looked askance at the English, and even refused to lodge them in their houses or stable their horses. On November 9 and 10 the great fight at St. Cloud took place- a bloody affray, in which Burgundian asked no quarter of Armagnac, and Armagnac none of Burgundian. It was Arundel's force which eventually turned the scales in Burgundy's favour ; and they won the admiration of the Frenchmen by the way in which they tended the wounded, when their own fellow-countrymen slew them. As the year 1411 was coming to a close Arundel and his men

> cam hoom agayn with grete giftis.

To them it had been a most successful adventure.

The point to be decided is at whose orders did this force proceed overseas. Undoubtedly, at the prince's. He was at that time the president of the council—his father's deputy, and that gave him the right to make decisions which he considered to be to the advantage of the realm. Subsequent events were to prove that the prince's policy was sound : as long as the English could rely upon the Burgundians remaining neutral in the struggle with the King of France they were able to keep a stranglehold on France, but when the Burgundian alliance was broken—as it was in Henry VI.'s reign —that hold was so weakened that the English forces were eventually driven back to their native land.

Henry IV. did not approve of the action taken by the prince and council. The incident is somewhat blurred and hazy, but the inference to be drawn from the scanty evidence available is that a definite breach was made between father and son. It has been suggested that Henry IV. favoured an alliance with the Armagnacs, but this can hardly have been the case, for at the time when the battle at St. Cloud took place they recognised as the rightful King of England the shadow in Scotland whom men called ' Richard II.' It is inconceivable that Henry IV. should coquet with men who looked upon him as a usurper. In January 1412, however, the Armagnacs changed their tactics : they announced their readiness to recognise Henry as the lawful king of England, and as a bait for English help against Burgundy they offered to restore in full sovereignty to the English the duchy of Aquitaine. There was, of course, the additional safeguard of a marriage alliance, to be secured by betrothing Prince Henry to an Armagnac princess ; and an embassy was sent to England to arrange the details. And by August an understanding was reached, and Thomas, now Duke of Clarence, sailed with a force to help the Armagnacs. Well might

Walsingham observe that many Englishmen won-
dered

> what could be the sudden change that in so short a space
> of time the English should support two opposite contending
> parties.

Incidentally, the expedition achieved nothing :
they had hardly landed in the country when another
reconciliation between the rival parties was made,
and the Duke of Orléans was obliged to offer a large
sum of money to Clarence to secure his withdrawal
from the realm of France.

An explanation of Henry IV.'s repudiation of
his son's action might be found in the very human
failing of jealousy. On all sides were evidences of
the prince's popularity. Tales, too, may have
been told to the king that the Beauforts were
working for his abdication : and they would be
true. Moreover, whatever suspicions which he
might have would be aggravated by his son's
detractors—notably by Archbishop Arundel, who
in 1411 had good cause to resent the prince's power
and influence. The archbishop had wished to force
upon the University of Oxford certain ecclesiastical
decrees against Lollardy, but the dons—true to
the Oxford tradition of dislike for all outside
authority—refused to accept them, even though
they hated Lollardy as vigorously as Arundel
himself, and in their opposition they were supported
by Prince Henry. Arundel would have been less
than human had he taken that rebuff kindly : he
was obsessed with the idea that heresy must be
rooted out, and he believed that it lurked—and
gained strength—in Oxford's halls. So it may well
have happened that he was able successfully to
turn Henry IV. against his son, by subtly suggesting to him that the young man was taking the
bit between his teeth, and might at any moment

accept the Beaufort plan of supplanting Henry IV.
on the throne. On the plea that the prince had
acted without the royal assent—indeed contrary
to the king's wishes—resignation was forced upon
him ; and when he went it followed that his friends
would go with him.

It must be admitted that during his retirement
the prince did not always act with discretion.
Although his father was pledged to support the
Armagnacs, he himself entertained with considerable
show the Burgundian ambassadors. He attempted
in June 1412 to win his way back into his father's
confidence, when he had an interview with him at
Westminster. On that occasion he behaved with
every show of filial respect : he would not allow
his retainers to pass beyond the great fire in Westminster Hall when he went to talk to his father,
and when he was on his knees before the king he
offered him his dagger and invited him to kill him
if he suspected his loyalty. Some time about the
middle of 1412 the prince came near to death by
assassination. He was asleep in the Green Room
at Westminster when his servants, awakened by
the barking of a spaniel, discovered a man concealed
behind the tapestries. He was racked in the presence
of the Earl of Arundel, but all the information he
would give was that he had been hired by Bishop
Henry Beaufort to make away with the prince.
The tale was so fantastic that Arundel appears to
have given it no credence, and the assassin was tied
in a sack, and hurled into the Thames.

It was in the summer of 1412 that the story
went round the country that the prince had appro-
priated to his own use money voted for the defence
of Calais. There is no doubt whatever that this
was a baseless charge, meant only to discredit the
prince in the eyes of his fellow-countrymen. He
was able to prove his innocence by producing the

account rolls ; and on September 23, at the head
of a great host of his friends, he came before the
council and demanded that his enemies should
either be dismissed or compelled to prove their
insinuations. The king told him that the whole
matter would be placed before the next parliament
and full justice would be afforded him. When
that parliament met, the prince had succeeded to
the throne.

CHAPTER FOUR

KING AND LOLLARDY

THE story of the physical suffering which Henry IV. endured in his last years makes most distressing reading. The syphilitic taint, inherited from lecherous old John of Gaunt, took terrible toll of a body which was never physically robust. Fainting fits, which at this distance of time look uncommonly like epileptic seizures, more than once made it necessary for the king to leave the direction of the business of the State in other hands. To his enemies his misfortunes were joyous tidings. In Scotland men believed that so wasted was the royal body that it had shrunk to the size of that of a child of twelve ; and in Paris the scandal-mongers gloated over the tales which purported to tell how Henry's hands were fingerless and his feet toeless. There is no doubt that the disease had disfigured his face most terribly : that is the burden of Hardyng's, the rhyming chronicler's, tale :

> Of which ryghte nowe ye poorest of this lande
> Wolde lothe to look upon, I understande.

He could no longer sit a horse, and he walked only with the greatest difficulty.

But torn though his body was by the ravages of that foul disease, agonising though the sufferings which he had to endure were, conscious all the time that his people shrunk from him as though he was leprous, Henry IV.'s indomitable courage—that finely-tempered spirit which had enabled him to face many and great difficulties in the everyday life of usurped kingship—never wholly left him. Within him was active that mystic force which makes the dying cling so tenaciously to life, and he dragged his body from place to place in order to perform his kingly duties—duties which were doubly hard when performed in the face of strong opposition and in the knowledge that traitors lurked even in unsuspected quarters. Sometimes physical suffering brought on fits of blank despair, and on these occasions the man within him became craven, and called forth in anguish for that relief which death alone can give.

Henry IV. was a very sick man when he journeyed to his manor of Eltham to spend what proved to be his last Christmas. It was typical of his courage, however, that he would not allow his own indisposition in any way to mar the customary festivities ; and we are able to prove from an examination of the account-rolls that the merrymaking at Eltham was conducted on a most magnificent scale. At the end of January 1413 Henry IV. removed his court to Archbishop Arundel's palace at Lambeth, but within a few days he had moved on to his royal manor of Mortlake. There he lay when the parliament-men rode into London ready for the meeting of parliament, summoned for February 3. But that meeting was destined never to take place in Henry IV.'s reign : obviously the king was shy of showing his face in public, and so the parliament-men hung about the capital ' at their own charges.' The loyal support which the Londoners gave to the house of Lancaster acted as a magnet, forcing Henry IV., even in his sickness, to remain in their midst ; and before February was out he had taken up his residence at the palace at Westminster. It was about Mid-Lent that he felt well enough to make an offering at the shrine of St Edward Confessor, the king-saint of England, which was situated immediately behind the high altar in the abbey church at Westminster. The king walked slowly, his companions finding it difficult to retard their steps so as not to press upon him. On a sudden he stumbled, and then crashed lifeless to the floor. Tenderly they bore him out and through the cloisters to the abbot's lodgings, where they laid him upon a ' pallet ' in front of a roaring fire, in a room called the Jerusalem or Bethlehem.

It requires no tricks of the imagination to envisage the scene in the sick man's room. Prince Henry, if he was not actually in attendance on his father, would be hastened to his father's bedside, and the principal officers of State would stand awkwardly silent, as though afraid to drown the sound made by the wings of the angel of death. Sadness there must have been—for few are able to stand unmoved in the presence of death ; but all around the dying king must have felt that death would bestow an inestimable boon upon the sufferer. Archbishop Arundel, constant to the end in the friendship which existed between them, and Dr John Tille, the Dominican friar who was chief of the royal confessors, were ready at hand to perform those last offices by which the Church solaces the departing soul. Near the bed, resting on a cushion of silk, was the iron Lancastrian crown of England, brought in great haste to the death-chamber as a precaution against theft by men with better claim to the throne —a reminder, too, that in a monarchy kingship is deathless, and the germ of the later practice of proclaiming that ' the king is dead, long live the king ! '

Henry IV. had not moved since they carried him in to that chamber. At last all present thought that he was dead, and an officer of the royal household brought in a ' silken towel ' and drew it over his emaciated face. That done, the young prince was urged to take up the crown. But the spark of life was rekindled in the dying man's frame : he sighed, they rushed to remove the cloth over his face, and his eyes wearily wandered to the place where the crown had lain. At once the prince came to his father's side, to explain that he had taken the crown only on the advice of those present in the room. There was no rebuke, but rather the voice of troubled conscience, in the words which the dying king spoke to his eldest son :

> What right have you to it, my son, seeing that I had none ?

That question called forth a spirited reply from the young man :

> Sire, as you have held and kept it by the sword, so will I hold and keep it while my life shall last.

The weariness which comes with death had taken hold of the king : he must now direct his thoughts from earthly matters :

> Do as you will, my son, I commend me to God, and pray that he may have mercy upon me.

His lustreless eyes fell upon Dr John Tille. He asked what he did in the room, and was told that he was there prepared to administer the Viaticum. The dying man painfully lifted up his body on the bed, in readiness for the Blessed Sacrament. Dr John Tille earnestly begged the dying man to confess whatever guilt he had in the business of Richard II.'s death and of his destruction of those of Richard's friends who had tried to thwart his purpose. Henry thereupon reminded him that he had already revealed to the Pope the innermost secrets of his heart, and had received the holy father's pardon. So the Viaticum was administered, and the king fell back exhausted on his pallet.

One last duty remained to be done—a dying father's injunctions to his son. The young Henry, at his father's command, came to the bedside. He bent down, and the king kissed him. Forgotten and forgiven were the old enmities between them. Henry IV. counselled his son to do right in all things —to pay his debts, keep faith with his friends, seek the solace of wise confessors and the counsel of wise ministers, to work for the honour and glory of the realm of England. And when he had done these things, so the chronicler tells us, Henry IV. ' made a happy end,' his last breath going out in asking God's mercy and blessing on his four sons. The king died on St. Cuthbert's Day (March 20), 1413.

It has always been the sacred privilege and duty of an eldest son to close his father's eyes in death, and to see that the obsequies are decently and fittingly carried out. Such a privilege and duty now devolved upon the young Henry. The customary preparation of the body—' washing, braining, bowelling, embalming '—was done by those skilled in such work ; and then the corpse was arrayed in the richest robes, and borne into the abbey church at Westminster to lie in state. For more than a week the citizens of London filed past the ' hearse,' and paid a last tribute to a king whom they had loved because he had saved them from the reckless government of Richard Redeless—a government which rifled rich men's pockets in its pursuit of senseless pleasures. In due course, the corpse was placed on a barge, and brought down the London River to Gravesend : there followed in its wake eight ships, on board of which were the young king, his brothers John and Humphrey, and a crowd of notables in Church and State, their draped shields hanging along the gunwales, and their pennons dipped in salute. The leaden casket was then taken on a horse-drawn bier from Gravesend to Canterbury, the mourners following on horseback and on foot ; and finally it was interred in a grave in the chapel of St Thomas Becket of Canterbury. Some years later Henry IV.'s queen and second wife, Joanna of Navarre, raised over the grave a magnificent tomb of stone and alabaster, the work of skilled masons of Derbyshire ; and in 1437, when the glories of Henry V.'s reign were overshadowed by the hopeless spectre of civil war, other hands laid Joanna's body in that self tomb.

The work of government did not stand still during the weeks given over to the funeral of Henry IV. Immediately on his death mounted messengers galloped madly out of London, riding to the north and the south, the east and the west, to command the sheriffs of the shires of England, and other royal officials in the wild hill country of Wales, that they must proclaim the ' King's Peace,' and warn the people that on no account would ' riots and assemblings ' be countenanced. It was imperative, too, that a certain number of royal officers should be appointed for the better safety of the realm. John, the king's brother, was duly confirmed in his office of Warden of the East Marches of Scotland ; and a similar confidence was shown to Ralph Nevil, Earl of Westmoreland, in respect of his wardenship of the western marches on the same frontier. The office of Steward of England, not filled since the death of its last occupant, the traitor Thomas Percy, Earl of Worcester, went to Richard Beauchamp, Earl of Warwick ; and since Thomas, Duke of Clarence and Constable of England, was on military service in France, Henry, Lord fitzHugh, was detailed off to act as his deputy in that office at the coming coronation.

9

It will be remembered that Henry IV. had summoned the parliament-men to meet him in February, but that owing to his illness no session was formally held. Many of the members had remained in London during the intervening weeks, and on the day following the king's death some of them rode over to Kennington and ' made their homage ' to the new king, at the same time protesting that this pre-coronation oath of allegiance must not be taken as a precedent. Undoubtedly there was some uneasiness in London at the time : people awaited the appearance of some one bold enough to declare himself for the fifth Earl of March, who by the law of primogeniture was the rightful heir to the throne. The parliament-men perceived that hesitancy on their part in recognising the young king might be wrongly construed by the populace—and they had much to lose by the fall of the Lancastrian dynasty.

It was typical of Henry V. that on the day preceding his coronation he should admit to the order of knighthood, so peculiarly Lancastrian— the Order of the Bath—Edmund Mortimer, Earl of March, his brother, Roger Mortimer, and at least two other members of the nobility whose fathers had been implicated in treasons against the house of Lancaster. The young king was not only generously minded towards his enemies, but he was wise enough to realise that hatreds are not eradicated by a visitation of the sins of the fathers upon the children ; and he was obviously prepared to trust these young men whose position in the feudal hierarchy made them important members of the feudal state. As subsequent events were to prove, Henry V. was wrong neither in his judgment of their characters nor in his estimate of their abilities.

The hallowing and crowning of the king took place in the abbey church at Westminster on April 9.

It was Passion Sunday : in years to come men
recalled that it was ' a sore ruggie and tempestuous
day,' when storms of snow and sleet swept over the
realm.   At the time some regarded these vagaries
of the weather with mixed feelings.   Were they the
signs of a harsh, cold rule ?   On the other hand,
might they not forecast happier things—the snow
promising purity of government, and the frost the
destruction of vice in high places ?   The sacred
ceremony was performed by Archbishop Arundel
—his right by virtue of his office of metropolitan
of the Church of England ; and as he laid the Crown
upon the young man's head he knew that his own
political career had ended.   It had been a long
and honourable one, and in these circumstances his
regrets were understandable.   So that the throng
of people might see every detail of the coronation
a stage was erected between the high altar and the
quire : it was draped with the costliest cloths of
gold, and the throne was set in the centre of it.

The religious ceremony was followed by the
customary riot of feasting and merry-making in
the great hall of the royal palace adjoining the
abbey.   Henry V., seated in a marble chair,
looked, so we are told, ' like an angel ' in his isolated
place on the raised dais at the upper end of the hall.
No expense was spared in making the feast worthy
of the occasion, and the royal cooks demonstrated
their art in the multitude of ' messes ' which were
borne from the kitchens to the crowded tables.
Dr Wylie has recaptured for us something of the
splendour of the royal tables on that coronation
day in 1413, and the picture which he draws enables
his readers to have ' a curious peep into the possibilities of the mediæval digestion.'   The ' subtleties '—' gastronomic triumphs . . . made of sugar,
paste, or jelly '—were garnished with trite counsel
on the art of government.   They begged Henry to

'Have pitee on the commonaltee' and to 'Keep the law and guard the *foi*'; some displayed the neat epigram — 'Out of court be banished tort.'

The dishes were brought in by servers mounted on horseback. They were preceded by the marshal, who cleared the gangways and arranged for the easy distribution of the courses. Mounted, too, was John Dymmok, the royal champion, who was dressed as St George. He challenged to battle any man who was in doubt as to the rightness of Henry's claim to the throne. No one in that company accepted his challenge. The minstrels in attendance cheered the company with merry songs, and served in some measure to drown the noise which was created by mediæval table manners and the hubbub of the talkers.

There was plenty for all at the banquet, and if contemporary evidence is to be relied upon (evidence which relates that the Englishman of that age was a devil when fighting and a wolf when eating) the fullest justice was done to the efforts of the royal cooks and scullions. Nor were forgotten the needs of the multitude of loyal subjects which thronged the streets leading up to the palace at Westminster. The fountains in the main courtyard poured forth a luscious stream of red wine from Gascony and white wine from the Rhineland principalities; and in the city of London the mayor and aldermen provided a variety of amusements for the journeymen and apprentices of the various gilds. For a moment the solemnity of the Lenten fast was completely overshadowed by the gaiety which attends a king's coronation.

More than one contemporary noted with dismay that the king himself took little pleasure in the festivities. Throughout the banquet he sat morose and preoccupied, not even tasting a mouthful of

the delicious things which they placed before him
on the table. A later biographer saw in this
behaviour evidence of his changed heart, and read
into his gloomy looks proof that all at once he had
become conscious of the sacred obligations of
kingship. This is pleasant speculation, which does
justice to the biographer's subject : it is more
likely that the royal behaviour was caused by the
disturbing news that many of his subjects still
believed that Richard was alive, while some held
that the Earl of March's claim was the better in law.
The newly crowned king, therefore, would ponder
on the tricks which treason can play in a state.
Would some of those who to-day were his guests
become his bitterest enemies ? Would his reign be
as ' unquiet ' a time as that of his father's ? Nevertheless, whatever force the opposition to his
accession may have had, it was quickly dissipated
or driven underground ; and not many days
after the coronation, John Burghersh, Prior of
Lewes, proudly informed his spiritual superior,
the Abbot of Cluni, that the new king had been
accepted with ' the universal acclaim of the whole
nation.'

In the mediæval state the ministers were the
personal secretaries of the monarch. They held
their offices literally at the king's pleasure, and
were subject only to his will—though it was now
becoming the custom (and an inconvenient one
from the monarch's point of view) for the parliament-men to claim that there was such a thing as
ministerial responsibility to parliament. Ministers
therefore, relinquished their portfolios on the death
of the monarch by whom they had been appointed,
and their chances of further employment rested
entirely with the new king. Even before his coronation Henry V. made one or two ministerial appointments : Thomas fitzAlan, Earl of Arundel, took

over the duties of Warden of the Cinque Ports and
Constable of Dover—offices which the king had held
as Prince of Wales, and regarded as of the highest
importance in the realm; and William Hankeford
replaced William Gascoigne as Chief Justice of the
King's Bench. Archbishop Arundel, who had
rendered such signal service to Henry IV. at the
Chancery, was replaced by Henry Beaufort, Bishop
of Winchester. The Earl of Arundel received the
office of Treasurer, lately held by Sir John Pelham;
and the king's youngest brother, Humphrey, was
installed as Chamberlain of England. Two
ministers of the previous administration were
retained in their offices : they were John Wakering,
Keeper of the Chancery Rolls, and John Prophet,
Keeper of the Privy Seal.

The real significance of these ministerial appointments should not be lost sight of. In Henry
Beaufort and Thomas fitzAlan the young king had
ministers who thought much as he thought : they
were young enough to have some of the enthusiasms
of youth, and old enough to appreciate the value of
caution in administration. They took their stand
upon the Lancastrian dynastic position : they were
resolved to prevent it being undermined or
threatened. The others were ' safe ' men—except
perhaps Humphrey, who had already given evidence
of his erratic charm.

On May 15, in the Painted Chamber at Westminster, Henry V. met the first parliament of his
reign. Bishop Beaufort opened the proceedings
with a sermon, preached from the text—' biforn
alle deed stable conseil.' The sermon did duty for
the speech from the throne, and it outlined the
royal purpose—to maintain ' his high and royal
estate,' to respect the law and give good governance,
and to cherish his friends and confound his enemies.
True to the tradition which had been created in his

father's reign—a tradition founded in the poverty
of the Lancastrian dynasty—Henry let it be known
through his chancellor that it was his intention in
the business of government to look for counsel and
advice from the lords and commons ; and he won
universal admiration from the parliament-men
with the announcement that he himself would
provide the money to enable the executors under
his father's will to carry out the dead king's wishes.[9]
Partly out of a sense of gratitude to their king for
this fine display of filial affection, and in accordance
with the custom of the times, parliament proceeded to vote the necessary monies ; and introduced an innovation by setting apart an annual
sum of £10,000 for the expenses of the royal household.   Henry V., however, never kept his promise :
perhaps, faced as he was with great financial needs
for his wars, he was quite unable to do so.

The business of parliament thereupon proceeded in its normal way.   Petitions were examined
and converted into laws, and the reign began under
auspicious circumstances.   Some slight stir was
caused when the news came that a certain yeoman,
named John Whitlok, had affixed to the doors of
certain of London's churches a document which
to-day would be styled ' an open letter.'   In it he
declared upon the most solemn of oaths that
Richard II. was alive and well in Scotland :

> I betake the devil ever to lie in helle, body and soul
> without departyng, but that person that was sumtyme
> kyng Richard be alive in Scotland.

His ' vapourings ' were not taken seriously.

It was early in Henry V.'s reign that an ominous
shadow fell across the path of his government.   In
a meeting of the convocation of the clergy of the
province of Canterbury pointed remarks had been
passed on the subject of the ' great men of the realm

who were favourers of the Lollards.' How powerful
Lollardy was at that time is a matter which cannot
be determined with accuracy, but it is certain that
a not inconsiderable body of opinion in the country
was more or less sympathetic towards its doctrines,
and as subsequent events proved it claimed
among its followers men of social and political
distinction.

Lollardy was the child of Wiclif's heresy, and it
had been saved from strangulation at birth by the
powerful patronage which its parent had received
from John of Gaunt. The worldliness of the
Papacy in the latter part of the fourteenth century
was inevitably reflected in the behaviour of the
clergy throughout the lands of Western Europe.
High ecclesiastical preferment too frequently was
reserved for those politically-minded clergy whose
spiritual other-worldliness was in inverse proportion
to their marked administrative abilities; and in
consequence saintliness was left to languish in
obscure country rectories and vicarages. In the
thumb-nail sketches which Chaucer made of the
clergy of his age we see the appalling state of the
fourteenth-century church. It may be argued that
Chaucer was a satirist, and therefore prone to the
exaggeration of satire ; but the popularity of his
Canterbury Tales lay in the fact that it told of
people whom every one knew in the flesh. The only
reputable figure in his ecclesiastical gallery was the
' povre persoun of a toun,' who, it will be remembered

> . . . wayted after no pompe and reverence,
> Ne maked a spyced conscience,
> But Christes lore, and his apostles twelve,
> He taughte, and first he folwed it himselve.

John Wiclif saw that the burdens of political
business were crushing out of the leaders of the
Church that fine spiritual feeling without which

the so-much-needed spiritual revival could not be effected ; and the shafts of his subtleties were directed with deadly accuracy against this type of ecclesiastic. His poor preachers, or Lollards, were established in order to give the ordinary people of the land the religious solace which was not easily to be had from the majority of the regular and secular clergy. In course of time they acquired immense popularity, chiefly because they took the trouble to preach to the people in the simplest of language. In their revolt against the Church these Lollards took their stand on the Wiclifian doctrine of *dominion*. In Wiclif's opinion *dominion*, whether in Church or State, could only be founded in grace. It followed conversely, therefore, that those who did not live in grace could exercise no *dominion* either in ecclesiastical office or secular jurisdiction. It will be seen immediately that this doctrine of *dominion* was pregnant with dangerously sub- versive implications. If a priest did not live in grace then he ought not to be regarded as the mediator between God and man : if a lay lord did not live in grace he ought not by right to exercise any form of jurisdiction over his tenants. It was ethically right for a man to challenge the sacer- dotal character of a priest who lived a worldly or immoral life ; and since Wiclif had never paused to reflect upon the difficulty of evaluation of character his teaching could only produce chaotic results. It made every Tom, Dick, and Harry the judge of priestly behaviour. The political implications of *dominion* made for anarchy. Indeed its echoes were heard in such upheavals as the Peasants Revolt, and in the murmurings of the workers in the countryside, when the landlords endeavoured to check the drift towards the collapse of villeinage caused by the Black Death and the rise of the woollen industry. It was a Lollard preacher who rambled throughout the land preaching from the text :

> When Adam delved,
> And Eve span,
> Who was then the gentleman.

Feudal society was profoundly shocked and angered by this communistic attack upon privilege ; and since privilege was politically powerful, it triumphed. Furthermore, the Lollards, following blindly the example of Wiclif, but lacking his schoolman's appreciation of philosophic subtleties, cast grave doubts on the doctrine of transubstantiation, the mighty pillar of faith upon which Catholicism is raised ; and it was characteristic of Lollardy that throughout it upheld a definitely Protestant conception of the sacraments and the priesthood.

When the members of the Convocation of Canterbury fulminated against ' the great men of the realm who were favourers of the Lollards,' they had in their minds chiefly the activities of one man. He was Sir John Oldcastle, or more correctly styled Lord Cobham, for he had married one of the Cobham heiresses and took that title by courtesy of his wife. Oldcastle had played a notable part in the Welsh wars, doing splendid service for the English king—more often than not at his own charges—in the dangerous heart of the rebel principality ; and his courage on the field of battle and resourcefulness and wisdom in council had won for him the love and confidence of the young Prince Henry of Wales. As a native of the county of Hereford he wielded considerable influence in that part of the realm, and through his Cobham connections he had come to be a man of great importance in Kent, London, Northamptonshire, and Wiltshire. How and when he was converted to Lollardy is not known, but before the accession of Henry V. he was under suspicion

by the ecclesiastical authorities because not only
did he maintain a Lollard preacher as his chaplain,
but he was a notorious champion of the poor
preachers in the dioceses of London, Hereford, and
Rochester.

One of the privileges which Convocation had was
a censorship of publications, and this carried with
it wide powers of search for illegal books and papers.
During a search of the premises of a certain
' lymnore ' (limner) in Paternoster Row the officers
of Convocation came across a particularly obnoxious
book.   The limner was questioned as to how it was
in his possession, and he replied that it belonged to
' Sir John Oldcastle.'   Some time in June 1413,
therefore, Oldcastle was commanded to come to
court to explain himself.   He came willingly enough.
Passages from the offending book were read out to
him in the presence of Henry V. and ' almost all the
prelates and nobles of England.'   Henry himself
said that he was painfully shocked by the heresies
which the book contained : he could hardly believe
his ears when the reading was taking place.   Oldcastle replied that he personally was unaware of the
contents of the book : he had read only one or two
folios, and he quite agreed that it was offensive and
worthy of destruction.

In all probability the matter would have ended
there, but there was a group of wild spirits in Convocation, and they refused to let Oldcastle's case
drop.   They reminded their colleagues that he was
the protector of the Lollards, that they resorted to
his houses in London, Herefordshire, and Kent ;
and they urged that he should be called to account
for his flagrant disobedience of ecclesiastical authority.   A warning note was raised : it came from
the lips of Archbishop Arundel, who throughout
the proceedings against Oldcastle acted with
commendable restraint and charity.   The old arch-

bishop, conscious of the services which Oldcastle
had rendered the State in the time of the previous
ruler and of his friendship with the new king, asked
leave to consult Henry V. on the matter ; and in
this he was supported by a number of the bishops.
Henry agreed to see Oldcastle in order to

> win him back by kindness from the maze of error to the
> straight path of truth,

but in the event of failure he would hand him over
to the ecclesiastical authorities to be dealt with by
them.   This plan had the unqualified support of
Archbishop Arundel and his friends ; but some of
the lower clergy in Convocation were boldly in-
dignant at what they regarded as a royal usurpation
of ecclesiastical prerogatives.   The truth of the
matter is that a section of the clergy were bent upon
having Oldcastle's blood : he was a heretic, a friend
and champion of heretics, and he must die a heretic's
death.
    We must digress for a moment.   Where precisely
did Henry V. stand in this business ?   The comrade-
ship of the battlefield is not easily broken or quickly
forgotten, and in his effort to ' win him back by
kindness ' it is obvious that Henry did his best to
save Oldcastle from the wolves of Convocation.   But
since his accession to the throne the king had given
proof of a piety which bordered on fanaticism ; and
the reason of this change must be sought in the
clerical influences which had been brought to bear
upon him.   His father on his death-bed had counselled him to choose wise confessors from members
of the religious orders, and he had obeyed that
injunction most loyally.   To his household were
attached two Carmelite friars, Stephen Patrington
and Thomas Walden or Netter.   The former was a
doctor of theology of the University of Oxford, and
had held office as provincial of his order in England.

His hatred of Lollardy dated back to his undergraduate days at Oxford—' when hot-headed partisans attended lectures in the schools with daggers under their gowns '—and he was zealous for the extirpation of heresy.   Patrington looked on Lollardy as the canker which would destroy both Church and State, and like a good surgeon he meant to cut out the offending tissues.   More unbending even than Patrington was Walden or Netter, who was the younger man.   He, too, was a product of the Oxford divinity schools, and he enjoyed great reputation as a fearless and eloquent preacher.   His dread of heresy clouded his powers of argument, so that his utterances were almost maniacal, and he lived only for achieving the triumph of orthodoxy.   Under the guidance of these two mentors Henry V. was quickly confirmed in the rigours of the faith ; and in the end their influence was strong enough to shatter a friendship formed in the perils of war and the lusty life of the camp.

Henry obviously did his best to persuade Oldcastle of the error of his ways ; but neither would compromise his opinions, and the discussion was broken up by the royal reminder of the dire penalties for ' contumacy.'   Oldcastle thereupon retired to his castle of Cooling in Kent, and, if the reports of his enemies are true, he immediately gave evidence of his intention to resist by force any ecclesiastical attempt to effect his arrest.   About the middle of August the king commanded Archbishop Arundel to proceed against Oldcastle, and at the same time the sheriffs up and down the country were ordered by royal writs to arrest all preachers who were known to favour the doctrines of the Lollards. Oldcastle was summoned by the archbishop to appear before him to answer a charge of heresy ; but the archiepiscopal ' sumner ' who bore the summons was bluntly refused admittance at

Cooling, and compelled to return with the summons in his pocket. On September 5, however, the archbishop had the summons affixed to the door of the cathedral church of Rochester : it ordered Oldcastle to appear within five days in the archiepiscopal court to be held in the castle of Leeds. Oldcastle again disregarded it, and Archbishop Arundel now had no alternative but to pronounce upon him the curse of the Church. At this stage of the proceedings Oldcastle's quarrel was solely with the ecclesiastical authorities : he had defied them because his conscience told him to do so. When the king, therefore, sent an officer to arrest him he made no show of resistance, but went willingly with him in obedience to the royal command.

On September 28, 1413, Oldcastle was brought into the chapter house at St Paul's to stand his trial. The court was most carefully constituted : Archbishop Arundel presided, bishops Beaufort and Clifford were the assessors, and the court had the services of ' twelve learned legists and theologians.' No praise is too great for the way in which Archbishop Arundel handled the prosecution : he showed every consideration to the accused, and promised to withdraw his curse and grant him plenary absolution provided that he would recant. Oldcastle was proudly defiant : to the archbishop's offers he turned a deaf ear, and asked permission to make a formal declaration of his faith. This privilege was accorded him : he read his statement in a clear, strong voice ; and at the same time handed a copy of it to the archbishop for the information of himself and the court.

It would be wearisome and quite unnecessary here to detail the lines of Oldcastle's arguments ; but in general terms his declaration showed no great divergence from catholic teaching, though he avoided most skilfully certain fundamental aspects of doctrine and dogma. The court at once admitted that it 'contained much good catholic truth,' but in order to bridge the gaps created by Oldcastle's omissions they asked him two vital questions : (1) Did he believe that after consecration the bread remained a material substance ? and (2) Was confession to a priest essentially part of the sacrament of penance ?

Orthodoxy had posed its 'murderous question.' Oldcastle, however, attempted to beg it, and stated that he could add nothing more to the statement which he had already made to the court. The archbishop gently reminded him that his refusal to answer the questions put to him left the court with no alternative but to pronounce him guilty of heresy ; and in order to strengthen him in the faith the learned doctors in the court were ordered to explain to the accused the Church's teaching on these questions, as given in the works of 'the foure greete doctoris '—SS. Austin, Ambrose, Jerome, and Gregory. There was no desire on the part of the court to rush Oldcastle either into orthodoxy or heresy : after the learned theological dissertation the archbishop announced that he would adjourn the court for two days so that the accused could think matters over.

When the court reassembled in the Black Friars, Oldcastle was ready to face his accusers. Now he neither attempted to beg the questions nor compromise his opinions. The bread was the material substance which veiled the invisible body of Christ, just as His humanity had veiled His divinity. Confession certainly might be beneficial to some people, and in consequence was permissible, but it was not necessary for salvation, for sin could only be purged by contrition. Oldcastle did not let the matter rest there : he wished to declare

upon other aspects of Catholicism. He said that
the cross, and not the image upon it, was worthy
of adoration ; and when asked how he would regard
that image he replied that he ' would keep it clean.'
Having cut the painter, and drifting out into the
sea of heresy, he was bold to the point of insolence.
He likened the Pope to the head of Antichrist, the
bishops to the limbs, and the friars (a direct hit
on Patrington and Walden or Netter) to the tail.
Then, turning to the crowded court, he shouted in
strident tones :

> Those who judge and mean to condemn me will seduce
> you and themselves also, and will lead you to hell. There-
> fore, beware of them.

Oldcastle's position was uncompromising throughout : the efforts to save him the indignities of con-
demnation for heresy had proved to be of no avail.
That he himself believed in the justice of his cause
is beyond the shadow of doubt ; and as a man
of the world he knew as well as any man in the
court the price which he must pay for his repeated
refusals to recant. He may have believed that
Lollardy was strong enough to save him from death :
men in their enthusiams have often misjudged the
power of their party. It is interesting, however,
to notice that nothing was said by Oldcastle during
the trial to indicate defiance of the secular authority :
he confined his opinions solely to religious matters,
although it can be argued that his final outburst
against the authority of the court was *ipso facto* a
defiance of the authority of the State which per-
mitted the functioning of such an ecclesiastical
court.

The archbishop's duty was a painful one. We
are told that when he pronounced Oldcastle guilty
of heresy he displayed ' great sorrow and bitterness
of heart,' and that there were tears in his eyes.

That done, Oldcastle was led away to the Tower
to await the punishment of the secular arm of the
law ; for while the Church condemned her prisoners
on charges for which the punishment was death
she shrank from the actual taking of life, and
bestowed that doubtful honour on the State.

One man still clung tenaciously to the faint hope
that Oldcastle could be won back to the fold of the
Church. He was old Archbishop Arundel. No
sooner was the trial ended than he went to see
Henry V. to beg him not to order the execution
until the customary forty days' grace had elapsed ;
and it was a request which the king found it impossible not to grant. Indeed, during the time that
Oldcastle was in the Tower the king and archbishop
sent visitors to him with the object of arguing him
out of his heresy ; and a form of recantation was
actually drawn out ready for his signature. Many
have believed that the king himself ordered the
guard set over the prisoner to relax their vigilance
so that he might make his escape. Be that as it
may, during the night of October 19, Oldcastle,
with the help of Richard Wrothe (undoubtedly a
Herefordshire man) and William Fisher, broke
prison ; but instead of fleeing the country—as the
king probably hoped he would do—he remained
some days in the capital, and then bolted for the
West country.

The inexorable law of self-preservation destroyed
the last vestiges of friendship which Henry had for
Oldcastle. He was the dangerous champion of
Lollardy, and the king now knew that among the
Lollards he was dubbed ' the priests' prince.' The
more reckless members of Lollardy vaunted their
imaginary strength by plastering the doors of the
churches with notices to the effect that 100,000 men
were ready to rise in arms against the monarchy ;
and for a time the excitement in the capital was

10

dangerously electric, despite the fact that with the Londoners Henry V., like his father, was intensely popular. The wildest rumours circulated throughout the country, and once again arose the spectre of a living Richard II. safe and well with friends in Scotland. One thing Henry V. could do : he could kill the force of that story by a reburial of Richard's corpse. Accordingly, in December 1413, with every mark of respect and all the pomp and ceremony due to royalty, the remains of Richard II. were brought from Chiltern Langley to Westminster, and laid reverently in the magnificent tomb which he had raised over the body of his beloved wife and queen, Anne of Bohemia. Henry attended the service in the abbey, being accompanied by a goodly array of notables of the realm—bishops, barons, and parliament-men—and the occasion was duly marked by a generous distribution of largesse among the poor, and Masses for the soul of the dead king were arranged for. So thoroughly were the details of the reburial carried out that Richard's body was placed in a new coffin—a most wise precaution, which enabled those entrusted with the gruesome task to see that the remains were those of the last Plantagenet king of England.

In the meantime Oldcastle had crossed his Rubicon, and was parading up and down the country as a traitor to his king. Under the cover of Lollardy he was able to conduct his treasonable organisation with considerable secrecy and efficiency; but by some means or other the details of his plot came to the ears of Henry V. and his ministers. Oldcastle had ordered his followers to rendezvous on the night of Tuesday, January 9, 1414, in Fickett's Field—then a favourite playground of the young clerks in the Chancery—and with this body of men he meant to force the gates of the city of London. The wildest tales of his intentions went round the city : he would despoil the city churches, murder the bishops, and take prisoners the king and his brothers. Then he would proclaim himself regent of the realm, pending the return of Richard II. from Scotland. Walsingham, drawing upon an earlier chronicle, has left a clear picture of the enthusiasm which prevailed among Oldcastle's supporters in this dangerous venture :

> You might see the crowds drawn by great promises, hastening along by footpaths, through villages, by cross-ways, from almost every county of the kingdom, to join together at the day and hour now at hand. And when asked why they thus hurried and ran themselves out of breath, they answered that they were hastening on to join lord Cobham, who had sent for them and retained them in wages.

On January 8, Henry and his brothers left Eltham, where they had been spending Christmas, for London. With them were Archbishop Arundel, Richard Courtenay, Bishop of Norwich, and a large number of 'lords and bachelors.' The king at once saw the danger of the situation : he ordered the city gates to be shut and guarded, and patrols were sent out to observe the movements of the rebels in the neighbouring countryside. Towards evening Henry met his council in his palace at Westminster, and stock was taken of the situation. Some members were for a cautious policy : they urged that the attack on the rebels ought to be deferred until daybreak. Henry himself counselled immediate action ; and there is good reason for saying that he carried his plan through the council in the face of the most determined opposition. At the head of a competent force Henry took up his position in St. Giles' Field, and awaited events. In the darkness some of the rebels mistook the royal force for their friends, and unsuspecting they marched into the camp, immediately to be disarmed and taken prisoners ; and when the others found that the promised support of the Londoners was not forthcoming they lost heart, and in their attempt to get back to their homes were roughly handled by pursuing royalist troops.

Dangerous though the plot had appeared, it ended in fiasco. Oldcastle himself—if indeed he actually was present at the muster in Fickett's Field—escaped, but many of his followers were prisoners in Henry's hands. On January 10 a special commission was set up to deal with the imprisoned rebels. No pretence was made at judicial trial : the accused were summarily condemned, and sent in batches to be hanged on the ' Lollers Gallows,' specially erected for the occasion on the high road near to St. Giles' Field ; and fires were piled beneath the hanging bodies of the more notorious rebels. Other commissions dealt with suspected persons in various parts of the realm ; and a price was put on Oldcastle's head.

On January 15 a solemn service of thanksgiving was held in London. Henry and his three brothers attended ; and the Litany was sung and the prayers for the extirpation of heresy were said by Archbishop Arundel. It happened that this was the old man's last triumph. He had already suffered some inconvenience from a quinsy, and he was far from well. On February 19 he died in the rectory of Hackington, near to his cathedral city of Canterbury.

And what was the fate of Oldcastle ?

After the disaster at Fickett's Field he returned to his Herefordshire estates—for on the Welsh border the king's writ ran imperfectly, and excellent sanctuaries were to be had in Wales for the king's enemies. For three years he remained a thorn in the side of Henry's government, although steps had been taken—particularly in the Leicester

parliament held in 1414—to arm the authorities
with wider powers for the overthrow of Lollardy.
Henry V., however, rightly believed that Oldcastle's
power was not sufficiently strong to compel him to
remain in England, and as we shall presently see
in 1415 the king began his great attack on France.
It is true that on the departure of the king Oldcastle made an attempt to marshal the Lollards in
treason.   He appears to have been lurking at that
time in the Malvern country—a country steeped in
the socialism of Langland—and he planned an attack
on Richard Beauchamp, lord of Bergavenny (Abergavenny), while he lay at his castle of Hanley.
Beauchamp had little trouble in beating off the
attackers, and the movement collapsed almost as
suddenly as it had begun.   In the following year
—1416—the hand of Oldcastle was seen at work
in the attack which the Scots made on the northern
districts of the kingdom ;   and it was currently
reported that he had actually had an interview with
William, Earl Douglas, at Pontefract, with the object
of persuading him to place ' Richard II.' on the
English throne.   Once he came near to capture by
the men of the Abbot of St Albans ; and in 1417
in a stiff engagement at Cae'r Barwn, near Welshpool, he was taken prisoner by Edward Charleton,
lord of Powys.   He had been wounded in the engagement, and in consequence was compelled to
journey to London in a horse litter.   On December
14 he was brought before parliament : the record
of his outlawry was read out to him, and he was
asked to show cause why he should not die for his
treason.   His defence was a long and rambling
sermon on the mercy of God.   John, Duke of Bedford, regent of the realm in his brother's absence
overseas, ordered him to keep to the point, and not
to waste parliament's time with irrelevances.   In
an instant Oldcastle's defiance returned, and to the

regent's remark he flashed back the Pauline utter-
ance :

> With me it is a very small thing that I should be judged
> of you or of man's judgment.

Again he endeavoured to lecture the assembled
parliament, but this time the Chief Justice inter-
vened, reminding him that he was there to give
reasons why he ought not to be put to death for his
contumacy. It was at this point in the proceedings
that he boldly declared himself to be Richard's man :
he would recognise no other king. Lords and
commons at once petitioned that he should be put
to death for his heresy and treason ; and the regent
gave his consent. The sentence—that he was to
be drawn on a hurdle from the Tower to the ' new
gallows in the parish of St Giles outside the bar of
the Old Temple,' and there put to death by hanging
and burning—was read out to him ; and he was led
away to prison. The record of his escape from the
Tower during his previous imprisonment was fresh
in the memories of parliament, and in order to avoid
a repetition the execution was fixed for later in the
day. John, Duke of Bedford, and the lords and
commons were present at the gallows ; and as they
brought the old rebel to be pinioned the regent sadly
told him that he grieved for him with all his heart.
Oldcastle told him that it would be better if he
grieved for himself. They then offered him the
services of a confessor, but he defiantly told them
that he would not confess his sins even to St. Peter
or St Paul if they were present. To Sir Thomas
Erpyngham, a gallant soldier whom he must have
known well in the days of the wars against Glyn
Dŵr (for Erpyngham had been in Prince Henry's
household), he said that he would rise from the dead
on the third day : this terrible blasphemy shocked
all who heard it, and the order was given for the
law to take its course.

If this last statement is true then charity compels us to see in Oldcastle the victim of a religious mania. Such a view does not detract from the splendour of his sacrifice in the cause of a reformed religion : throughout his later life he showed in his adherence to Lollardy the same grim determination which had won for him the highest praise in the Welsh wars.   He was courageous even in his treason, for it is inconceivable that he could have been actuated by personal dislike for the king under whom he had soldiered ; and his championship of the cause of Richard II. was due solely to his belief that Henry V. was a puppet in the hands of Antichrist—the bishops and clergy of the realm.   At the same time justice demands fairness for his enemies.   They acted against him because they sincerely believed that his doctrines were subversive to good governance in Church and State ; and—a fact which is too often forgotten—they regarded the Lollards as men who had departed from the scriptural interpretation of religion.

CHAPTER FIVE

THE GATHERING OF THE WAR CLOUDS

THE motives which prompted Henry V. to break the twenty-five years' truce made in 1396 and continue the war with France are confused and difficult to follow. In a later age Englishmen believed that the clergy, headed by Henry Chichele who succeeded Thomas Arundel in the metropolitan see of Canterbury, purposely fostered in the king's breast a spirit of hostility towards the French in order to divert his attention from a matter which touched them nearly—disendowment; and the story was given more permanent form by Shakespeare in his *King Henry the Fifth*.

The question of disendowment had certainly been discussed. Many Englishmen believed that riches were choking the spiritual life of the Church, and in 1410 a petition had been presented in parliament with the object of vesting the property of the bishops and abbots in the king. Here can be seen the influence of Wiclif and his Lollards; but it should be remembered that the country generally did not accept the Wiclifite position. The young king Henry had certainly given no indication that he favoured such a policy; and it was not long before he emerged as an uncompromising champion of orthodox religion. It is true, however, that early in his reign a measure of disendowment had passed through parliament; but it is significant that it aroused no great outcry in clerical quarters; and there was good reason why it should not. For long enough wealthy French monastic foundations had derived incomes from dependent houses in England ; and in many cases these alien priories were peopled with men and women from overseas. When the alien priories were attacked in the Leicester parliament of 1414, and eventually deprived of their income, the country generally applauded what to them was only an attack on the hated Frenchmen.

The fact that the clergy gave Henry their un-qualified support once he had embarked upon war with France has been thought to lend colour to the story. Why were they so eager to see their king at war with the French ? The answer is not far to seek. The English clergy hated the influence which the French court exerted in the affairs of Christendom, and believed that that influence was hurtful to the interests of religion. The memory of the enforced residence of the popes at Avignon was fresh in men's minds : the more recent schism had largely been brought about by French intermeddling in papal affairs. In attacking France, therefore, Henry was attacking the power which created so much confusion in the Church— at least that opinion was firmly fixed in the minds of English churchmen ; and it was only natural that they should support Henry to the utmost of their ability.[10]

Is this story of the clergy's attempt to divert the attention of Henry from disendowment abso-lutely without foundation ? It would be dangerous to say that it is. It must be remembered that the story was told by a generation which lived nearer to Henry's times than we do, and it may possibly contain the germ of historical truth. Henry V., like his father before him, was always in desperate need of money. His parliament gave him its confidence, and endorsed his warlike schemes ; but the grants which it voted were totally inadequate to meet the charges of a great war, and were barely sufficient for the ordinary expenses of government. Aware of the king's poverty, therefore, the clergy may have feared that the time would come when the king would be tempted to lay hands upon the wealth of the Church, and they would not have to be reminded that such an act would meet with a large measure of popular approval. The easiest way of meeting the danger was to join the war-party which clamoured for a renewal of hostilities. War would keep the king's hands full : he would have little time for such matters as ecclesiastical reform. But this explanation cannot be sup-ported by historical evidence : it is advanced merely to explain the origin of a story which was every-where told and universally believed in the sixteenth century.

In some quarters it has been the fashion to accuse Henry of wilfully provoking a quarrel with France in order to satisfy his megalomaniacal ambitions. That he was ambitious is undeniable : he was young and had youth's capacity for dreaming dreams of greatness and fame. His whole life had been devoted to warlike pursuits : he could not fail to know that he had acquitted himself well in the field, and as a keen soldier it was natural that he should seek to rise to the heights of his pro-fession. His critics will admit all this : the sting of their criticism is to be found in the charge that Henry sought to win renown at the expense of a neighbouring state at a time when it was torn by internal dissensions. In other words, they accuse him of taking a miserable and cowardly advantage of the misfortunes of the French people. While it is impossible to say that Henry would have made war against a united France, the record of his career proves that he was not wanting in personal courage. The king who could march his little army from Harfleur to Calais, through the heart of a hostile countryside and in the knowledge that the French would almost certainly bar his path, was quite capable of hurling defiance at the strongest power in western Europe.

On his death-bed he murmured words about his intention of regaining from the infidel the Holy Land ; and it has been suggested that his attack on France was a well-planned stage in this scheme. He meant to conquer France in order to unite the military powers of the two kingdoms, and then at the head of a mighty crusading force to challenge the Turk's hold on Palestine.

It is more probable, however, that Henry embarked upon the French war in the interests of his own dynasty. He knew that the Lancastrian title was weak ; he might strengthen it by a successful war. Men still talked of the glorious achievements of Edward III. and the Black Prince : how at Crécy and Poitiers a handful of English soldiers rolled up and destroyed the magnificent armies of the French kings ; and the popular delight in these memories was due to no indecent and unnatural bellicosity on the part of the people of England, but to the fact that these victories had been won by the yeomen of England—simple people who neither bore arms on their shields nor wore richly plumed basnets on their heads. Henry V., after his experience in Wales, felt it within his power to follow in the footsteps of Edward III. and the Black Prince ; and he was no doubt aware that in making this decision he would divert the warlike spirits of his realm into channels which would not converge in an attack on the House of Lancaster.

Once he had embarked upon this policy he did not lack the enthusiastic support of his people. War in the Middle Ages, from the nobleman's point of view, was a pleasant and profitable undertaking. It afforded him with an opportunity of displaying his skill in the use of weapons ; and by booty and ransoms his income could be appreciably augmented. The ordinary soldiers—the archers particularly—shared these feelings with their noble captains. Men, who Sunday after Sunday at the butts in their respective parishes shot with deadly accuracy, would welcome a chance to try out their marksmanship against living targets ; and, as will be presently seen, they were well paid for their services. War was a great adventure in an age which had few diversions : and a love of adventure was the Englishman's heritage even in the fifteenth century.

Soon after he came to the throne Henry found plenty of evidence of the popularity of a French war. Such notable merchants of London as Dick Whittington and John Hende were ready to advance him money for that purpose ; and many of the clergy and nobles followed their example. In the summer of 1413 envoys from Burgundy came to ask the king to help the duke against the Armagnacs, and at the end of July Henry Chichele, Bishop of St. David's, Richard Beauchamp, Earl of Warwick, Henry, Lord Scrope of Masham, and William, Lord Zouche, went overseas to continue the negotiations. Later in the year they had an interview with the duke himself, during which there was talk that Henry should marry one of his daughters and that the duke should help the English to seize certain French towns. And yet in December of the same year an embassy from the Armagnac government in Paris was in London : it was led by Guillaume Boisratier, Archbishop of Bourges, and Charles d'Albret, Constable of France.

The truth of the matter is that both factions in France were eager to secure Henry's friendship for the advancement of their own selfish ambitions, and the king must not be blamed for skilfully playing off one party against the other. It was imperative that they should not compose their differences and unite against him : once that happened they would seek to regain the lands which the English already held in France. So envoys from both sides came and went with baffling regularity ; and it is now well-nigh impossible to present the story of the double negotiations in an intelligible form. One common principle ran through the negotiations with both parties : Henry must marry a wife. At one moment she was to be a daughter of the Duke of Burgundy : at another, the daughter of the king of France. Henry himself undoubtedly preferred the latter arrangement. Every one who had seen the Princess Catherine praised her beauty and grace, though she was still merely a child, and opinion was sharply divided on the attractiveness of the other Catherine, the Duke of Burgundy's daughter — a fellow-countryman likened her to a featherless owlet, and was promptly punished for his lack of consideration for a lady's feelings !

While the parliament which met at Leicester was in session (it was opened on April 30 and broke up on May 29, 1414) Armagnac and Burgundian embassies were in the country ; and the old game of double dealing was played by Henry's representatives. But the king had obviously come to the parting of the ways. The Armagnacs were in the ascendancy in France, and to them must be stated his demands : at the same time he was shrewd enough to realise that in the coming struggle he must secure either the neutrality or, better still, the active support of the Duke of Burgundy. Burgundy was thereupon promised English help in his struggle with his Armagnac enemies, and a force was sent to his country. Coincident with this move was the appointment of envoys to treat with the king of France and his Armagnac friends.

On June 1, therefore, Cardinal Thomas Langley, Bishop of Durham, Richard Courtenay, Bishop of Norwich, Thomas Montacute, Earl of Salisbury, Richard, Lord Grey of Codnor, John Pelham, Henry Ware, and Robert Waterton were commissioned to proceed to the court of the king of France. On their arrival in Paris on August 8 they were received in state by the Duke of Berri, Charles VI.'s representative, and for the next eight days were feasted and entertained in a sumptuous manner. Time came for the negotiations to begin. The Duke of Berri invited the English envoys to state their case, which was done by Bishop Courtenay in the form of a sermon, preached from the text—' We be come from a far country to make a league with you.' He asked for the hand of the Princess Catherine, and coupled with this most reasonable request the preposterous demand that the king of France should surrender his throne and kingdom to Henry. This claim to the French throne was not seriously meant, for the bishop quickly informed the French delegates that Henry might be satisfied with less, and proceeded to define what he meant by calling upon the French to cede in full sovereignty to the king of England the territories specified in the Treaty of Brétigni,[11] and recognise the English suzerainty over Anjou, Maine, Brittany, Flanders, Touraine, and Normandy. But Bishop Courtenay did not stop at that : he further demanded the lordships of Beaufort and Nogent in Provence, and asked for the payment of 1,600,000 crowns due under the arrangement made for the ransom of the French king John in 1360.

The Duke of Berri adopted a surprisingly conciliatory attitude. He said that the French king would cede in full sovereignty the duchy of Aquitaine as it had existed at the time of the English king Henry II. His royal master would do this in the interests of peace, and prevent further unnecessary effusion of Christian blood. As regards the lordship of Beaufort and Nogent in Provence these were not his to give ; and Henry must thrash out his claim with the Duke of Anjou, who was also Count of Provence. He further observed that his government would be prepared to give the Princess Catherine as her dower 600,000 crowns—a much larger sum than was usually given to a king's daughter ; and suggested that the question of King John's ransom might be left over for further discussion. The conference thereupon broke up ; and the English embassy was dismissed with the object of reporting to its royal master. Before the envoys left Paris, however, the duke presented them with costly presents of gold and tapestry.

About this time is supposed to have occurred an incident which did more than anything else to arouse the anger of the English people against the French. The tale went round that the dauphin had sent Henry

> a tonne full of tenys ballis because he wolde have somewhat for to play wt all for hym and for hys lordis, and that became hym better than to mayntain any Were.

The nation received a thrill of pride when they heard that Henry had answered the dauphin to the effect that,

> as sone as Good wolde send hym grace and myght,

he would return the compliment with ' grete gonne stones ' made in London, and they would bring the power of France tumbling about his ears.

It is unbelievable that the dauphin should have acted so foolishly. It is true, he was a thoroughly irresponsible young man ; but the code of chivalry set limits even to the bad behaviour of a reprobate ; and in the face of this insult Henry would have no alternative but to break off all negotiations with the French government. Nevertheless, negotiations were continued, and in the official documents connected with them there is no record of the tennis balls incident. On the other hand, it finds its place in chronicles which can be more or less regarded as contemporary ; and there is evidence to show that it was popularly believed by the king's subjects. The whole business of what was called ' the bitter mock ' is shrouded in mystery.

About Michaelmas Henry summoned a great council of the magnates of the realm to confer with him at Westminster on the subject of his claim to the French throne. His case was put ; and they answered that while they had every confidence in his judgment they hoped that he would do all in his power to prevent an effusion of Christian blood, and suggested that further negotiations should be opened with the French. On November 19, parliament met. Bishop Beaufort's text was, ' While we have time let us do good,' and he proceeded to elaborate it with customary pedantry. For every natural thing there were proper seasons : with the tree there was a time to bud, a time to flower, and a time to bring forth fruit ; and so with man there was a time for peace and a time for war and work. The realm of England had enjoyed the blessings of peace, and in view of the French refusal to recognise the justice of the king's claim, the time was now at hand for war. To this end three things were necessary : wise and faithful counsel, strong and loyal support, and a generous subsidy. The parliament-men were subtly reminded that the more the king's dominions were extended the less would be the charges upon the people of England—incidentally a curious piece of logic—and that as a result of a successful war great honour and glory would accrue to the nation.

Could the king's determination to go to war with France be more clearly put ? The parliament-men gave the bishop a patient and enthusiastic hearing : his hint that no great charges would fall upon the nation doubtless met with murmurs of approval, for Lancastrian parliaments were re-nowned for their parsimony ; and when the time for deliberation came they showed their agreement with the royal plans by voting two-fifteenths and two-tenths. They were at pains, however, to explain that the taxes were intended for the defence of the realm and the safety of the seas ; and at the same time they said that in their opinion the king would be well advised to send further envoys to the court of France in the hope that right might be done by peaceful means. When the routine of parliamentary business had been completed the members returned to their homes (December 7).

Henry respected parliament's wishes, and before the session was ended he appointed another embassy to negotiate with the French. Cardinal Langley and Bishop Courtenay were the chief plenipo-tentiaries ; but they were accompanied by Thomas Beaufort, Earl of Dorset, Richard, Lord Grey of Codnor, Sir William Bouchier, Sir John Phelip, William Porter, Philip Morgan, and Richard Holme. With them went a bodyguard of 600 armed horse-men, and they arrived in Paris on February 9. The dauphin himself gave strict orders that the English envoys were to receive the best of hospi-tality; and before the actual negotiations opened Charles VI. asked them to dine with him. They saw the Princess Catherine, were charmed by her appearance and graciousness, and took away with them a painted portrait so that Henry might see what manner of woman he had chosen for his queen.

The French envoys were Guillaume Boisratier, Archbishop of Bourges, Pierre Fresnel, Bishop of Noyon, Charles, Count of Eu, and Guillaume Martel, Seigneur of Bacqueville.

It was not until March 12 that the actual discussions opened. ' Let but peace and truth be made in my days ' was the text from which Bishop Courtenay preached ; and a very subtle sermon did he deliver. It was a good sign, he said, that the people of France wished for peace, and he reminded his hearers that the saintly Brigit had foretold that there would be no peace between the two kingdoms until their royal houses were united by marriage. His own people wanted peace no less sincerely than the French ; but there could be no peace without justice. Thereupon the bishop detailed the *just* demands of the English king. Once again were stated the claim to the French throne, Henry's rights in certain French lands, and the desire for a marriage with the Princess Catherine : the latter was accompanied by the usual details about the value of the princess's dower.

The French categorically rejected Henry's claim to the throne and realm of France. They were willing, however, to make concessions in the matter of the duchy of Aquitaine ; but in doing so they considered that they had more than satisfied the English king, and therefore put forward the view that the concessions might be regarded as wiping out the arrears of King John's ransom. They were as anxious as the English for a marriage alliance ; but the English demand that the Princess Catherine should have a dowry of 2,000,000 crowns was quite unreasonable. So some time was spent in haggling over the value of the dowry. The English envoys dropped their demand first to 1,500,000 and finally to 1,000,000 crowns : the French raised their offer from 600,000 to 800,000 crowns.

Nothing further could usefully be done in the conference. The English embassy made it clear that they were not empowered to make terms on the basis suggested by the French, and said that they must report back to the king. The French expressed the hope that even if a deadlock ensued on the territorial issues the English king would receive a further embassy in order to conclude the marriage alliance which both parties so obviously desired. With the courtesy traditional of their race the French showered valuable presents upon the English envoys, and wished them godspeed. These reached London at the end of March, and at once reported to the king that the conference had been abortive, though they had gone out of their way to be conciliatory, and in the interest of peace had considerably modified the *just* demands of their king.

For some months Henry had been preparing for an attack on France. In September 1414 he ordered a certain Nicholas Merbury, one of the masters of Ordnance, to engage artificers for the manufacture of ' gonnes ' and other engines of war ; and about the same time an ordinance was issued making it illegal to ship gunpowder out of the realm. In the following March at the king's command Richard Clyderow and Simon Flete travelled to Holland to hire ships to be at his service in English ports in May ; and there is abundant evidence to prove that vast stores of ordnance and arrows were being accumulated in London.

Some of Henry's critics have endeavoured to make these warlike preparations the proof of his insincerity and hypocrisy. They maintain that he smugly talked peace, and yet all the time made ready for war ; and sometimes it is suggested that

the peace talks were deliberately planned to prevent
the French from attacking him before he was ready
to attack them. This view is wrong. England
and France were still at war when Henry V. came
to the throne. By the terms of a truce actual
fighting had ceased ; but at any moment a truce
might be broken or not renewed, and fighting would
then be continued. Even under modern conditions
of warfare an armistice does not require belligerents
to cease their warlike preparations : nor is it
necessarily a prelude to peace. In the great
European war of 1914 to 1918 fighting on the
western front actually ceased by the terms of an
armistice to become operative in November 1918 ;
but peace with Germany was not concluded until
the end of June 1919 ; and in the interval, between
the armistice and the Treaty of Versailles, allied
ships maintained, as they had a right to maintain,
a strict blockade of the German ports. And a
blockade is as much an act of war as a naval or
military engagement.

The breakdown of the negotiations in Paris in
March 1415 made a renewal of the war inevitable ;
and as a capable soldier and statesman Henry
speeded up his warlike preparations. On April 16
he met a great council of notables in his palace at
Westminster, and through the mouth of Bishop
Beaufort he announced his intention to invade the
realm of the king of France. On the following day
he appointed John, Duke of Bedford, to be the
regent during his absence from England. He was
to have at his disposal the services of a council of
nine ; and among the members of this council
would be such wise and capable men as Archbishop
Chichele, Cardinal Langley, and Bishop Beaufort.
The arrangements for the defence of the realm were
outlined : they were concerned with the defence of
the Anglo-Scottish border and the holding down of

Wales. On April 18 Henry announced the rates of pay in his expeditionary force, and settled the method of raising men for service abroad.

The rates of pay are interesting. A duke was to receive 13s. 4d. a day ; an earl, 6s. 8d. ; a baron, 4s. ; a knight, 2s. ; a squire or man-at-arms, 12d. ; and an archer, 6d. Henry's army was to be raised by indentures or contracts. He could require all the tenants-in-chief of the Crown to serve overseas for forty days at their own cost ; but at the end of that period they were free to return home, or if they continued to serve they did so at the king's cost. That was the old feudal idea. Henry knew its inherent weaknesses and decided to rely upon a paid army. Many of the indentures or contracts are extant, and it is, therefore, possible from them to see how the system worked.[12]

A noble or knight undertook to raise so many men-at-arms and archers at the stipulated rates of pay. He himself was responsible for the payment of his company ; but by the terms of the indenture received from the king, payment at definite periods in the campaign, or pledges that payment would be made by given dates. A special ' regard ' or bounty of 100 marks was paid to every captain in respect of every thirty men-at-arms in his company. The king undertook to convey the companies and their horses overseas at his own expense, and to provide the necessary provisions for the voyage ; but once the campaign commenced each man provided his own food out of his pay, or, if necessity demanded, procured it by foraging in the countryside. All prisoners taken during the campaign belonged to the captains of the companies by whom they were captured ; but the king of France, his sons, nephews, uncles, cousins-german and chief officers of the French army were to be regarded as royal captives, though the king would make a compensation to

the actual captors. All booty or ' gagnes of war '
belonged to the captains of the companies, who
distributed it as follows : one-third to the king,
one-third to the men of their respective companies,
and one-third to their own use.

Henry found no difficulty in raising a well-
trained army under these conditions. The pay
was good. Captains found that they could turn
company-raising into a profitable business ; and
the ordinary soldiers were quite satisfied with the
condition of their service. When Henry put a
stop to looting there were murmurs : he had
deprived his men of a source of income, and they
not unnaturally resented it. But his injunctions
against looting did not necessarily mean a loss in
booty : what Henry tried to do—and by force of
character succeeding in doing—was to prevent his
men perpetrating acts of violence against the non-
combatant population. They were free to strip
the dead and rob the armouries in captured towns,
even though they were denied the satisfaction of
raping young women and robbing churches.

The Duke of Clarence contracted to raise 240
men-at-arms and 720 archers—the largest company
in the expeditionary force. Both the Duke of
York and the Earl of Dorset came with 100 men-
at-arms and 300 archers ; and the numbers were
graduated downwards until we come to one surgeon
having in his train only three archers. All the
fighting men were mounted—even the archers ;
and this explains the rapidity with which Henry
was able to move through hostile country.

In addition to the men-at-arms and archers
there were gunners, many of whom were recruited
in Germany or Flanders, sappers and miners,
chirurgeons and physicians, chaplains and minstrels ;
and all were put upon the pay-roll of the army.

Throughout the months of April, May, and June

Henry and his ministers were busily engaged in making ready for the coming expedition to France. On April 11, a sergeant-at-arms, Nicholas Maudyt, was authorised to impress into the royal service all vessels of twenty tons and upwards ; and a few days later Nicholas Frost, a bowyer, was commanded to provide bows and bow-staves from the royal lands and elsewhere. In May, Robert Hunt, who was the sergeant of the waggons of the royal household, was told to collect a commissariat train ; and Stephen Ferrour, sergeant of the royal farriers, was set to work to gather together a supply of horseshoes and nails. On June 6, orders were issued to Simon Lewys and John Benet to recruit 100 of the best and most able masons ; to Thomas Mathew and William Gill to find 120 carpenters ; and to William Mersh and Nicholas Thokyngton to raise 40 smiths. Great quantities of bows, arrows, and goose quills were moved from the arsenals to the seaports ; ships were refitted in the royal dockyards ; and master gunners tested and proved the newly cast ' gonnes.'

So great an undertaking required considerable financial backing ; and that is what Henry could not get from his parliaments. The taxes voted in the parliament of the previous autumn were quickly exhausted ; and he found himself at his wits' end for ready money. By the terms of the contracts he had to pay the captains of the companies the first quarter's pay in advance ; and many of the contingents were mustered at the seaports of the south coast as early as the middle of June. There was nothing for it but to use every known means of raising money. Loans were raised. In many cases corporations or subjects offered them voluntarily : in others they were asked for in such a way that the lender dared not refuse to part with his money. Security was given, and in many cases repayment was made within a very short time of the lending of the money.   Even the Crown jewels had to be put into pawn.   The *Harry Crown*, for example, was broken up, and the parts held as security by four creditors :

> To sir John Colvyl, a great flower de lys part of the said Crown, garnished with one great balays, and one other balays, one ruby, three great sapphires, and ten great pearls.
> To John Pudsey, esq., a pinnacle of the aforesaid crown, garnished with two sapphires, one square balays, and six pearls.
> To Maurice Brune a pinnacle of the said crown garnished as the former.
> To John Saundish, another of the pinnacles garnished as those above.

Another creditor, Sir Thomas Hanley, received as pledges ' a pair of gold spurs ' and the sword, ' garnished with ostriches' feather,' which had belonged to Edward, Black Prince ; and even the sacred vessels of the royal chapels were made to do their duty as security in that feverish scramble for money.

On June 16, Henry left Westminster in order to be nearer the scene of the mustering of his expeditionary force.   After having bidden his stepmother, Queen Joanna, farewell, he rode to Paul's Church where he made an offering ; and as he rode with his retinue through the principal thoroughfares of the city he was escorted by the mayor, aldermen, and between 300 and 400 citizens.   They rode with him to the Church of St George, which stood at the junction of Kent Road and High Street in Southwark.   Henry made another offering in the Church of St George ; and then dismissed the Londoners.   Gazing upon the city he said :

Christ save London !

That done he rode along the road which passed

through Kingston to Winchester, which was reached on June 20. Bishop Beaufort had placed at his nephew's disposal his episcopal palace ; and there Henry waited to receive the embassy which was already on their way from Paris to make one last effort to avoid war.

It was in the city of Winchester that the curtain went up on the last act in the drama which ended in a renewal of hostilities between England and France. On June 30 there rode into the city a French embassy, consisting of the Archbishop of Bourges, the Bishop of Lisieux, the Count of Vendôme, and the Seigneur of Ivry. Henry himself received them almost immediately after their arrival, being accompanied at the audience by his three brothers, Cardinal Langley, bishops Beaufort and Courtenay, the Duke of York, and Sir John Holland. His manner was exceptionally gracious ; and the envoys were invited to dine with him on the following day, after which the formal negotiations would begin.

The peace conference was opened with a sermon from the French archbishop. Taking as his text, ' Peace be to thee and to thy house,' he emphasised the need for peace between the two realms, and assured his English hearers that no man desired peace more sincerely than his royal master, Charles. Bishop Beaufort replied on behalf of the king of England. He said that the archbishop's sermon had created a favourable impression upon the English, but they were at a loss to understand why there were so many delays, and hoped that in the present negotiations the French would act with greater expedition.

On July 2, when the conference was resumed, Bishop Beaufort asked the French envoys to table their proposals in concrete form. The archbishop replied that in order to secure peace Charles VI. was

ready to make great concessions—to hand over
territory in Aquitaine and to provide the Princess
Catherine with a dowry of 800,000 crowns ; and in
return he hoped the English king would dismiss
the army which was being mustered for an attack on
France. The English reply contained the old
stumbling-block—Henry meant to have his *rights* ;
and the French were baldly told that he would be
put off with nothing less. Why had they not
mentioned Normandy and other French lands to
which Henry laid claim ? Before the day was out
tempers were badly frayed, and both sides indulged
in heated arguments.

On the next day the English announced one
modification in their demands : they were ready to
accept the princess with a dowry of 900,000 crowns
instead of 1,000,000 crowns. The French archbishop replied that his government's offer was the
limit, but in order to secure peace they would offer
800,000 francs instead of crowns—a concession of
about £50,000. So for that day they haggled over
the princess's dowry ; they could come to no agreement on the matter, and it was little discussed
during the further negotiations.

Henry himself then decided to take a hand in
the conference. On July 4 he asked the envoys to
meet him, and pressed them to explain to him their
proposals. The archbishop stated his government's
case, as he had already stated it to the English
plenipotentiaries ; and it is said that Henry appeared
to be fully satisfied. For a moment it seemed as
though peace was in sight ; but when the formal
conference met on July 6 a deadlock almost immediately ensued. The English asked that the Princess
Catherine should be sent to England to marry Henry
not later than November 30, 1415 : the French
replied that this left them with insufficient time to
raise the necessary monies for her dowry. The

English immediately suspected the French of playing for time ; and once again tempers were lost.

Henry apparently was present during the arguments on that day. When he saw that his representatives could not pin down the Frenchmen to definite promises and actual dates he flew into a rage, and reminded them that he was the *rightful* king of France, and that he was resolved to have his *right*. At the king's words the Archbishop of Bourges threw caution to the winds, and blurted out :

> Sir, the king of France our sovereign lord is true king of France, and over those things to which you say you have a right ; you have no lordship not even to the kingdom of England, which belongs to the true heirs of the late king Richard ; nor with you can our sovereign lord safely treat.

In an atmosphere, so charged with threats, further negotiations were impossible. In a terrible rage Henry told the French envoys to get back to their own country, adding that he would soon follow them ; and with this threat he flung himself out of the conference chamber. Before the French embassy left Winchester on July 9 Bishop Beaufort handed to them a written ultimatum ; and on reading it once again the archbishop's temper deserted him. Let Henry of England come to France : he would quickly find that the Frenchmen were more than a match for his men. The concessions which the French king had made did not mean that he was afraid of the power of England. Henry would soon find out his mistake : he would either be killed in battle or taken prisoner.

After the archbishop had reminded Henry that he was not lawful king of England, the king decided that his presence in Winchester was no longer necessary ; and in the evening of July 6 he left for Southampton to meet his army and to super-

intend personally the final preparations for the
departure of the expeditionary force. Nothing
must be left to chance in the coming trial of strength
with the French king ; and with his customary
thoroughness he saw to it that every branch of his
army was ready for the struggle. On July 24 he
made his last will and testament, and in his own
hand wrote on it :

> This is my last will, subscribed with my own hand,
> R. H. Jesu Mercy and Gremercy Ladie Marie help.

And then came a most unexpected and painful
blow. The young Earl of March came to the king
with the information that a plot was on foot to
murder Henry and his brothers and to place him
(the Earl of March) on the throne. The chief
conspirators were Richard, Earl of Cambridge,
who was a brother of the Duke of York, Henry,
Lord Scrope of Masham, and Sir Thomas Grey of
Heton ; and they were to be supported by Oldcastle and his Lollards and disaffected persons in
Wales and Scotland.

Henry acted quickly and relentlessly. The
conspirators were arrested and thrown into prison.
Sir Thomas Grey was summarily executed after he
had confessed his fault. The Earl of Cambridge
also admitted his guilt, and threw himself on the
king's mercy ; but the Lord of Masham denied
treasonable complicity in the plot, and attempted
to persuade the king that he had merely tried to
learn the details in order to warn him at the proper
time. Both the Earl and the Lord of Masham
claimed to be tried by their peers. They were
promptly found guilty and sentenced to death.
As royal blood flowed in the veins of the Earl of
Cambridge he was spared some of the indignities
which were attached to a mediæval execution, and
was merely beheaded. Scrope of Masham could

expect no pity from the king. He had been his friend—and had even shared the royal bed ; and had been employed on some of the weightiest business of State. So like a common felon he was drawn on a hurdle to the place of execution ; and his head was sent to adorn one of the gates of York —and to remind Englishmen in the country where the Scropes exercised great power that the king would make a sharp end of traitors. Incidentally the incident had no repercussions in the country, though help was promised by Oldcastle and his Lollards.

CHAPTER SIX

HARFLEUR AND AGINCOURT

IN the roadsteads hard by Portsmouth lay 1500 ships
of all shapes and sizes, awaiting the coming of
Henry V. On August 7 he went on board *La
Trinité Royale*, the pride of the royal navy. Two
magnificent figures of the Trinity and Our Lady
were her protection against wind and weather, and
on her wooden walls were painted the arms of St
Edward Confessor, St George, and England. As
soon as Henry was aboard he signalled the other
ships to get into position astern of *La Trinité
Royale* ; and a contemporary states that ' a goodlye
syghte it was to see ' this armada—for the gunwales of the vessels were bedecked with shields of
the knights ; and their banners, and the pennons of
the bannerets, floated in the breeze. And even so
there were not enough transports to take over all
the troops who had come to Southampton and
Portsmouth.

The departure was delayed by a mishap : three
ships took fire, and were gutted. Many men said
that it was the hand of God, shewing Henry the
wrongfulness of invading the lands of his neighbour ;
and when this went the round of the army, men
grew afraid at the thought of the unknown dangers
awaiting them. The king, however, was in no
mood to hearken to divine disapproval of his
cherished plans, and on the afternoon of Sunday,
August 11, the fleet put to sea. The gloom occasioned by the popular interpretation of the incident
of the burnt-out ships vanished when near the

Isle of Wight a large number of swans were seen swimming among the ships ; from classical times the swan was regarded as an emblem of purity and justice, and the optimists in Henry's force at once believed that these birds endorsed the justice of the king's cause.

Navigation in the Middle Ages was not an exact science ; ships were set a course, but the winds and storms often upset the shipmaster's calculations. Few, if any, of the company knew where they were bound for ; but during the voyage Henry ordered his admiral to set his course for Harfleur ; and in the afternoon of August 13 the ships came to anchor near that town, opposite to a headland called Chef de Caux. (The English seamen, as indifferent then to the niceties of foreign pronunciations as their descendants now, knew the headland as *Kidcocks* or *Kidcaus*.) The king at once gave orders that no one—'under pain of death '—was to land that night ; he had no intention of seeing a fine army melt away beneath his eyes because isolated parties of soldiers were anxious to fill their bellies with looted French wine and Norman cider, or to secure creature comforts from the forced caresses of captured women.

It was the vigil of the Assumption of the Blessed Virgin (August 14) when the disembarkation of the invaders began. In the night a patrol of daring men—Sir John Holland (later to be rewarded for his services with the earldom of Huntingdon, forfeited by his father for treason in Henry IV.'s time), Gilbert Umfraville, John Cornwall, John Grey, and William Porter—had reconnoitred the countryside in order to ascertain if any hostile demonstration was to be offered to the landing-party. But all they could say was that the French kept behind the walls of Harfleur.

It was a glorious August morning when, between

six and seven o'clock, Henry V. of England stepped ashore on land which he regarded as his by right of inheritance—the duchy of Normandy. One of his fifteenth-century biographers tells us :

> Then forthwith the king falling upon his knees, devoutly prayed unto God, that to the honour of his divinity he would give him justice of his enemies.

He then told off the men who were to carry the banners and standards of the royal army—' men whom he knew to be of great strength and prowess ' —and before moving off he dubbed as knights ' divers gentlemen ' in the host.

Henry selected as his headquarters the Priory of Graville, perched on

> an high hill dificile and uneasie for armed men to mount upon.

There were installed the officers of the king's household and their servants. There, too, were billeted Thomas, Duke of Clarence, and Humphrey, Duke of Gloucester. Indeed one is amazed at the strangeness of the company accommodated in the Priory of Graville. A French prisoner, for example, was much struck by the beautiful singing of the ' king's choristers,' who were brought all the way from England to sing the offices of Church ; and for the entertainment of the headquarters staff in the evenings or at meal-time were companies of minstrels.

The landing of the horses, stores, and ordnance kept the troops and seamen busy until the following Saturday (August 17). It was a dangerous foreshore, and the utmost care had to be exercised in the beaching of the ships. While this work was going on scouts were scouring the surrounding countryside : the inactivity of the French was unbelievable, and Henry was concerned lest a

hidden force might pounce down upon him. At
the same time it was imperative that he should
have the fullest information to enable him to
encircle the town of Harfleur.

Henry made it clear that he would have the
strictest discipline in his army. The men were
drawn up, and to them was read this proclamation :

> that no one, under pain of death, should set fire to any
> place, that the churches and sacred places with their goods
> should be left untouched ; that no one should lay hands
> upon a woman, nor upon a priest or minister of the people,
> unless armed or offering violence or attack.

These were injunctions which certainly deprived
war of many of its glamorous attractions for the
mediæval soldiery.

Much praise has been given to Henry for this
proclamation, because it is thought to mark a new
departure in the business of war in the Middle Ages.
Was it not the age in which a famous soldier should
say that had God Himself been a man-at-arms He
would have looted like the rest of the soldiery ?
It was an age in which the track of an army was
marked by the smoke from burned homesteads
and byres, sad-eyed maidens forced to surrender
their maidenhood not to one, but perhaps to scores
of rough soldiers, old women raped by drink-sodden
libertines, and ill-treated priests. These were the
grim realities of mediæval warfare : evidence of
their existence abounds on the pages of the history
of the period.

Nevertheless, some critics have argued that
Henry's action was dictated not by humane considerations, but solely from self-interest. An army
demoralised by looting and womanising would be an
ineffective weapon of warfare, and an easy prey for
a watchful enemy. Henry, appreciating this truth,
was not the man to jeopardise the achievement of

12

his boundless ambition by allowing his men to
become a rabble. Moreover, it is also pointed out
that proclamations similar in content and purpose
had been issued by military commanders from
remote time, and that it was a widely accepted fact
that no man need obey them !

These arguments are historically sound ; but
do they detract in any way from Henry's military
greatness ? It does not greatly matter that the
common good and self-interest are coincident
factors in the creation of motive : the point to be
decided is, Was the common good benefited ?
Henry did his utmost to preserve the discipline of
his army, and in doing this he humanised warfare
at a time when it was diabolically inhumane. The
people of France appreciated his efforts, and it can
be argued that his desire to deal humanely with
non-combatants contributed in no small measure
to the ultimate success of his military plans.
Frenchmen undoubtedly hated Henry and his men,
because they were the enemies of France ; but
they could not refrain from observing that these
English ' midges ' treated them with far greater
consideration than their own troops. Not many
years before Henry's invasion, during the faction
fights of Armagnac and Burgundy, French soldiers
had staggered the world by their brutal excesses
in the neighbourhood of Soissons ; and when the
English envoys appeared before the walls of Harfleur
they assured the garrison that they had no intention
of treating them to ' another Soissons.' It must
not be supposed, however, that such a revolution
in the business of war was effected by the reading
of a simple proclamation. There is abundant
evidence to show that Henry had on more than one
occasion trouble with his men ; but he did not
allow these reverses to damp the ardour of his
intentions, and throughout his military career he

disciplined his men as no contemporary commander thought worth while to do.

Henry decided to take Harfleur by assault : he could not afford the time to conduct the customary siege, thereby forcing the garrison to surrender for want of victuals and stores.   The Duke of Clarence and the Earl of Salisbury were sent with a large force to block the entrances to the town from the east.   Their march lay through difficult country : the marshes and intersecting rivulets and ditches forced them to make a wide detour, for they had with them some of the great ' gonnes ' which Henry had brought out with him from England—the *London*, the *Messenger*, and the *King's Daughter*. Fortunately for them the French made no attempt to impede their progress, and by the evening of August 18 they had successfully done what Henry meant them to do—closed Harfleur from the east.

The French must not be too hardly blamed for their inactivity. Harfleur itself was hopelessly under-garrisoned, even after Ralph, Seigneur de Gaucourt, and some 400 men-at-arms slipped in by an eastern gate almost immediately before Clarence and Salisbury had put their men into position. The men in charge of the defence had stout hearts ; and even in the face of desperate odds they refused to abandon hope that their friends would come to their rescue.   These French captains were the seigneurs of Blainville, Clères, Estouteville, Hacque-ville, and Quitry, the castellan of Beauvais, and Lionnet de Braquemont ; and their courage was a fine example to their men.   To Henry's offer of peace—conditional, of course, upon the surrender of Harfleur—they returned the contemptuous but chivalrous reply : they would fight.   So the attack on the town of Harfleur began.

Henry ordered the ' gonnes ' and missile-throw-ing engines of mediæval warfare—arblasts, bricoles, mangonels, robinets, scorpions, springalds, and trepgets—to be brought as close to the walls as practicable ; and preparations were made for the bombardment. But do not imagine that Henry's ' gonnes ' were overwhelmingly superior to the older missile-throwing engines. When they did work they were capable of doing a terrific amount of havoc to life and property ; but they often did not work—flaws in casting resulting in the destruction of gun and gun-team, damp powder refusing to ignite, and ranging by rule of thumb producing erratic shooting. It was a difficult business to position these cumbersome weapons ; and loading was a highly complicated and lengthy operation. At the commencement of the attack on Harfleur the greatest value of the English artillery was its effect on the morale of the defenders, for the ' thunder-boxes ' rent the air with the most unearthly roar, and struck terror into the hearts of those who had never before been under gun fire.

When a mediæval commander decided to take a castle or town by assault he resorted to mining— that is, if he adhered rigidly to the rules of warfare as laid down in the mediæval manuals of tactics and strategy. The ' sappers ' and ' miners ' dug underground tunnels below the foundations of the walls ; and they held those foundations temporarily in place by timber structures in the mines. At the appointed time the timber was tarred and pitched, and then fired ; and as a result the walls were breached, ready for the attack. Mining was met with counter-mining ; and at Harfleur some desperate fighting took place in the underground workings when miners and counter-miners came to grips with one another. The English ' miners ' were among the most heavily worked men in the royal army ; and what must have been most galling to them was the fact that no sooner did they breach the wall than the defenders repaired the damage by means of temporary fortifications, and beat off every attack.

Even the English were not stingy in their praise of the defence ; and the following contemporary account gives a fairly good picture of the ding-dong character of the struggle.

> And although our guns had disarmed the bulwark, walls, and towers during the day, the besieged by night, with logs, faggots, and vessels full of earth, mud, sand or stones, piled up above the bulwark and walls, and faggots with clay, earth and mud, within the shattered walls, and with other barricadoes, refortified the streets ; and even stopped up the lanes with this sort of clay, earth and mud, in great thickness ; so that the stones of our guns, coming down upon them, might be swallowed up in them, lest the besieged who were in the lanes and streets, should suffer damage, hurt or death, from the sudden and unexpected violence of the stones or the fragments of them. They had also warily provided on the walls an abundance of pots full of combustible powders of sulphur and quick-lime, to cast into the eyes of our men, if an assault should be made, and vessels of scorching earth and oils, and fat combustibles, for the burning and destruction of our ranks, when they should approach to the walls for an assault. Nor could the besieged, in the judgment of man, have resisted our attacks more prudently or more cautiously than they had done.

To the eternal shame of the authorities in Paris and Rouen, nothing was done to send succour to this gallant garrison.

During the operations outside Harfleur, Henry was everywhere—in the trenches, in the mines, in the gun-pits. Every night he visited the sentries, gave them a cheering word of encouragement, and then, like an ordinary soldier, lay down on the ground to snatch a short sleep. More than one assault was led by the king in person, and his friends felt that he was running unnecessary risks ; but no one dared to remonstrate with him. And herein lies the great secret of Henry's military

successes—he never once lost the confidence of his
men. They had seen him playing a soldier's part,
doing work which they themselves had to do,
risking his life as they risked theirs ; and in consequence they were not afraid to follow him to the
ends of the earth. Clarence and Gloucester, too,
won golden opinions from their comrades ; and
throughout they co-operated loyally with their
elder brother.

Soon another enemy made its appearance—
disease. The low-lying swamps, over-indulgence in
new wine and fresh fruit to slake a thirst caused
by strenuous work in oppressively hot weather,
chilly nights, brought on what to-day would be
called dysentery, but was then known as 'the
bloody flux.' It spared neither dignity nor age,
man-at-arms, nor archer ; and soon thousands of
Henry's men were stricken down with it. It is
estimated that more than 2000 died.

Among the victims was Richard Courtenay,
Bishop of Norwich, who died on September 15.
He was Henry's dearest friend—they shared the
same tent ; and when death claimed him it was
the king who closed his eyes and bathed his feet.
He was without question one of the most brilliant
men of that age—a scholar of distinction and a
competent diplomat ; and it was largely through
his efforts that Archbishop Arundel was prevented,
in 1411, from interfering with the rights and liberties
of the University of Oxford.

Three days after Courtenay's death the ' flux '
claimed Michael de la Pole, Earl of Suffolk. He
was a man in the middle fifties—about twenty years
older than Courtenay ; and his service to the House
of Lancaster dated from the time when he accompanied Henry V.'s father, then Earl of Derby, on
adventurous journeys into foreign lands. And
with them died many useful knights and archers.

As a sidelight on war in mediæval times it might be mentioned that the bodies of Courtenay and Suffolk were sent to England for burial, a special ship from the fleet at anchor in the Seine being detailed off for that purpose.

On September 16 the garrison of Harfleur made a desperate sortie. They burnt some of the English stores ; but after terrible hand-to-hand fighting they were driven back within the walls. In accordance with the age-old military rule that the best form of defence is attack, Sir John Holland, John Cornwall, and Gilbert Umfraville (whose men had borne the brunt of the sortie) hurled themselves against the fortifications ; but the Frenchmen held on like grim death, and the English were compelled to withraw to their lines.

The Frenchmen, however, had nearly come to the end of their tether. Messenger after messenger had slipped through the enemy lines with messages asking the authorities to send the garrison help, but in a capital so hopelessly divided against itself as Paris, where men accounted the rights of Armagnac and Burgundy of greater importance than the expulsion of an invading army, these entreaties fell upon deaf ears. It is true that an army had been marshalled for the relief of Harfleur, but it never marched more than a score of miles from Paris. On September 18, therefore, the leaders of the garrison sent a message to Clarence to the effect that they would surrender Harfleur if help did not reach the town by noon on the following Sunday (September 22). At first Henry refused to listen to these peace overtures : the garrison must surrender unconditionally not later than September 19. Clarence talked his brother round, and Henry thereupon sent the Earl of Dorset (Thomas Beaufort), Lord fitzHugh, and Sir Thomas Erpyngham to draw up the customary articles of surrender with the Frenchmen. Fighting now ceased : both sides sat and watched each other, waiting for the turn of events within the stipulated time. At noon of September 22, when no news came of a French relief, a force of 500 English soldiers marched to the gates and demanded admittance. The siege of Harfleur was over.

In the Middle Ages the surrender of a town or fortress was always looked upon as a proper occasion for a display of pageantry ; and so it happened at Harfleur. To Henry, ' clad in gold and *caparsites* ' and seated on his throne in the midst of a goodly company of nobles, came Ralph de Gaucourt and thirty-four prominent Frenchmen. They were clothed in penitents' shirts, and had halters hung round their necks ; and as soon as they came before the king they prostrated themselves at his feet, humbly begging mercy and proferring him the keys of the town. Henry reminded them that they were somewhat late in coming to this conclusion, but although they had kept him from ' a noble portion of his inheritance '—a subtle reminder that he claimed Normandy of right—he was ready to be merciful ; and he promised them their lives. They then accompanied the English king to his pavilion tent, and were

> entertained . . . magnificently enough at the approaching supper, with what dainties he had.

That done, they were handed over to certain of his company to be kept as prisoners until the king could arrange for their release.

The Earl of Dorset was at once appointed captain of Harfleur. It was an admirable choice, for he had already held a similar post at Calais, and knew what was expected of him. On September 23 Henry made his triumphal entry into the captured town. He dismounted at the main gate, unloosed his shoes, and walked barefooted through the streets to the Church of St Martin, where he attended a solemn service of thanksgiving.

The clemency of the English king had a profound impression upon the people of Harfleur. They had expected no mercy from the conquering army, and were surprised when Henry announced that 2000 ' of the poorer sort ' were to be allowed to depart from the town in peace to find homes in other parts of France. Each received a sum of money—from five to ten shillings ; and an armed escort took them out of Harfleur, so that they should not run the risk of being spoiled by the soldiery. But spoiled they were, not by the English, but by their own countrymen. The wealthier townsmen were given the alternative of swearing allegiance to Henry—their lawful duke, or were fined for their refusal ; and in the latter case were sent away from the town. Henry had resolved that Harfleur must be transformed into a ' second Calais ' : he needed a good base for future operations in the Seine country.

In due course Henry dealt with the French captains who had been in his hands since the capitulation. They were released on parole, having first promised to present themselves before Henry at Calais ' on the feast of St Martin in the winter ' (November 11). One special condition was attached to the release of Ralph de Gaucourt : he was to escort the Guienne herald to the presence of the dauphin, to whom Henry addressed a challenge :

> Henry, by the grace of God, King of England and of France, and Lord of Ireland, to the high and puissant Prince, the Dauphin of Vienne, our cousin, eldest son of the most puissant Prince, our cousin and adversary of France. As, for the reverence of God, and to save the effusion of human blood, we have many times, and in many ways, sought peace, and notwithstanding that we have not been able to obtain it, our desire to possess it increases

more and more. And well considering that the effects of our wars are destruction of countries, the deaths of men, lamentations of women and children, and so many general evils, that every good Christian must lament it and have pity, and we especially whom this matter more concerns ought to seek diligently for all possible means to avoid the above-mentioned evils, and to acquire the approbation of God, and praise of the world. Whereas we have considered and reflected, that it has pleased God to visit our said cousin, your father, with infirmity ; that with us and you lies the remedy, and to the end that every one may know that we do not prevent it, we offer to place our quarrel, at the will of God, between our person and your's. And if it should appear to you that you cannot agree to this offer on account of the interest which you think our said cousin your father has in it, we declare to you that if you are willing to accept it and to do what we propose, it pleases us to permit that our said cousin, from the reverence of God and that he is a sacred person, shall enjoy that which he at present has for the term of his life, whatever it may please God to happen between us and you, as it shall be agreed between his council, our's and your's. Consequently, if God shall give us the victory, the crown of France with its appurtenances shall be immediately rendered to us without difficulty, as our right after his decease, and so that all the lords and estates of the kingdom of France shall be bound in manner as shall be agreed between us. For it is better for us, Cousin, to decide this war for ever between our two persons, than to suffer the unbelievers by means of our quarrels to destroy Christianity, our mother the Holy Church to remain in division, and the people of God to destroy one another. And we pray that you may have such anxious desire to avoid them, and to seek for peace, that you will neglect no means by which it can be obtained. And we trust in God, that a better or shorter way of effecting it cannot be found ; and therefore in discharge of our soul, and in charge of your's, if great evils follow, we propose to you what is above said. Protesting always that we make this our offer, for the honour and fear of God, and for the reasons above-mentioned, of our own motion without our loyal relations, counsellors, and subjects being around us, having in so high a matter dared to advise us ; nor can it at any time to come be urged to our prejudice ; nor in prejudice of our good right and title which we have at present to the said crown with its appurtenances ; nor to the good right and title which we have now to other our lands and heritages on this side the sea ; nor to our heirs and successors, if this our offer does not take full effect between us and you, in the manner above said.

Given under our Privy Seal, at our town of Harfleur, the xvi day of September.

The contents of this letter of challenge have caused men to question the sanity and sincerity of Henry. Did he for a moment believe that the dauphin would do battle for a kingdom ? Was he really so concerned about the ' effusion of blood ? ' It is certain that these questions cannot be answered satisfactorily : Henry's admirers will scorn the imputation of insanity and insincerity ; his detractors will emphasise them. What can be said is this : a letter of challenge had to be written in a certain conventional form, and part of the technique demanded an appeal frequently to the justice of the challenger's cause. Without a doubt Henry V. believed in the justice of his cause ; but whether he would have faithfully abided by the trial by combat, had the verdict gone against him, is another matter ; and he was not so ignorant of affairs in France not to know that the dauphin was a prince who was unlikely to enter the lists against him. He cannot have been surprised, therefore, when he received no answer to his letter.

The magnificent army which Henry had led out of England had melted away. Death and disease had literally decimated the English force ; and there are records of serious desertions. After he had made arrangements for the government of Harfleur more than 5000 men were invalided home ; and with them the Duke of Clarence, the Earls of Arundel and March — the former so seriously weakened by the ' flux ' that he died shortly after reaching home. A force of ' ccc. lances and nine hundred archers on pay ' was left as a garrison in

Harfleur ; and all that remained with Henry were 900 men-at-arms and 5000 archers.

What was to be his next step ?   In defiance of the advice of the majority of his barons and captains he resolved on one of the most hazardous marches in the history of warfare.   He would lead his men to Calais ; and he justified that decision in a speech to the council.

> I have a great desire to see my lands and places that should be mine by right.   Let them assemble their great armies, there is hope in God that they will hurt neither my army nor me.   I will not suffer them, puffed up with pride, to rejoice in misdeeds, nor unjustly, against God, to possess my goods.   They would say that through fear I had fled away, acknowledging the injustice of my cause. But I have a mind, my brave men, to encounter all dangers, rather than let them brand your king with word of ill-will. With the favour of God we will go unhurt and inviolate, and if they attempt to stay us, victorious and triumphant in all glory.

Posterity cannot hope to understand Henry's real motive in making this seemingly reckless decision.   It may be that he thought the French, so absorbed in the stupid quarrel of Armagnac and Burgundy, would not attempt to bar his progress to Calais.   It may be that, obsessed with the belief that he was the chosen of God, he was unable to contemplate defeat.   It may be that personal pride—the fear of being branded a craven —overcame his better judgment as a soldier.   These are the possibilities : readers must therefore make their own decisions.   Had the English force been annihilated at Agincourt it is certain that Henry's plan would have been held up to the world as a terrible tactical blunder.

On October 6, the English army marched out of Harfleur.   Sir John Cornwall and Gilbert Umfra-ville commanded the vaward.   Henry, assisted by his brother Humphrey, Sir John Holland and John,

Lord Roos, followed with the main army. In charge of the rearward were the Duke of York and the Earl of Oxford. The king had resolved to march light, and only the essential baggage, packed on the backs of sumpterhorses, was taken forward. Each man took with him provisions sufficient for eight days' marching.

The road to Calais hugged the coast, but it passed over a number of deep and swiftly-moving rivers, and it was at the bridges and fords that Henry expected to meet with opposition. Henry was not greatly concerned about the castles which were dotted along this route : they could be avoided if necessary ; and even if the garrisons showed fight the superiority of the English force would crush that kind of opposition. His insistence on the strictest discipline saved his men from the wrath of an infuriated peasantry : orders were given that there must be no looting or destruction of property, and if in dire necessity food had to be taken the country people were to supply only the barest necessaries of life. The English were soon to find that these barest necessaries of life were hard to come by ; on hearing of Henry's intention to march to Calais the French authorities had ordered the wholesale wasting of the country through which his route lay.

The garrisons of the castles at Montivilliers and Fécamp made attempts to close with the advancing army, but these were quite futile, and the English easily brushed them aside and passed on their way northwards. It was October 11 when they reached Arques, which guarded a passage over the Béthune ; and there they found a large French force gathered together to resist their crossing. Henry immediately informed the seigneur of the district that unless he was allowed to cross the river without hindrance he would order his men to waste the town of Arques

and the surrounding country ; and so successful
was the threat that not only did the French resistance crumple up, but the people of the town gave
the invaders ' a certain quantity of bread and wine
for the refreshment of the army.' Scouts had come
in with the news that another French force awaited
Henry at Eu, so he passed by it, ' leaving it half a
mile on the left.' The Frenchmen showed fight, and
near Eu a regular skirmish took place ; but the
issue was never for a moment in doubt, and the
English drove them ' hastily back to the town for
protection.'

Henry had now reached a critical stage in his
advance. Before him lay the Somme ; behind
him a hostile country. The Somme was a difficult
river over which to transport an army ; but near
the estuary was a famous ford known as Blanque-
taque or Blanche-tache, over which Edward III.
had forced his way immediately before Creçy.
This ford, however, was negotiable only at low tide.
Before Henry reached Blanque-taque on Sunday,
October 13, he had been told by a prisoner—' a
gentleman, a native of Gascony, servant to messire
Charles de Labreth, then Constable of France '—
that stakes had been driven into the bed of the ford
and that a French force under the Marshal Boucicaut
lay on the opposite side. Whether this information
was true or was wilful misrepresentation with the
object of impeding Henry's advance it is now hard
to say ; but the latter was generally believed ; and
when the disaster of Agincourt had wounded
France's national pride and sent her chivalry into
mourning, the blame was shifted on to the shoulders
of this ' gentleman of Gascony,' for had he but told
the truth the English would have reached Calais
without interference !

There was nothing for it but to march south-
east up the Somme until a crossing could be

effected ; and all that Henry knew when he made
this momentous decision was a hearsay report that
a ford existed 'upwards of lx. miles from that
place ' (Blanque-taque). There were bridges not
so far distant, but it was hardly to be expected
that they would be left unguarded ; and the
English soon learnt that the tales about a French
army being on the other side of the Somme were
only too true. This army made a passage across
the bridge at Bailleul-en-Vimeu, about three miles
distant from Abbéville, impossible ; and a similar
experience awaited the advancing army at Pont
Remy. The plight of the English was now
desperate. The eight days' supply of provisions
had run out ; a wasted countryside could provide
them with nothing ; and disappointment at being
unable to bring the French to a decisive battle ate
like a canker into the hearts of the English soldiers.
Strong men prayed piteously to Our Lady and St
George to intercede for them. Thus wrote one—a
chaplain—who marched with Henry from Harfleur
to Calais :

> Many of the rest of the people looked bitterly up to
> heaven, unto the clemency of the celestial regard ; and
> we besought the glorious virgin and the blessed George,
> under whose protection the most invincible crown of
> England had flourished of old, for mediation between God
> and our people ; that the supreme Judge, who beholdeth
> all things, might in mercy spare the desolation of all Eng-
> land, at the expense of our blood ; and that He might, of
> His unbounded justice, rescue from the swords of the
> French, to the honour and glory of His name, and lead to
> Calais with triumph, our king and us, whose object has
> been peace not war.

The fires of hope burned low in the army which
plodded wearily upstream. At Boves the men were
somewhat cheered : though they could not use
the bridges over the river there they had a good
meal of bread and wine—wrung from the lord of

the castle after the usual threat of laying waste his town and lordship—and enjoyed a good night's rest in billets. But Henry was none too pleased with the behaviour of his army at Boves. There was much shoving and pushing as the men crowded round the wine vats, and there was danger that blood would be shed. The king thereupon ordered them away from the vats. One of the captains, however, remonstrated with his leader :

> The brave fellows are only filling their bottles.

In disgust Henry retorted :

> Their bottles ! they are making big bottles of their bellies, and are getting very drunk !

Was this the first manifestation of that aversion to drink which in later years caused Henry to contemplate the destruction of the vineyards of France and the suppression of the drink traffic in our own country ?

At Corbie on October 16 a sharp fight took place between the French garrison and the English. The Frenchmen managed to capture the Guienne standard, borne by Hugh de Stafford, son of the Earl of Stafford ; but it was won back by John Bromley, a squire of the county palatine of Chester, who was one of the Grooms of the Chamber. After Corbie the English army marched across country to the headwaters of the Somme. This was a wise move on the part of Henry, for it removed his force from the observation of the French army under d'Albret and Boucicaut operating on the northern bank of the river. Nesle was reached on October 18 : there the resistance of the castle garrison compelled Henry to lay waste the surrounding countryside. It was probably with a desire to be rid of these English ' midges ' that countrymen told Henry that ' about a league off there was a convenient ford.' There was no time to be lost. Sir John Cornwall and Gilbert Umfraville, with a strong detachment of horsemen, were sent post-haste to hold the ford until Henry could bring up the main body of the army. Very early in the morning of October 19 a detachment of archers went across the river with orders to beat off any hostile attack, made while the approaches to, and bed of, the ford were being repaired ; and this advance guard was later strengthened by 500 lances, commanded by Sir John Cornwall and Gilbert Umfraville. Henry himself stood all day long by the ford to ensure the orderly crossing of his men ; and by an hour after nightfall the whole of the English force was across the river.

On the morning of October 20 three heralds from the Dukes of Orléans and Bourbon were brought by the Duke of York before Henry. The incident is recorded by Titius Livius :

> The heralds . . . addressed him in these words : " Right puissant prince, great and noble is thy kingly power, as is reported among our lords. They have heard that thou labourest by thy forces to conquer towns, cities, and castles of the realm of France, and of the Frenchmen you have destroyed. For which causes, and for perform-ance of the oath which they have taken to the king, many of our lords are assembled to defend this realm, the king's right and their own, and they inform thee by us, that before thou comest to Calais they will meet thee, to fight with thee, and to be revenged of thy conduct." To which Henry, with a courageous spirit, a firm look, without anger or displeasure, and without his face changing colour, mildly replied, that " all would be done according to the will of God." When the heralds inquired what road he would take he answered, " Straight to Calais, and if our adversaries attempt to disturb us in our journey, it shall be at their utmost peril, and not without harm to them. We seek them not, neither will the fear of them induce us to move out of our way, or the sight of them cause us to make the greater haste. We advise them, however, not to interrupt our journey, nor to seek such an effusion of Christian blood."

13

Such were the courtesies of mediæval chivalry that
when the three French heralds left the English
camp they bore with them a present of a hundred
gold French crowns.

The French were not in a hurry to carry out
their threats, and the English army marched along
without much sign of armed opposition. It is true
that at Péronne, which was reached on October 21,
French cavalry tried to draw the English within
range of the artillery positioned behind the town's
walls ; but this ruse failed lamentably, and, badly
mauled by the English cavalry, they retired. The
ordinary soldiers did not share the king's desire
to put the Frenchmen in their place : the possibility
of a pitched battle hung over them like a Damoclean
sword and filled their hearts with terror ; and
nowhere was this fear of an impending doom more
real than in the little group of non-combatants—
the chaplains and sumptermen—who marched with
the army. They raised, so we are told, their
hearts and eyes to heaven, and cried with voices of
deep earnestness for God to have compassion on them,
and to spare them from the power of the French.

On October 22 Henry and his men crossed the
Canche at Frévent ; and two days later saw them on
the other side of the Ternoise. Scouts brought in the
news that the French were in the locality ; and as the
English marched along the Calais road from Blangy
they suddenly came in sight of the Frenchmen.

> We saw three columns of the French emerge from the
> upper part of the valley, about a mile from us, who at
> length being formed into battalions, companies, and
> troops, in multitudes compared with us, halted a little
> more than half a mile opposite to us, filling a very wide
> field, as with an innumerable host of locusts ; a moderate-
> sized valley being betwixt us and them.

Henry had already drawn up his men in battle
array. He himself took command of the main
army or battle ; the Duke of York, of the vaward ;

and Thomas, Lord Camoys, a captain with a long military experience, was put in charge of the rearward. The chaplains were sent among the men to hear their confessions ; and we learn that the only need of the English army at that moment was priests. The sight of the overwhelmingly large French army brought from one of the knights in the army, Sir Walter Hungerford, the remark that he wished there were present ten thousand archers who were away in England, but who would wish that they could be with their king. Henry answered :

> Thou speakest foolishly, for by the God of heaven, on whose grace I have relied, and in whom I have a firm hope of victory, I would not, even if I could, increase my number by one ; for those whom I have are the people of God, whom he thinks me worthy to have at this time. Dost thou not believe, that the Almighty with these, his humble few, is able to conquer the haughty opposition of the French, who pride themselves on their numbers, and their own strength, as if it might be said that they could do as they liked ?

Under no circumstances would Henry tolerate pessimism in the ranks of his army.

The road along which the English must march to Calais lay midway between the villages of Agincourt and Tramecourt, both of which were screened by woods. Henry at once perceived the military possibilities of these woods. On the one hand, they might be used by the enemy to cover a movement executed with the object of encircling the English force. On the other hand, they narrowed down to about two miles the front along which an attack could be developed. Henry, therefore, set himself two tasks : first, he must push his army far enough forward to prevent an encircling movement being carried out ; and, second, he must induce the French to attack him in the country between the woods, for his flanks would then be defended from the enemy cavalry.

The first objective was achieved when the Duke of York and the vaward, by sundown on October 24, reached the edge of the Tramecourt woods. There they bivouacked for the night ; while the main battle and rearward lay between the Tramecourt woods and the village of Maisoncelles. The French were at Agincourt and Tramecourt, and in the intervening country.

Rain fell incessantly during the night of October 24–25. Since there was only limited accommodation in billets, the majority of the English spent the night in the open under what must have been most dismal conditions. Henry gave strict orders that there must be no noise in the English lines : a knightly offender would lose his horse, an archer or knifeman, the right ear. The noise from the French camps shattered the stillness of the night. Knights bawled for their attendants or diced for the prisoners to be taken on the morrow. Indeed so ominous was the silence in the English lines that the Frenchmen began to think that their enemies had stolen away under cover of darkness ; but when the Comte de Richemont and more than two thousand cavalry came out about midnight to see if this was the case they found the English wide awake, and capable of giving them a nasty mauling.

Mediæval chroniclers never concerned themselves with accuracy of numbers, and in the contemporary records of mediæval battles the variations in the numbers of men engaged is often so staggering that posterity cannot hope accurately to know the strength of the armies. In the case of the battle of Agincourt, for example, the number of Frenchmen engaged is variously estimated from 10,000 to 200,000, and the English from 4000 to 26,000. This is not the place to examine these figures :

sufficient is it to say that the English force almost certainly did not exceed 6000, while the French may have had as many as 60,000 men engaged.

Moreover, there was a marked difference in the personnel of the two armies. The French, despite the lessons of Creçy and Poitiers, relied with pitiable tenacity on the shock tactics of feudal cavalry. The English depended entirely upon the missile action of the archers, of whom there were about 5000 in Henry's army. Edward I. had learnt that lesson during his Welsh wars : his grandson and great-grandson, Edward III. and the Black Prince, had pitted successfully their archers against the flower of the French chivalry. A brilliant French captain like Bertrand du Guesclin knew only too well the inherent weakness of the traditional feudal tactics, and under his capable leadership Frenchmen fought the English in the English way —and with great success. But in a state so highly feudalised as France in the beginning of the fifteenth century the traditions of caste were not lightly to be discredited : it was a gentleman's business to ride down the enemy, and archers and men-at-arms of baser sort had no claim to posts of honour in battle.

The French cavalry was heavily armed. The knights wore cumbersome armour which impeded their movements when they came to fight on foot. The English archers, on the other hand, were lightly armed. They wore a loose-fitting tunic or jerkin belted at the waist ; and in this belt they carried their stock of arrows, daggers, weighted clubs, and axes. On their heads they wore simple brain-caps, some of which had stout leather or an iron framework stretched across the crown for greater protection. They seldom wore shoes, but went barefooted ; and were as nimble as cats. The accuracy of the shooting of these English archers was well-nigh uncanny : they could strike down a man at two hundred yards with a well-aimed shot through a chink in his armour ; and they could volley with terrifying rapidity.

Few in the great French army drawn up between Agincourt and Tramecourt believed that a handful of Englishmen would sweep them from the field : the fifteenth-century Frenchman thought that he was a better fighting man than half a dozen Englishmen. When dawn broke, therefore, on October 25 —a Friday and the feast of the cobbler saints, SS Crispin and Crispinian—the Frenchmen marshalled themselves into the usual mediæval military formation. In the vaward were the dismounted knights —the flower of the nation's chivalry. They stood, so some said, thirty-one deep. Behind them were the men of less important social status ; a division hardly less numerous than the vaward. And in the rear were the varlets, the attendants of the knights, who remained mounted, and held their masters' horses in readiness for the pursuit.

In the English lines reigned the quiet confidence of men who, not caring to ponder upon the issue of the battle, were resolved to do their duty. News had come that the Frenchmen meant to give no quarter to the archers : their hands were to be cut off and their fingers sold as souvenirs. It was not with the kindliest of feelings that these simple yeomen of England went into battle with the French. The king himself was up before dawn, and when he had donned his armour—emblazoned with the arms of England and France—he quietly heard Lauds and Mass. He then mounted a grey palfrey, had his crown placed upon his basnet, and went forward to marshal his host. Every man knew his place, and went quietly to it : the banners were unfurled, and the captains gave their final orders.

The king commanded the main or centre battle.

On his right was the division under the Duke of
York ; and on his left, Lord Camoys and the rearward. Protecting each of these divisions were
wedges of archers. Each little group contained
about 200 men ; and each man protected his station
by a sharpened stake driven firmly into the ground.
These stakes were meant to break the rush of the
French cavalry. A small number of archers took
post on the edges of the Agincourt and Tramecourt
woods.

About a mile to a mile and a quarter separated
the two armies, and from six to nine in the morning
they stood facing each other without making the
slightest attempt to join the battle. For a moment
it appeared as though the French meant to starve
the English force into surrender. Fight or surrender : no other alternative remained for Henry.
Would Henry surrender ? Never ; and with the
object of making the French stand their ground
and fight he gave the famous order :

> Forward banner ! In the name of Jesus, Mary, and St
> George.

It was as they were preparing to carry out this
order that the English saw the Frenchmen advancing
towards them.

Every man in the English army prostrated
himself, and kissed the ground three times. A
morsel of soil was placed in every mouth. This
was the earth-housel, without which no good soldier
would go into battle, for later in the day he might
die and it was imperative that he should carry in
his body some of the earth to which that body
would then return. Then every man commended
himself to God's mercy and pity.

When the men stood to their posts there walked
out in front of the English ranks Sir Thomas
Erpyngham, a gallant soldier who was growing grey

with age ; and in the sight of the whole army he hurled his warder into the air as a signal for battle to commence.

Forward came the French chivalry, plugging their way with the utmost difficulty across the rain-sodden field ; and on either side of their line were the cavalry, whose orders were to charge down the archers. The Frenchmen put their horses to the gallop. Suddenly from the captains of the archers came the order :

Knee !   Stretch !

A terrible volley of arrows struck the advancing French horse. Another, and another, and another followed with relentless rapidity. Saddles were emptied, and riderless horses dashed madly back, ploughing lanes through the oncoming dismounted French knights. The archers now turned their aim on this body ; but weight of numbers told, and the two armies came to grips. For a moment the English line recoiled ' a full spear's-length.' The English knights and men-at-arms fought their way back ; and all the time the archers volleyed death into the Frenchmen's flanks and rear.

> And when the arrows were exhausted, seizing up axes, poles, swords, and sharp spears which were lying about, they prostrated, dispersed, and stabbed the enemy.

Early in the fight the Duke of York was killed : a French knight—perhaps the handsome young Duke d'Alençon—had cleft him to the teeth. Dead, too, was the boy Earl of Suffolk, whose father had died only a few weeks before at Harfleur. Humphrey of Gloucester went down with a wound ; but his royal brother stood across his body, warding off French attacks, until the wounded man could be carried from the fight. The carnage was inde-scribable. The front French ranks would have broken and retired, but they could not, for their friends behind forced them forward to death at the hands of these English ' midges.' The French chivalry lay piled in heaps of living, dead, and dying, as high as a man's shoulder ; and on the top of these mounds of stricken humanity stood groups of English archers and men-at-arms, smiting down the enemy as they came near them. Wrote an eye-witness, the chaplain, who had watched the progress of the fight from the rear :

> Nor was it ever seen in former times, mentioned in chronicles of history, that so many choice and robust soldiers, made so sluggish, so disorderly, so cowardly, and so unmanly a resistance. For they were seized with fear and panic ; there were some, even of the more noble of them, as it was reported in the army, who on that day surrendered themselves more than ten times. But no one had leisure to make prisoners of them, but all without distinction of persons, as they were cast down to the ground, were put to death without intermission, either by those who threw them down, or by others that followed after.

Throughout the fight Henry himself was hotly engaged. Like the other knights in his army he fought on foot, and in years to come old soldiers told stirring tales of the havoc which he made with his sword on that dread field of Agincourt. In the French army was a band of sworn companions— eighteen strong : they were resolved to seek out and cut down the king of England. Not one of that little band escaped alive. Some one cleft a part of Henry's crown ; and his armour was dented with the blows which he had received.

For three long hours the slaughter continued ; and between three and four in the afternoon the Frenchmen drew off. The victorious English sorted out the prisoners, pulling many a distinguished gentleman of France from the piles of dead and dying ; and the ordinary soldiers searched the dead for valuables. Suddenly the news spread through the English force that the French had rallied and were about to counter-attack. The crisis was emphasised by the fact that bands of peasantry had fallen upon the English baggage line. A mighty cheer went up from the French captives : they thought the lost fortunes of the day might be retrieved.

It was at this juncture that Henry gave an order which has done more than anything else to sully his fair name. Every man must slay his prisoners. His men held back. Were they to lose so easily the ransoms of men whom they had taken after such a stiff fight ? But the threatened danger was too great in Henry's opinion to allow such selfish motives to govern : two hundred of his bodyguard—picked archers—lined up the prisoners and shot them down.

Though the attack on the baggage line was not a serious military movement, it is certain that the French had counter-attacked, and since the prisoners were more numerous than the fighting men Henry had no alternative but to dispatch them. The counter-attack was led by Anthony, Duke of Brabant, brother of John, Duke of Burgundy ; and at the head of the second French division he dashed forward against the English, shouting " Brabant ! Brabant ! " The Frenchmen had little stomach for fighting that day ; and the counter-attack was a miserable failure. As the afternoon light weakened into dusk Henry and his men found themselves the masters of the field.

He called his men around him, and thanked them for the gallant service which they had rendered to him that day. He warned them that on the morrow they would continue their march ; and no man must burden himself with too much loot. Then he sent for his heralds, and the French Montjoie king-at-arms, who was a prisoner in his hands ; and he asked them what was the name of the castle which he could see in the distance, through the rain and falling light. They told him that it was called Agincourt.

Then let this be called the battle of Agincourt.

France had never suffered a greater disaster. Among the dead were the flower of her chivalry—the dukes of Alençon, Bar, and Brabant, the Constable (Charles d'Albret), the Admiral (Jacques de Châtillon, Seigneur de Dampierre), the counts of Blamont, Fauquembergues, Grandpré, Roucy, Vaucourt, and Vaudémont, and—so the English chaplain wrote—

upwards of ninety barons and standard-bearers, whose names are written in the Book of Records, and more than one thousand five hundred knights, according to their own computation.

Between four and five thousand men-at-arms—every man a French gentleman with the right to bear arms—were slain ; and no one stopped to count the dead among the men of baser sort. Without exaggeration the French losses can be taken as more than 10,000 dead. Prisoners in the hand of the English were the Duke of Orléans and Bourbon, the Marshal de Boucicaut, the counts of Eu, Richemont and Vendôme, ' and but few other noblemen.'

The English casualties were unbelievably low. The chaplain present at the battle mentions only 15 : a French chronicler, Monstrelet, writing after the event and from hearsay, fixes the losses at 1600. This latter figure is undoubtedly wide of the mark : modern opinion inclines to the view that not more than 80 Englishmen died that day. Among the English dead was Dafydd ap Llywelyn ap Hywel or Dafydd Gam, the Welshman who had tried to assassinate Owen Glyn Dŵr at Machynlleth in the

days of the Welsh rebellion and regarded by many
as the original of Shakespeare's Fluellen.   Dafydd
Gam was knighted by Henry as he lay dying on the
stricken field, as some say, because he had saved
the king's life during the engagement.

On the morning following the battle the English
army began its march to Calais.   Their passage over
the battlefield moved the chaplain to bitter
reflection :

> And I firmly believe there is not a heart of flesh nor
> of stone, if it had seen and contemplated the dreadful
> destruction and bitter wounds of so many Christians, but
> would have dissolved and melted into tears from grief.
> Not even had the illustrious or distinguished on our
> return, any covering whatever, save only in the secrets
> parts of nature, beyond what they had received at their
> very birth.

As there was no longer any possibility that the
march would be opposed, the knights and men-at-
arms took off their coat armour,   The wounded lay
in carts or hobbled along as best they could between
the vaward and the main army.

On October 29, the eve of All Souls, Henry
made his entry to Calais.   He was met at the gates
by the Earl of Warwick, the Governor of the town,
who was accompanied by a host of clergy.   These
clergy headed the procession through the town's
thoroughfares, chanting " This is the day that the
Lord hath made."   The children screamed madly
" Noel ! Noel ! " and their parents cried " Welcome
to our sovereign lord the king."   But they were
not kindly disposed towards the ordinary soldiers,
whom they robbed right and left by selling them
food and drink at exorbitant prices ; and these
men—the men who had made the victory at Agincourt possible—were forced to sell their loot so that
they could keep body and soul together until the
time the transports arrived to carry them back to
their native land.

Henry himself contemplated a further campaign, but his men were eager to be back in their homes ; and the project was postponed. On St Martin's Day the Seigneur de Gaucourt and the other captains of Harfleur came to surrender themselves to Henry ; and the majority of them were sent across to England to wait until they could purchase their release by ransom. Henry himself set sail for home on November 16. A terrible storm overtook the ships as they made the crossing, and two were lost, while a number of others were driven ashore on the coast of Holland. We are told that Henry's behaviour during this storm won the admiration of the French prisoners : to them the experience was even worse than the fight at Agincourt, but Henry was quite unconcerned, and, marvellous to relate, he made the crossing

without accumbrance and disease of his stomach.

On arriving at Dover in the evening the barons of the Cinque Ports waded into the water and carried Henry shoulder-high to land, while the men of the Channel seaports, lining the slopes of Barham Down, cheered and cheered again. Henry remained at Dover one day ' to enable his prisoners to recover from the voyage ' ; and then he moved on to Canterbury. There he was met by the cathedral clergy, headed by Archbishop Chichele ; and after two days' stay he resumed his progress. All along the route—through Rochester and Eltham —people pressed to see the king who had won such a wonderful victory over the French.

At Blackheath the mayor of London (Alderman Nicholas Wolton, called by the quick-witted Londoners 'Witless Nick') and twenty-four aldermen met Henry early in the morning of November 23. They had with them 20,000 Londoners, bedecked in the many-coloured liveries of their craft gilds ;

and it is said that the wily city fathers had staged
this splendid pageant so that the French prisoners
could see what kind of men guarded England during
their king's absence! At ten o'clock the procession moved towards the city which was to be
entered by way of London Bridge. On either side
of the gateway stood two figures, ' as if man and
wife ' : the man held a huge axe in one hand, and
the keys of the city in the other ; the woman was
arrayed in fine apparel. Upon the city wall was
the inscription : CIVITAS REGIS IUSTICIE ; and
figures of heraldic emblems—the antelope and the
lion. ' Over the foot of the bridge ' and protected
by a pavilion ' stood a most beautiful image of
Saint George, armed, excepting his head, which
was adorned with a laurel wreath, studded with
pearls.' On his right hand hung ' his triumphal
helmet ' ; and on his left his arms—the red cross
on a white ground. In his right hand he held the
hilt of his sword ; and in his left a scroll on which
was written SOLI DEO HONOR ET GLORIA. Boys
' arrayed in white and with countenances shining
with gold ' were placed in adjacent houses to
represent the angelic host ; and as Henry approached they sang ' with organs ' the English
anthem :

DEO GRATIAS ANGLIA REDDE PRO VICTORIA !

Owre kynge went forth to Normandy,
With grace and myght of chivalry ;
The God for hym wrought marvelously,
Wherefore Englonde may calle, and cry
          Deo gratias :
Deo gratias Anglia redde pro victoria.

He sette a sege, the sothe for to say,
To Harfleur toune with ryal aray ;
That toune he wan, and made a fray,
That Fraunce shall rywe tyl domes day.
          Deo gratias, etc.

Then went owre kynge, with alle his oste,
Thorowe Fraunce for all the French boste ;
He spared ' for ' drede of leste, ne most,
Tyl he come to Agincourt coste.
Deo gratias, etc.

Than for sothe that knyghte comely,
In Agincourt feld he faughte manly ;
Thorow grace of God most myghty,
He had bothe the felde, and the victory.
Deo gratias, etc.

Ther dukys, and erlys, lorde and barone,
Were take, and slayne, and that wel sone,
And some were ledde into Lundone,
With joye, and merthe, and grete renone.
Deo gratias, etc.

Now gracious God, he save oure kynge,
His peple, and all his well wyllynge,
Gef him gode lyfe, and gode endynge,
That we with merth mowe savely synge.
Deo gratias :
Deo gratias Anglia redde pro victoria.

When the procession reached 'the tower of the
conduit in Cornhill' a wonderful spectacle awaited
them.

That tower was found decked with crimson cloth,
spread out after the fashion of a tent upon poles covered
with the same cloth. The middle of the tower below, was
surrounded with the arms of Saints George, Edward,
Edmund, and of England, in four elevated places, with
intermediate scutcheons of the royal arms ; amongst
which was inscrted this inscription of pious import, QUON-
IAM REX SPERAT IN DOMINO ET MISERICORDIA ALTISSIMI
NON COMMOVEBITUR. But higher of the turrets the arms
on the royal family were raised for ornaments on halberds.

In this pavilion itself 'was a company of prophets,
of venerable hoariness, dressed in golden coats and
mantles ' ; and when Henry passed by they loosed
a number of sparrows as an emblematic thank-
offering for victory. Some of the little birds
perched on the shoulder of the king ; and the

prophets burst into praise, chanting the psalm
CANTATE DOMINO CANTICUM NOVUM, ALLELUIA :
QUIA MIRABILIA FECIT ALLELUIA : SALVAVIT, etc.

At the entrance to the Cheap was more
pageantry, and more ' men of venerable old age,'
but this time they represented the Twelve Apostles
and the twelve kings, 'martyrs and confessors of
the succession of England.' They chanted an
anthem, and when Henry passed by

> they sent forth upon him, round leaves of silver mixed
> with wafers, equally thin and round, with wine out of
> pipes of the conduit, that they might receive him with
> bread and wine, as Melchisedeck received Abraham, re-
> turning with victory from the slaughter of the four kings.

' The cross of Cheap ' was concealed by a wooden
castle, over the four gates of which were the words
GLORIOSA DICTA SUNT DE TE CIVITAS DEI. It
was such a beautifully constructed castle that men
thought ' the whole had been cemented together of
squared and polished stones.' As Henry approached
there trouped over the drawbridge of this mock castle

> a chorus of most beautiful virgin girls, elegantly attired
> in white and virgin dress, singing with timbrol and dance,
> as to another David coming from the slaughter of Goliath
> . . . this song of congratulation, WELCOME HENRY THE
> FIFTE. KYNGE OF ENGLOND AND OF FRAUNCE.

Boys ' decked with celestial gracefulness ' hung
out of the window and dropped on the procession
' minæ of gold with boughs of laurel,' all the time
singing TE DEUM LAUDAMUS, TE DOMINUM
CONFITEMUR.

On the procession passed to the great centre of
the nation's religious life—' the Church of Peter
and Paul ' or, as we know it, St Paul's. The great
bells were ringing a merry peal, and at the door
no less than eighteen bishops awaited the arrival
of the hero-king. He entered, kissed the sacred
relics, and joined in the service of solemn thanks-

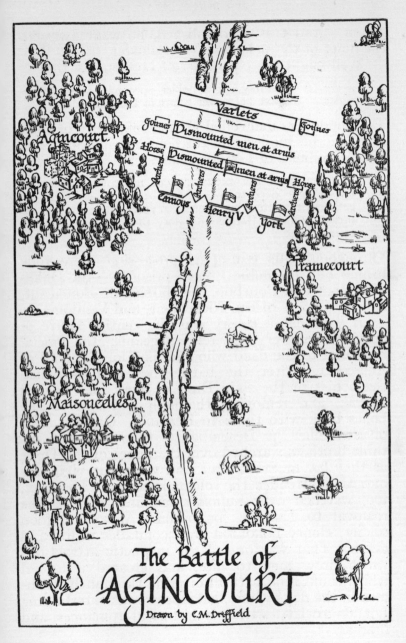

The Battle of
AGINCOURT

Drawn by C.M. Driffield

giving. And this accomplished, he went away to the quiet of the palace at Westminster.

Well might the chronicler of London say that

> a greater assembly, or a nobler spectacle, was not re-collected to have been ever before in London.

The Londoners marvelled at the composure of their king, and his modesty in the hour of triumph. The same chronicler of London relates :

> Even from the taciturnity of his countenance, his unassuming deportment, and sober step, it might be gathered that the king, secretly revolving the affair in his breast, rendered thanks and glory to God alone, and not to men.

Throughout this triumphal procession there rode behind him his noble French prisoners—the Dukes of Orléans and Bourbon, the Marshal de Boucicaut, and the Counts of Eu, Richemont, and Vendôme.

A week later Henry was the central figure of another, but very different, pageant : the official memorial to the dead who had died for England at Agincourt. After the battle they had parboiled the bodies of the slain Duke of York and Earl of Suffolk, and removing the flesh had carried the bones back with them to England. On the night of November 30–December 1, the king and his three brothers watched over the bones of the Duke as they lay in St Paul's ; and when the vigil was over they attended the solemn requiem. The king, too, watched over Suffolk's remains prior to the removal to Ewelme for burial. Always a good soldier, Henry honoured loyal comrades in life and death. That was one of the magnetic attractions which drew men to him, and created a legend which could send a thrill of pride through Englishmen in the days when Shakespeare was entertaining London society with his historical romances and dramas.

CHAPTER SEVEN

REGAINING THE 'ANCIENT HERITAGE'

HENRY V. was too astute a man of affairs, and too great a realist, to believe that the victory at Agincourt would bring the French government to their knees. While he was in Calais, before his return to England in November 1415, he toyed with a scheme for attacking Boulogne in order to secure another seaport base for operations against the French ; but his men, anxious to see their families and friends in England and forget the experiences of that terrible march from Harfleur, murmured against an extension of their service ; and Henry wisely, though reluctantly, allowed them to have their way.

Short though his stay in France had been it was long enough to let him take stock of the position and to arouse a longing again to possess what he regarded as his own. He had trodden the soil of the 'ancient heritage' of England's kings— the duchy of Normandy ; and he could hardly fail to observe that the misgovernment of the French had created a sullen and discontented peasantry in that province. All that was required to seduce these hard-working people from their allegiance to the French kings was just government and fair taxes ; and it is significant that Henry, when he had conquered the duchy, gave the Norman peasants what they wanted, and he gained rather than lost by such concessions. On the other hand, as a soldier, he must have known that the complete conquest of France would be a lengthy business, to be undertaken by a well-disciplined and well-equipped army. The country was dotted with castles and walled towns, in each of which lurked a small fighting force, always eager either to give battle to, or harass the movements of, an invading army. His next campaign, therefore, must be devoted to a systematic attack against these castles and walled towns.

Henry, like Chatham in a later age, had the gift of choosing brilliant lieutenants. On returning to England after the Agincourt campaign he found that his choice of regent was everywhere applauded. John of Bedford, during the short time he held that office, had ruled wisely and well ; and although the Lollard Oldcastle was still at large and a general uneasiness prevailed (as was always the case when England and France made war in the Middle Ages) on the Anglo-Scottish border, the king's peace had never once been seriously challenged. John of Bedford had been tried and not found wanting : it was a source of great encouragement for Henry to know that in this brother he had a man who could control the destinies of England while he himself pursued his warlike ambitions in France.

Nor did Henry hide from his people those warlike ambitions. In the parliament which met in the Painted Chamber at Westminster on March 16, 1416, his intentions were stated in the plainest language by Bishop Henry Beaufort in the customary opening sermon. The very text had a warlike ring about it—' He hath opened for you a way.' In expanding it the bishop explained that Henry was the instrument whom God had selected for the punishment of the stiff-necked people of France, the sinfulness of whose lives was offensive to all good Christian people ; and since they had not listened to the voice of God in times past it was now plainly Henry's duty to proceed with the war. Then, with true Lancastrian deference for the prerogatives and authority of parliament, the bishop went out of his way to assure the members that the king looked to them for advice and help in such a grave business.

Help the king certainly needed—financial help. His men were still unpaid, and the royal resources were mortgaged up to the hilt. Parliament graciously though none too generously relieved the royal necessity; and then proceeded to transact the normal business of government. One item of business was concerned with the Great Schism, of which we must presently speak. Since there was no lawful Pope, parliament decided to accept confirmation of all episcopal appointments by the Archbishops of Canterbury and York as equivalent to the customary papal confirmation as long as the disastrous schism continued. It was during the meeting of this parliament that Henry healed another old sore : he accepted back into grace young Henry Percy, Hotspur's son and heir, and restored to him the titles and lands of his grandfather and father. Within a little time young Percy was holding high office under the Crown on the Anglo-Scottish border. And it was in this same year (1416) that Sir John Holland was given back the earldom of Huntingdon, forfeited on his father's treason. Sir John had proved his loyalty to Henry up to the hilt, and he was destined to become one of the main pillars of the Lancastrian cause.

About Easter, while the parliament-men were in recess for the purpose of honouring the greatest of Christian festivals, Sigismund, king of the Romans, arrived in England.[13] He was one of the outstanding figures in Europe at that time, and had had an exceptionally adventurous and chequered career. He had been compelled to fight

for his life against the great Magyar landlords of
Hungary ; he had been hopelessly defeated by
the Turks at the battle of Nicopolis—a battle in
which Henry IV., as Earl of Derby, had taken a
prominent part ; he had been poisoned by political
enemies and then saved from death by hanging
from his feet for twenty-four hours. Nevertheless,
despite all these inconveniences, Sigismund had
built up for himself a great reputation as a patron
of learning and a ruler with high, if superficial,
ideals of Christian unity.

Sigismund had set himself the seemingly
Herculean task of bringing order out of chaos in
the Church. It was a shrewd move on his part,
for popes had long enough argued that they were
above princes, and Sigismund perceived that if
a prince could heal the schism which divided the
Church against herself he would seriously undermine that papal pretension.

In order that readers can understand the
ecclesiastical situation in Europe it will be necessary
to outline the events leading up to the ending of
the Great Schism.

From 1309 to 1377 the Papacy had been a
satellite of the French kings. The popes lived in
the town of Avignon, and the papal authority was
repeatedly used to bolster up French policy and
advance French ambitions. This association of
the Papacy with one great power was bound to
weaken its authority. This happened in England ;
it was not so much the popes' attempt to exercise
papal patronage in England in the fourteenth
century as the fact that the Papacy was under the
thumb of the French court, which aroused the anti-
papal legislation of the English parliament in that
period. The pious protests of St Catherine of
Siena persuaded Gregory XI. in 1377 to take the
papal court back to Rome, the ancient centre of the

Church in western Christendom; but in the following year Gregory died, and in a very short time a scandal even worse than the ' Babylonish Captivity ' was destined to overtake the Church.

As Gregory's successor the cardinals elected Bartolomeo Prignano, Archbishop of Bari, who took the title of Urban VI. Six months later, acting under the influence of the French court, they declared that election null and void, and elected Robert of Geneva, Bishop of Cambrai, to be Pope Clement VII. Urban, refusing to acquiesce in this arrangement, remained in Rome, and received the obedience of the Holy Roman Empire and England : Clement, as a good Frenchman, set up his papal court at Avignon, and was recognised by France, Spain, and Scotland. So Christendom witnessed the distressing spectacle of the seamless robe of Christ rent in twain by worldly self-seekers.

In 1409 the confusion was worse confounded by a third occupant of the chair of St. Peter. The Council of Pisa in that year deposed Gregory XII. (Angelo Coriaro), the Roman pontiff, and elected as his successor Baldassare Cossa, who was known as John XXIII. Gregory refused to accept the decision of the council, and continued to exercise papal authority, being strongly supported by adherents in Sicily and Naples. At Avignon was Pedro de Luna, claiming to be Pope Benedict XIII. : and he had the support of France, Spain, and Scotland. John XXIII. could claim that he had the backing of the greater part of the Empire.

He was a strange occupant of the papal throne.[14] As a young man he had adopted the career of arms, and the greater part of his life was lived as a *condottiere* in Northern Italy, where there was always fighting to be had. There seems little doubt that he changed his profession because he saw that the Church offered more lucrative rewards than the camp ; and so great was his ambition that he was resolved to rule over an undivided Church. In the end it was the ambition of this *condottiere* which saved the Church from herself ; for John XXIII., knowing that alone he could never hope to realise his ambition, turned to Sigismund for help, and persuaded him that it was his duty as emperor-elect to end the Great Schism through a general council of the Church.

The opportunity of presiding over such a council was one which Sigismund was not likely to let pass ; and on November 16, 1414, he was the central figure in the formal opening of the famous Council of Constance. The trend of events at the protracted meetings of this council do not fall within the scope of this book : it is enough for the readers to know that one of the chief obstacles in the way of a settlement of the schism was the enmity which existed between England and France. It was not likely that France would accept a pope whose position had been largely secured by English help ; and for long enough Englishmen had demonstrated to the world their contempt of the papal puppets of France. So the delegates at Constance talked and argued, negotiated and intrigued : for one moment, however, they forgot their differences, and even their disloyalties to the Church which they had so hopelessly divided, when they sat in judgment on, and condemned to death at the stake, the Bohemian John Hus, whose only crime was his desire to teach the Gospel of Christ in a way which the poor people could appreciate.

It was soon made clear at Constance that the first step towards healing the schism was the resignation of the three so-called popes. John and Gregory were ready to accept this decision, provided that Benedict did the same ; but there was some doubt about Benedict's attitude, and consequently

Sigismund decided to visit France to talk matters over with him. They were in conference at Perpignan at the very time when Henry V. was trying to take the town of Harfleur.

Benedict, however, was not to be won over as easily as Sigismund imagined ; and the conference broke down. Sigismund thereupon went to Paris, hoping that by personal contact with the French government he would be able to persuade them to bring pressure to bear upon Benedict, and also to allow him to mediate in the quarrel between their country and England. Unfortunately he was none too discreet during his stay in the French capital : his poverty prevented him from treating the Parisians to the displays of generosity which they expected from all visiting monarchs ; and, worse still, he seriously offended French pride when he conferred the order of knighthood on a Frenchman —an obvious assertion of imperial suzerainty over the French king's realm. Sigismund's mission was a complete failure : he came no nearer mediation between France and England, and the French were disinclined to persuade Benedict to do what the Council of Constance wanted him to do.

Sigismund now turned his eyes on England. He must have known that Henry was a seriously-minded monarch, with strong inclinations towards piety ; and from the behaviour of the English delegates at Constance it was clear that he was eager to heal the schism which divided the Church. Henry welcomed the opportunity of talking matters over with so important a person as Sigismund, and consequently he invited him to visit England. Sigismund sailed from Calais on April 30, and was escorted to Dover by a magnificent fleet, specially sent from England for the purpose. But Henry was determined that his visitor should make no pretence to exercise imperial suzerainty over the realm of England ; and, wiser than the French, he decided to have this matter settled actually before Sigismund set foot on English soil. The incident is recorded in *The Life of Henry V*.

> The Duke of Glowcester, and all the other estats of England that were present, went into the water against the Emperor, wth their swordes drawen in there handes, and by the mouth of the said Duke they saide vnto him : That if they intended to enter the lande as the Kings friends, and as a mediator to intreate for the peace, he shoulde be suffered to arryue, and if he woulde enter as an Emperor as into a Realme as vnder his Empire, or any-thinge of his Imperiall power therein to commaunde, they were ready to resist his entrie in the Kings name. And this was thus deuised for sauinge of the Kings Imperiall Maiestie, wch is an Emperor wthin his Realme. And when the Emperor had answered that he came as the Kings friend, as for a mediator of peace, and not as an Emperor of this Realme : then the Duke with all his lordes went out of the water and receaued the Emperor wth the most honnor he coulde, and that might he deuise.

Henry V. had a showman's appreciation of a grand spectacle, and as Sigismund journeyed to London he was treated to a continued display of the military power of England.

The desirability of peace between France and England was the chief topic of the conversations which took place between Henry and his imperial guest. The English king may have sincerely hoped for a settlement of the old quarrel with France : he certainly listened with the utmost patience to Sigismund's proposals. But in view of the happenings on the other side of the Channel, peace between the two countries was as remote as ever ; and Henry must not be too hastily blamed for taking up a warlike attitude in the face of Sigismund's peace talk.

On the death of Charles d'Albret on the ill-fated field of Agincourt the office of Constable of France became vacant : it was immediately granted to

Bernard, Count of Armagnac, the leader of the anti-Burgundian faction in France. Bernard was an implacable enemy, and he was resolved to retrieve the honour which his country had lost at Agincourt by the recapture of Harfleur—and, if luck was with him, of Calais. With this object in view, therefore, a great *aide* was levied throughout the dominions of the king of France ; and men were mustered for service in the field against the hated English 'midges.' A daring, though ill-conceived, raid north along the coast, carried out by the Earl of Dorset, John Blount, John Fastolf, and a thousand men of the Harfleur garrison in March 1416, nearly ended in a serious disaster for the English. Near Ouainville a French force caught the raiders and cut their line of communication with Harfleur. Had the French captain held his hand until the Count of Armagnac (he was at Valmont not far away with a force of 5000 men) could come up things would have gone badly with the English ; but with typical French confidence in the military superiority of their forces, the French captain at once gave battle ; and after a stiff fight, Dorset and his men were able to extricate themselves and beat a hasty retreat to Harfleur.

The treacherous activities of Burgundian sympathisers in Paris made it necessary for the Count of Armagnac to return to the capital, and consequently he lost the chance of following up the advantage which he obviously had gained through this ' brush ' at Ouainville. The English garrison in Harfleur at once put their house in order, and the defences of the town were strengthened to meet the threatened French attack.

The Count of Armagnac laid his plans carefully : he decided to starve the garrison into surrender ; but he realised that in order to do this he must close the mouth of the Seine to relief ships from

England. About Easter, French envoys were at
Genoa negotiating for the loan of ships of war for
this purpose ; and by the end of April nine two-
masted carracks and eight galleys took up their
position opposite the mouth of the Seine. With
them was a motley collection of shipping, hired by
the French from the king of Castile and the
merchants of the towns on the Bay of Biscay.

Thus, while Sigismund talked peace to Henry,
the garrison in Harfleur was in a desperate plight.
Outside the mouth of the Seine was a great mer-
cenary fleet under the command of Guillaume,
Seigneur of Montenay, and a large force invested
the town on the landward side. Some of the enemy
ships raided the south coast of England, and
inflicted a considerable amount of damage on
certain seaport towns. Only one English sea-
captain managed to run the blockade ; but the
supply of provisions which he landed was pitiably
insufficient for a garrison which had already lost
500 men from famine, and was reduced to eating
rats and mice. It seemed that it was only a matter
of time before the Frenchmen regained Harfleur.

Sigismund suggested that the town should be
handed over to him pending a settlement of the
dispute between the two countries ; and Henry
was not unimpressed by the suggestion. The great
relief force which he had collected as soon as he
heard of the plight of the Harfleur garrison was
held up : it was a gesture of his sincere desire to
bring peace to a distracted Christendom. His
subjects, however, took a very different view of the
delayed sailing of the relief force : they began to
say openly that Henry was being fooled by the
peace talk of Sigismund, and as a result their
fellow-countrymen in Harfleur were being sacrificed
needlessly to the French. All of a sudden Henry
saw that he was in danger of losing the confidence

of his people. That was something which he could not afford to do. He was at once all activity : in July he was at Southampton personally superintending the final arrangements for the sailing of the relief force. But at the last moment Sigismund's influence over Henry brought about a change of plans. Henry had resolved to lead the relief on Harfleur in person :

> But the Emperor discouncelled him from that, sayinge that the Kinge, in whome the common wealth resteth, ought not so lightlie to submitt himself to eueric perrill ; and thereto he added sayinge, that the assiege might as well be dissolued of some of his princes as by his commaunment as by himself.

Henry bowed to the Emperor's wishes, and on July 22 the command was given to John of Bedford. There were still delays : this time they were caused by the hostile activities of the Genoese and French sailors, who forced some of the English ships to keep close within their harbours.

At last Bedford got his fleet of three to four hundred ships under weigh ; and on the evening of August 14 they anchored in sight of the enemy ships off the mouth of the Seine. The news of the fleet's departure was flashed by beacon fires from the coast to London, and as soon as Henry learnt that his brother's great adventure had begun he went to his private chapel at Westminster and spent the night in prayer. Early in the morning he sent messengers to the Carthusian houses in London and Sheen to beg the monks ceaselessly to pray for the success of the undertaking and the safety of his brother and his men.

When the morning came, the two fleets made ready for battle. The sailors and fighting men on both sides committed themselves to the protection of Heaven, praying earnestly to the Blessed Virgin for her special intercession on their behalf—for that day was the feast of her most glorious Assumption. After a conference of captains on board Bedford's flagship, the signal for the engagement to begin was run up ; and the English ships weighed anchor and bore down upon the enemy, drawn up across the mouth of the Seine. In a short time both sides were hotly engaged.

It was a typical mediæval sea-fight. The attacking English did their best to grapple the French and Genoese ; but even when they succeeded they were at a great disadvantage :

> The English shipps were soone fastened to the greate carricks, wch exceeded so much the English shipps in height, that from the decks of theire carricks, where they stoode to fight, they might scarcely reach downewards the highest of the English shipps wth the longest spare they hadd.

This superiority in height enabled the enemy to pour into the attacking ships a deadly fire. ' They fought cruellie ' on both sides, and the losses were unbelievably great. The English certainly had the severest mauling. Bedford was badly wounded ; 700 of his knights were either killed or wounded ; and more than 2000 seamen and soldiers perished. The sea was thick with corpses, and many ships were sunk. But the pertinacity of the English told in the end, and the enemy drew off, leaving the passage to the town of Harfleur open to the English ships. The success of Bedford at sea was sufficiently great to compel even the French land forces to withdraw. Indeed, as a contemporary chronicler put it, the Frenchmen were ' sore bet,' and it requires no trick of the imagination to appreciate the ' grete joie ' of the Earl of Dorset and his men in Harfleur when they saw the English ships making fast alongside the town's quays.

It was not until August 21 that Henry learnt of the victory which his brother had won at the battle of the Seine. The news reached him at Smallhythe, and his first act was to fall on his knees and give thanks to God for the success which had attended English arms. Then, taking horse, he rode with all speed to Canterbury, where in company with Sigismund he attended a solemn thanksgiving in the cathedral church. Again God had demonstrated that He had chosen Henry and his people as the instruments for humbling the sinful people of France ; and although now this thought may appear to be a hypocritical obsession or perhaps even a manifestation of religious mania, the fact remains that it was sincerely and irradicably fixed in Henry's mind. In the hour of his rejoicings he remembered his duty to Our Lady, on the feast of whose Assumption the efforts of his subjects had been crowned with such magnificent success, and we read that

> the Kinge commaunded that euerie daye shoulde be sungen in his Chappell an anthem and a collett of the Assumption of our Ladie, wch was continually used duringe his life.

On the same day as Bedford smashed the French blockading force, Henry and Sigismund concluded a treaty of alliance at Canterbury. Sigismund realised that his efforts to seek peace were lost upon the French ; and so convinced was he that Henry had suffered grievous hurt at the Frenchmen's hands that he declared himself ready to conclude with the English king a

> perpetuall allyance and freindlie confederacion, as well of the oppressinge of the pride of the Frenchmen as for the moouinge and reforminge of the Sisme.

The claims of commerce were not forgotten : the merchants of England and the Empire were to be allowed uninterrupted rights of trading in the realms of the contracting parties, provided that they paid the customary dues and obeyed the

existing laws. In many respects this Treaty of
Canterbury is one of the most comprehensive
treaties of alliance concluded in the Middle Ages.

The time came for Sigismund and Henry to take
leave of each other. The emperor-elect had landed
in England as a peacemaker : he left as a sworn
friend and ally of the English king, and had even
pledged himself to support Henry in arms against
the proud Frenchmen. No doubt Sigismund was
conscious of the prestige which would be his when
Europe learnt that the victor of Agincourt was his
friend and ally : prelates and princes might in
the future be more disposed to respect his opinions
and purpose. Sigismund cannot have failed to
have taken away with him the pleasantest memories
of his stay in England. Henry had treated him
right royally. There had been the customary
round of chivalrous entertainment. He had received from his host's hands the coveted distinction
of the Garter. Poverty made it impracticable
for Sigismund to return these compliments with
splendid entertainments ; but he showed his
gratitude in a way which would endear him to all
Henry's loyal subjects ; and in return for that
coveted Garter he gave into his friend's keeping
the heart of St George.

Arrangements were made for Henry to escort
Sigismund as far as Calais ; but the activity of
French fighting ships in the Channel resulted in a
modification of the programme ; and Sigismund
and his suite sailed from the shores of England alone
on August 25. Ten days later, however, Henry
joined him in Calais ; and there they remained for
the next six weeks.

While Henry and Sigismund were in Calais they
were visited by John, Duke of Burgundy—the man
whose bitter hatreds of the Armagnacs plunged
him into the foulest treasons against his king and

country. At this interview Burgundy recognised
the justice of Henry's claim to the French throne,
but he prayed to be excused from doing formal
homage for his fiefs until such a time as Henry had
the greater part of France in his hands. His
reservation is understandable, if thoroughly dishonourable : he could not afford to burn his boats
by openly declaring himself the ' man ' of the
English king. At the same time Burgundy undertook to further the cause of the English ' by all
secret means ' ; and even went so far as to
promise that at the opportune moment he would
come in arms to his support. Precisely what
Henry promised in return for Burgundian help
is not known—doubtless a liberal share of the
conquests.

On October 16 Henry returned to England to
meet a parliament summoned to assemble on the
19th. Sigismund went on his way to Constance,
again to worry out the problems of a united Church.
A year was to pass before he found the solution :
on November 11, 1417, under the ægis of the Council
of Constance the cardinals elected one of their
college—Otho Calonna—Pope ; and he took the
title of Martin V.[15] But at the very moment when
this momentous decision was being made in
Constance, Henry V. of England was marching
through the realm of France, resolved to place
himself and his heirs on the throne of the
Capets.

It was in the autumn of 1416, soon after his
return from Calais, that Henry received strange
overtures for peace from the prisoners whom he
had taken at Agincourt. The Duke of Bourbon
secured an interview with the English king, during
the course of which he frankly admitted that
Henry's promise to renounce his right to the
French throne provided that he was allowed to

15

retain the territorial gains of Brétigni was ' a great and reasonable proffer.' The duke undertook to return to France to use his influence at the court to get these terms accepted ; and as an earnest of his sincerity and a pledge for his safe return he offered to leave as hostages in England his two sons and to deposit a bail of 200,000 crowns. At the same time the English king was informed that the majority of the French prisoners endorsed the duke's action ; and should their government refuse these terms then they would do homage to Henry as the rightful king of France.

The duke failed to raise the stipulated surety, and consequently he did not leave England ; but Ralph, Seigneur of Gaucourt, the gallant defender of Harfleur, went as his deputy, and it would appear that he presented in the proper quarters the prisoners' case. Nothing came of these peace overtures : the dominant Armagnacs, concerned only with a desire to crush their hated Burgundian rivals, had little time to devote to peace negotiations or the misfortunes of the prisoners ; and as true Frenchmen (for with all their faults the Armagnacs were more or less loyal to France—possibly because the Burgundians were disloyal to her) they were not going to accept the Brétigni arrangement as a settlement of the dispute between their country and England. And it is difficult to believe that Henry took these overtures seriously : when the negotiations were proceeding he wrote to his agent, Tiptot, at the court of Sigismund :

I wol not leve my voyage for any Tretee that they make.

His mind was made up : he was divinely appointed to conduct a war of conquest against the French ; and his loyalty to the Christian faith would never allow him to abandon that purpose.

The parliamentary session of the autumn of 1416

was short and uneventful. In the opening sermon, preached from the text—' Study to be quiet,' Bishop Beaufort told the Lords and Commons that since the French had wilfully thwarted every peace move the matter must now be settled by the sword ; and parliament, heartily agreeing with this sentiment, made a generous vote of money. On the last day of the session (November 18) Henry honoured one who had served him loyally—his half-uncle, Thomas Beaufort, Earl of Dorset. He was granted the title of Duke of Exeter, and provided with an annuity of £1000 : the dukedom, however, was only to be his for life. When parliament was asked if they approved of the royal action they frankly replied that they did, though they thought that the duke's services merited greater rewards ! It was the kind of rebuke which delighted the heart of Henry V.

Henry could not forget that the fate of Harfleur had depended upon the command of the sea. He had come within an ace of losing that important foothold in France, because the French had mustered sufficient ships to cut its communications with England ; and what had been done once might easily be done again—and perhaps with greater success. In 1416, therefore, he made it quite clear that he meant to give his country the command of the seas ; and in many histories he is paraded as the ' founder of the Royal Navy ' as a result of the steps which he took to make his country the dominant maritime power. This honour is greater than accurate history can allow him : he was not the ' founder of the Royal Navy,' but he certainly did a great deal to increase his country's prestige at sea.

Strictly speaking, there was no navy in Henry V.'s reign. The country possessed a number of royal ships, designated ' of the Tower ' (in February

1417 they numbered 3 carracks, 9 barges, and 10 balingers) ; but at best they were only armed merchantmen ; and in time of war they were reinforced by a motley array of shipping provided by the seaport towns. The three carracks which Henry possessed in February 1417 were *la Trinité Royale*, the *Holy Ghost*, and the *Nicholas* ; but later in the year two new ships of the carrack class —the *Jesus* and the *Grace Dieu*—were added to the fleet ; and throughout the reign the dockyards turned out a number of smaller craft. So great was Henry's interest in naval development that Englishmen in a later age (looking back, as a later age must always do, to ' the good old days ') commemorated the king's work in popular song :

> Henry the Fifte, what was hys purposynge,
> Whan at Hampton he made the grete dromons,
> Which passed other grete ships of the Commons,
> The *Trinitie*, the *Grace Dieu*, the *Holy Ghost*,
> And other moo whiche as now be lost.

The hopeless condition of their own times made men yearn for the strong hand of government such as their fathers had known ; and the mighty achievements of ' king Harry Fifte ' were completed by the popular tale that he had founded the kingdom's naval power.

Henry's naval programme could not possibly be completed in time to provide him with sufficient ships to convey his army overseas for the conquest of Normandy. Consequently early in 1417 his agents were actively at work in the Dutch ports hiring ships to act as transports ; and when some of the Venetian fleet—the great fleet which bore the luxuries of the Orient to the lands of western Europe—took shelter in English ports they were promptly pressed into the royal service. The protests of their owners merely called forth from the king the curt reply that he would pay well for their use — poor consolation for the Venetian merchants whose chief interest was in trade and not the quarrels of the king of England.

Henry knew that the success of his schemes depended on his ability to land a great army in Normandy. It was imperative, therefore, that the Channel should be kept reasonably free from enemy shipping ; and with this end in view Sir John Mortimer and Sir Thomas Carew were commissioned in February 1417 to ' keep the seas ' for six months. Apparently they did their work well (though they could not always drive away raiding Genoese and French ships) for in May of that same year a writer informed a friend that the two captains were effectively blockading ' the strait ' with a force of sixty ships.

From the commencement of 1417 Henry's attention was directed towards the preparation of the expeditionary force, and he hoped to be on the move at the end of May, for he had heard that his friend Sigismund meant to march with him in that month. In January, therefore, the returns of men-at-arms and archers were completed ; and in the following month the sheriffs all over England were ordered to draw up the necessary indentures. The men were to be at Southampton by early in June, when ships would be ready to carry them across to France. On April 25 Henry took his leave of the loyal Londoners, having first attended divine service in ' Paul's Church ' ; and the enthusiasm of his people left no doubt in his mind as to the nation's desire to prosecute the war against the French.

It was no easy matter to get a mediæval army under marching orders, and July was well advanced before Henry was ready to make a start. On July 23, he embarked on his ship, called the

King's Chamber. And what a splendid vessel she
was :

> the sayle thereof was sylke of purple couller, right boun-
> teouslie embrodered wth both the Arms of England and
> Fraunce.

A sister carrack, the *King's Hall,* accommodated
the royal brothers, Clarence and Gloucester, and
their staffs ; and the remainder of the captains
and their contingents were scattered about in the
1500 ships which had come together for the purpose
of transporting the expeditionary force to the other
side of the Channel.

Never had a greater or better equipped army
left the shores of England. It is estimated that no
less than 16,400 men were on board the transports ;
and many were left behind, because there was not
sufficient shipping to convey them over to France.
Henry had thought of every need :

> . . . there was no manner of occupacion or crafte absent
> from that hoast, that coulde be thought necessarie for
> them.   Neither Myners to vndermyne the grounde,
> Carpenters to make and rayse engins, laborers to delve the
> grounde, and to lade ditches, Masons to hewe stones for
> shott to breake walls, to subuert strong holdes, nor gunners
> to shutt gunnes ; nor briefely to accompt there fayled
> them no manner of occupacion or scyence that coulde be
> thought necessarie for them.

Incidentally some of the miners in the royal retinue
came from Liège, and the gunners from Germany.
In addition to the craftsmen mentioned in the
extract above were surgeons, leeches, chaplains,
minstrels, and farriers or veterinary surgeons.

Just at the moment when the fleet was ready
to put to sea there came the news that French ships
were hanging about the Channel ready to pounce
upon the transports. The Earl of Huntingdon
was sent out to scatter them, and a desperate
engagement ensued. The French, commanded by

Percival, the bastard of Bourbon, were numerically the superior force ; but Huntingdon fought his ships cleverly ; and after three hours gained a notable victory, capturing a number of carracks, a goodly sum of money for the payment of the French crews, and the bastard of Bourbon himself.

Once again Henry kept secret the destination of his expeditionary force, and the transports were commanded to follow closely the ' two shipps Royall, whithersoeuer they woulde sayle.' On August 1, after a pleasant crossing, the great fleet cast anchor off Touques at the mouth of the Seine, and hard by the present-day pleasure resort of Trouville. The Frenchmen on the shore

> at the first perceauinge so greate an navye, whose streingth they knewe themselues not able to resist, left there stations and fledd to saue theire lyues.

As a result the English landing was not challenged.

Immediately on landing Henry gave God thanks for the safe passage : he then dubbed forty-eight young esquires knights, and

> proclaimed all those ordynaunces and edicts that were published tofore the besieginge of Harefleet, and also diuers others such as he thought to be good and proffitable for his hoast.

The main part of the fleet went back to England under the command of the Earl of March ; the ships carrying the guns and the siege train lay quietly at anchor in the Seine.

Henry lost no time in opening his campaign. The Earl of Huntingdon marched to the castle of Bonneville, a mile distant from Touques, and demanded its surrender : the commander promptly made the usual arrangement to strike his flag if help did not reach him by August 9. No French relief force ever went to Bonneville, and a Yorkshire knight, Sir John Keighley, took possession of that great castle in the name of the rightful Duke of Normandy, Henry V., king of England.

Some of the English captains advocated an attack on Honfleur ; but Henry himself was resolved to seize Caen, one of the most important commercial centres in fifteenth-century France ; and on the 13th the main body of the English army began its advance on that place. Clarence, with a picked force of 1000 horse, was ordered to dash to Caen by the shortest route. He arrived outside the town on the 14th ; seized the suburbs before the garrison had time to fire them, and took up his headquarters in the Abbey of the Holy Trinity. This religious house, founded by Matilda, the queen of William the Conqueror, stood outside the town walls, and occupied a commanding position on the north-east of Caen. Outside the walls on the south-west was the Abbey of St Stephen, founded by the Conqueror himself, and it literally dominated the whole town. The French, therefore, as soon as they saw that the English were determined to attack Caen, hastened to destroy this abbey. One of the monks, his heart torn with anguish at the thought of the destruction of so magnificent a religious house, went by night to Clarence, and promised to lead him secretly into St Stephen's if he would spare it. Clarence accepted the offer, and was quickly in possession of this important position.

Just before he left Touques, Henry sent a letter to the king of France. In it he protested that he had always sought peace, whereas Charles had sought war ; and he told his royal cousin in the plainest language, that, unless he surrendered his Crown and kingdom, divine punishment would descend upon him.

Henry and the main army followed a circuitous route to Caen, passing through Dives, Grentheville, St André de Fontenay, Allemagne, and Éterville ;

and on the 18th, he appeared before Caen. The king made his headquarters in the Abbey of St Stephen's, and at once deployed his forces. As the southern part of the town was almost un-approachable, owing to the many channels of the river Orne, Henry concentrated his attack around the northern walls, from St Stephen's to the Holy Trinity. On the east was Clarence; on the north, Gilbert, Lord Talbot, Robert, Lord Willoughby, Gilbert Umfraville, and John Neville; on the north-west, the Earl Marshal and Lord Maltravers; and on the south-west, the Earls of Huntingdon, Salisbury, Warwick, Sir John Cornwall, and Lord Grey of Codnor. The weight of the English artillery was concentrated along the western wall; and the Duke of Gloucester was ' ruler and overseer ' of all ' the gunns and ordinance.'

Within the town was an old enemy of the English, Guillaume, Seigneur of Montenay—the man who had commanded the French and Genoese fleet in the battle of the Seine; and he had with him a large number of Genoese crossbowmen. But Caen was not a strongly fortified town, and it was ill-provisioned to withstand a long siege. Montenay had done his best to strengthen the walls with earthworks; and with the limited amount of ordnance at his disposal he defended the town.

Henry made great use of artillery. So fierce was the bombardment that the windows in St Stephen's were shattered; and one chronicler tells us that

within the Towne also manie olde edifices, not by the stroke onelie but by violent noyse of the gunns, were ouer-throwne and caste to the grounde.

The gunners in the English force ingeniously invented a flame shell. It was a hollow iron ball into which was stuffed straw and other inflammable material, and in its flight through the air it was ignited ; and it is said that much of the town was burnt by these shells. At the same time sappers and miners worked below the ground to undermine the walls ; and by September 4 all was ready for the great assault. This was most skilfully planned.

> At the first appeeringe of the day, trumpets were blowne in the Kings tents.

The French imagined that the main attack was to be delivered against the western walls of the town, and they concentrated their forces there. But the main attack was made by Clarence. Shouting " a Clarence ! a Clarence ! a Seynt George ! " his men dashed forward, supported by the Earl of Warwick and his men ; and after a desperate struggle they won their way into the town. Hand-to-hand fighting took place in the streets : the French were determined to sell their lives dearly. But numbers told, and the Frenchmen were beaten. The streets were piled high with dead, and, un-checked by the king, the English soldiery sacked and plundered the town, though every consideration was shown to women, children, and churches. It has been said that Henry deliberately allowed his men to run loose in Caen in order to strike fear into the hearts of the inhabitants of his duchy ; and the record of the behaviour of the English in Caen makes it difficult to refute this suggestion.

When the shouting and the tumult had ceased, Henry made a formal entry into the town ; and his first act was to go to the Church of St Peter to give thanks to God for his victory. That done, he turned his attention to the castle, whose garrison continued to hold out. But resistance was futile, and the commander at last agreed to surrender on September 19 if he was not relieved by that date. On September 20 the commander and his garrison marched out : Caen was completely in Henry's control.

From the outset Henry acted as the rightful Duke of Normandy. He promised free pardons to those who would return to their allegiance. Many of the poorer people accepted this offer : so, too, did the clergy ; but the men of substance and the nobles preferred exile to recognition of the enemy of their country. Henry remained in Caen until October 1.

During the time that his army had been investing the town, detachments of English troops had been busily engaged in breaking the resistance of the Normans and French in the surrounding country. Creully, Villers-Bocage, Lingèvres, Tilly-sur-Seulles, Thury-Harcourt, and Lamotte-de-Cesny had all surrendered by the middle of September ; and on the very day that the garrison of the castle of Caen marched out the English were in possession of Bayeux.

The next task which Henry set himself to accomplish was the conquest of lower Normandy. On October 1 he marched his men out of Caen, which was left in the capable hands of Gilbert Umfraville ; and by the 22nd he had advanced as far as, and taken, Alençon. All along his line of march, and in the neighbouring countryside, a great many castles capitulated ; and what was more important, during his stay at Alençon he was able to effect by treaty the neutralisation of the great fiefs of Brittany and Anjou.

By all the rules of mediæval warfare, Henry ought to have called a halt to his campaigning after the capture of Alençon. Mediæval armies seldom operated in winter months : they went into winter quarters, or more usually were disbanded until the following summer. Henry broke with this tradition : he meant to pursue his military schemes relentlessly and without intermission. One great Norman stronghold defied his power—Falaise, where once had lived the laughing and seductive Arlette, whom Duke Robert of Normandy had brought to child-bed of William the Conqueror ; and although Arlette was but a tanner's daughter, the kings of England were jealously proud of their descent from the bastard to which she had given birth.

At the beginning of December 1417, therefore, Henry and his men were before Falaise. The king himself was particularly active in providing for the creature comforts of his troops : huts were built to shield them from the wet and cold ; arrangements were made for their provisioning ; and the English camp was strongly protected by a trench. On January 2 the town opened its gates to Henry ; but the castle, perched high on a rocky cliff and commanded by a gallant French soldier, Olivier, Seigneur of Mauny, fought on. The solid rock on which the castle was raised defied the efforts of the miners ; and the English were compelled to fight their way to the very foundations of the walls. They did this by filling the ditch with faggots and earth, and then working in shelters at the foot of the walls ; and all the time they were subjected to a hail of enemy fire and downpours of molten metal, pitch, lime, and fired torches. In the end their tenacity was repaid : the garrison perceived that they were beaten, and on February 16 they surrendered the castle into Henry's hands. Soon afterwards Henry returned to Caen to direct the organisation of his Norman conquests and make ready for the great blow which he meant to deliver against Rouen.

While Henry himself had been actively engaged in advancing through lower Normandy, detachments of his army were operating in other parts of the duchy. Gilbert, Lord Talbot, had raided the

Cotentin in the latter part of 1417; but he was badly mauled by enemy forces; and early in 1418 Humphrey of Gloucester, with a larger force, took charge of operations in the western districts. By the middle of April he had more or less dominated the district of the Cotentin; and only the great castle of Cherbourg—acclaimed to be the strongest fortress in France—held out against the English advance. In the eastern districts of Normandy, Clarence and his captains were busily engaged in opening up the road to Rouen, which Henry was resolved to attack in the summer months.

Henry at once consolidated his conquests in lower Normandy. The district was divided into four *bailliages* — Alençon, Caen, Cotentin, and Evreux, over which were placed such trusted men as John Popham, Robert Lenthall, John Ashton, and John Radcliff. The *bailliages* were divided into fourteen *vicomtés*, which—with few exceptions —were left to be administered by the native-born Normans. Caen was the centre of the government. There Philip Morgan, the chancellor of the duchy, and John Tiptot, the president of the *chambres des comptes*, had their headquarters; and they were surrounded by a host of English and Norman officials.

Henry made every effort to win the confidence of the Norman people. He was too wise a ruler to run the risk of leaving in the rear of his advancing army a disaffected province, and too just a man not to endeavour to give the Normans a taste of good government. He had come to them as their lawful duke : he would show them by the justice and wisdom of his rule that there were positive advantages to be gained from a return to their rightful allegiance. The Normans had suffered ' grievous taxes, made worse by tyrannous magistrates ' while they were ruled by the French king.

Henry at once reduced taxation—particularly the *gabelle* or salt tax, one of the most odious exactions of the French government ; and steps were quickly taken to put an end to the lawlessness which pre-vailed throughout the duchy and was so hurtful to life and property, agriculture, and commerce. The poorer peasants and the lower clergy cheerfully accepted the change of masters : the nobles and higher clergy had little or no truck with the con-queror. They spurned Henry's offers of restoration of estates and sees ; and so conscious was Henry of his failure to bring them back to their lawful allegiance that towards the end of 1418 he wrote somewhat bitterly to his council in London :

> In substance there is no man of estate come in to the king's obeisance, the which is a thing that causeth the people to be full unstable, and is no wonder.

But he never lost hope : one day they would recognise him as their rightful duke, and have to accept him as the king of France.

Cursed with a king whose mind was diseased, the prey of factious noblemen whose hatreds were infinitely more important than the national safety, the people of France had to stand patiently by and watch the successes of the English. Poor Charles VI. was most unfortunate in his sons. In the December following Agincourt, Louis, the dauphin, a hopeless wencher and glutton, had died under circumstances which clearly indicated poison. His brother, John, was owing to marriage a catspaw in Burgundy's hands. He died in April 1417, and again men said that a poisoner had been at work. The new dauphin, Charles, was quickly seized upon by the Armagnacs as one who would advance their inter-ests ; and under their influence he was persuaded to imprison his mother, the Queen Isabella, first in the castle of Blois and then at Tours. Profligate and extravagant Isabella may have been ; but she was a woman of spirit and action. She became the bitter enemy of her own son, and aided by the Duke of Burgundy (who rescued her from the prison in which she had been lodged) she set herself up as regent of France. The scales were now turned in Burgundy's favour ; but their triumph brought only a renewal of the civil strife in France. Neither Armagnac nor Burgundy dared to resist the English invaders : each knew that the other would turn such patriotism to his own advantage ; and each was quite ready to treat with the invader in order to secure the triumph of his own cause.

At the end of May and in the beginning of June 1418 the senseless quarrel between Armagnac and Burgundy blazed forth with terrifying violence in Paris. The Armagnacs took as their warcry :

> Long live the king, the dauphin, and the king of England !

Their intrigues with Henry led them to think that he would intervene on their behalf to the discomfort of their rivals. The Burgundians replied with the blunt :

> Slay, slay all the Armagnac dogs !

And they made good their threat with a bloody reign of terror in the capital. Hundreds of Armagnacs were brutally slain, and among the victims was Bernard, Count of Armagnac, himself. In a little time Burgundy found himself at the helm of state in France : in that rôle it would be his duty to clear his country of the invading English. Could he play that part ? But the recent triumphs of the Burgundians did not mean the collapse of the Armagnacs. They were still a force to be reckoned with, and were led by the Breton Tanneguy du Chastel, a man of great ability and reckless determination. His party had the advantage of having the dauphin in their possession, and the dauphin was the heir to the throne of France.

Such was the state of affairs in France when Henry and his men were consolidating their conquests in the duchy of Normandy. Peace negotiations, it is true, had been fitfully carried on with the French government ; and the newly elected pope, Martin V., had sent two of the leading cardinals —Orsini and Fillastre—to France with the object of composing the quarrel between Charles and Henry. But there could be no peace, so long as France was torn by internal dissensions ; and Henry V. showed not the slightest sign of willingness to modify his demands.

By the summer of 1418 he was ready to make his thrust at Normandy's capital—Rouen. In the duchy few strongholds held out against him—the more important being Cherbourg, Domfront, and Mont-St-Michel ; and Henry had taken steps to effect their capitulation. The Earl of Warwick was hotly besieging the French in Domfront ; Gloucester's men were around Cherbourg ; and for the moment Henry deemed it unnecessary to waste time and money in reducing Mont-St-Michel. Domfront and Cherbourg put up a magnificent resistance. July was well advanced before the former surrendered, and Cherbourg held out until Michaelmas. In the eastern districts of Normandy Clarence was actively engaged in making ready for the advance against Rouen. He took Harcourt and Bec—the latter place put up a determined resistance—and it was not until the beginning of June that he was free to meet his royal brother outside Louviers. Three weeks passed before the English had that place. Henry came very near to death during the siege of Louviers. He was talking in his tent to the Earl of Salisbury when a stone shot from one of the town's guns crashed into the tent and smashed the pole. To the eternal shame of Henry, when the place was taken, he ordered the hanging of nine of the captured gunners ; and eight of them suffered death, the ninth owing his life to the intervention of one of the papal peace legates, Cardinal Orsini.

On June 27, Henry and the main body of the English army were at Pont de l'Arche, the key to the advance on Rouen. The town stood at the junction of the Eure and the Seine. It guarded one of the few crossings of the latter river ; and it was strongly defended. For a fortnight the English attacked Pont de l'Arche, but gained no advantage. Henry at once saw that he could not capture this strategic position until he held the opposite bank of the Seine. This was not an easy task to accomplish : on the other side was a large French force. Henry had with him pontoons and portable boats, but they could not be used until the French were removed from the opposite bank. His problem, therefore, was how to effect this : he solved it by a ruse. A party of men was sent to a spot three miles down the stream with orders to splash about in the water in the darkness. The French at once thought (as Henry meant them to think) that a crossing would be made at that place, and hurried there to contest it. Sir John Cornwall and eighty men were thereupon sent by boat to seize a small island near the opposite bank. They took with them some small cannons : these were put into position, and used to cover the crossing of the main English detachment. It was a most successful undertaking : not a man in the English army lost his life. Once on the other bank the English tried to take the bridgehead. Their efforts failed, though on one occasion they came within an ace of success, when Sir Gilbert Umfraville and sixty men trounced

16

a force of 5000 men sallying out of the town. The garrison at last knew that further resistance was hopeless, and arrangements were made to surrender the town on July 20.

The road to Rouen was now open, and Henry could place his army between that town and Paris. But in France affairs had taken a strange and unexpected turn. The papal envoys had succeeded in patching up the quarrel between Armagnacs and Burgundians, and the leaders of the rival parties had agreed to make common cause against the English attacking Rouen. Fortunately for Henry, old enmities were most lasting than papal blessings, and by the time he had reached Rouen (July 29) the two parties were again hopelessly at variance.

Rouen was the second largest town in France, and a great commercial centre. Its walls, built in the thirteenth century by Philip Augustus, extended for five miles, and were strengthened by towers and bastions. Except on the south-west side of the town, which fronted the Seine, a ditch ran in front of the walls ; and it in turn was protected by a complicated system of earthworks. The river Seine was spanned by a splendid bridge, built by the Empress Matilda, from the Pont du Porte to the suburb of St Sever ; and the southern end of the bridge was protected by a fortified post called La Barbacane. On the landward side there were five gates : Porte Cauchoise, Porte de Bouvreuil, Porte Beauvoisine, Porte St Hilaire, and Porte Martin-ville. Near the Porte de Bouvreuil stood the castle. On the south-east of the town, opposite the Porte Martinville and near the main road to Paris, was the fortified abbey of St Catherine.

A year before Henry appeared before Rouen, the town had been the scene of bitter faction fights between Armagnacs and Burgundians ; but in the face of the hostile English force the towns-

men decided to forget the past, and to co-operate
loyally in defence of their town. The organisation
of the defence was shared between Jean Segneult,
the mayor, Guy le Bouteiller, Guillaume Houdetot,
Alain Blanchard, Jean Jourdain, and Canon Robert
de Livet. Before the arrival of the English they
had razed the suburbs, thus depriving the attackers
of cover near the walls, and done their best to
protect the vital spots in the defensive *enceinte*.
Their resolve to fight to the finish was shown when
the Duke of Exeter, shortly before Henry's arrival,
appeared before the town and called for its surrender : they

> gave no answer but their guns.

On August 1, 1418, Henry ordered his captains
to take up their positions around the town. He
himself had his official headquarters in the
Carthusian Abbey of Notre Dame de la Rose : his
fighting headquarters were hard by Porte St
Hilaire. On the south of the river lay the Earl of
Huntingdon ; and he had with him that most
capable soldier Sir Gilbert Umfraville. Over
against Porte Cauchoise was the Duke of Clarence ;
and on his left, opposite Porte Bouvreuil, the
Earl Marshal. The Duke of Exeter watched Porte
Beauvoisine. On the king's left were Sir Philip
Leche, Sir Thomas Carew, and a Gascon captain,
Janico d'Artas. To the Earl of Salisbury was given
the task of reducing the Abbey of St Catherine,
strongly garrisoned by soldiers from Rouen.
Henry's first objective was the capture of this
stronghold. This was accomplished on September 1.
In the meantime his men had been busily at work
connecting by trenches the various English
divisions, and guns were placed in position ready
for the bombardment of the walls. Little food
was to be had in the locality ; and consequently

Henry made arrangements for supplies to be sent
to the army from England. The stores were
shipped to Harfleur, and then transferred to smaller
craft for passage up the Seine. Between Harfleur
and Rouen was the castle of Caudebec, strongly
held by the French ; and the convoys were therefore open to hostile attack from the garrison of
this place. Henry at once decided that Caudebec
must be taken, and the Earl of Warwick and Gilbert,
Lord Talbot were detached from the main army
to carry out this plan. It has been said that so
serious was the resistance of Caudebec that Henry
himself left Rouen to direct operations against the
garrison. Whatever happened by September 9,
the garrison had come to terms, and the danger
to the convoys was removed. With the object
of preventing the French sallying out by water
to attack the convoys, and friends from attempting
to run supplies into Rouen, Henry isolated the town
by placing a number of armed ships downstream
and a boom of chains about a gunshot above the
bridge.

His main concern was for the safety of Huntingdon's division on the south of the river. The earl
was not in communication with the other divisions
of the army : at any moment he might be attacked
by a hostile force, and cut up before help could be
sent to him. Henry soon overcame this difficulty :
he

> caused to be made a stronge bridge of tymber ouer the
> same riuer, that when neede shall require they might haue
> free passage on foote and on horse and carriage.

This was a great achievement. The bridge was
made by driving piles into the bed of the stream,
joining up the piles by chains, and then laying
planks of wood across the chains.

The garrison within Rouen made frequent
sorties ; but the English were always able to

repulse them with heavy loss; and in order to prevent the French and Normans from carrying any of his positions, Henry ordered his men to protect the trench encircling the town with a hedge of sharpened stakes. The king was indefatigable in supervising the attack. He visited the outposts, spoke cheering words to his men, and was particularly solicitous about the provisioning of his army. His enforcement of discipline was as rigid as ever; and those who were foolish enough to disobey the royal ordinances and commands were punished by death.

With the coming of autumn the plight of the garrison in Rouen became desperate. Bread was made from bran, and there was little enough of that—so little indeed that the maidens in the town were willing to sacrifice their virginity to secure a slice of it. Dogs, cats, rats, and mice supplied the townsmen with what little flesh meat they had; and vinegar and water did duty for wine. Hundreds died of starvation and disease; and none suffered worse than the non-combatants — the women and children, the aged and infirm. Many of them came out of the town to beg the English to let them depart elsewhere. Henry ordered his men to feed them, and then drove them back to their friends in the town. The townsmen, glad to be relieved of the obligation of feeding so many useless mouths, would not admit them; and for days these wretched creatures lived in trenches between the walls and the English lines. There, poor mothers gave birth to children : the men hauled up the babies over the walls so that they might be christened in the town's churches, and then returned them to their mothers. When Christmas came Henry's heart softened. He sent his heralds to tell the captains of the garrison that he would give sufficient food for the festival to all who cared to come out for it. They spurned his offer, and merely agreed to one day's truce so that the religious ceremonies of Christmas might be properly celebrated.

That was the act of desperate men, believing maybe that at the eleventh hour succour would come to them. The Rouen garrison knew that a mighty relief force had been mustered by the queen and the Duke of Burgundy to come to their rescue. They knew that in the middle of November poor Charles VI., momentarily sane, had taken the *oriflamme* from St Denis—the symbol of the invincibility of French arms. They had greeted this news with a mad ringing of the town's bells and services of thanksgiving. When Henry learnt the meaning of the commotion he called his captains to him and said :

Fellows, be merry !

At last he was going to meet the French in pitched battle : he was confident that he would repeat the crushing victory of Agincourt. He quietly posted his troops to meet the threatened attack. But the attack never came : the French relief force never marched farther than Pontoise, where, paralysed by lack of money and the jealous differences of the leaders, it melted away.

At the end of 1418 the garrison of Rouen decided to make a last bid for victory. Two thousand men flung themselves out of Porte St Hilaire against Henry's headquarters : another force dashed out of the castle gate. Both sorties failed lamentably ; and the failure completed the discomfort of the garrison. In the darkness of night on New Year's Eve the end came. At La Barbacane the English heard a commotion. Sir Gilbert Umfraville went forward to see what it was all about, and found that a party of townsmen had come out to ask for a parley. He rushed to his commander, Clarence, with the news ; and then sped round the divisions to tell the other commanders. In the morning he saw Henry himself. The king was willing to receive a deputation from the townsmen, and ordered Sir Gilbert to acquaint them of his decision. On January 2, therefore, four knights, four clerks, and four burgesses, dressed in black, were escorted by Sir Gilbert to Henry's pavilion. Sir Gilbert warned them to use their words carefully : he knew the royal temper, and was anxious that negotiations should not break down. When the deputation came to the royal pavilion they found that Henry was hearing Mass : it was some time before they were admitted into his presence.

He met them with a haughty scowl, and kept them kneeling before him for some time before he gave them permission to speak. They asked the king to have pity on the wretched people who lay dying in the ditches between the walls and his lines. The request called forth a spirited retort :

> Fellows, who put them there ? They abode in the city while they might.

Then he upbraided them for keeping him from his town of Rouen—his own ' heritage.' They mildly replied that they had held the place at the orders of the French king and the Duke of Burgundy, and that many of them were willing to swear allegiance to him (Henry) if the king and the duke would allow them to do so. This reply infuriated Henry : it was a gentle reminder that they did not readily accept his position as Duke of Normandy. And when a member of the deputation suggested that Rouen was a town worth winning he burst out :

> It is mine, and I will have it. Let those within prepare themselves, for men shall speak of me until the day of doom.

It was Clarence who calmed him. Then Henry
dismissed the envoys with the announcement that
Rouen must be surrendered unconditionally and
without delay.

At first the townsmen were inclined to refuse
the English king's terms. They thought of firing
the town, and then breaking out under cover of
darkness. But wiser counsels prevailed ; and on
the following day formal negotiations were opened
between the garrison and the besiegers. For days
both sides argued. The French would concede
little ; the English asked for much. Finally
negotiations broke down. When the envoys went
back to the town they were met by a mob at Porte
St Hilaire : they were told unless they made terms
with the English they (the mob) would open the
gates to the besiegers. So negotiations were again
opened, and on January 13, 1419, a settlement was
reached. Rouen was to be surrendered to Henry
if not relieved by the French by midday on the 19th ;
the townsmen were to pay a money indemnity of
300,000 crowns ; and the garrison was to be held
as prisoners. The envoys were plainly told that
Henry would allow the town to retain its ancient
privileges ; and all who swore allegiance to him
could retain their property.

At midday on January 19, the gates were thrown
open, and the Duke of Exeter, newly created
captain of the town, led the advance guard of the
English army through the streets which were still
littered with corpses. The banners of St George,
Our Lady, and the Trinity were hoisted on the
principal vantage-points ; and guards were posted
to check looting by the soldiery. Early on the next
morning Henry entered through Porte Beauvoisine. He rode a great black horse, and was led
by the principal clergy of the town to the cathedral.
As he entered the building the choir sang the

antiphon : ' Who is so great a lord ? ' Before the
high altar he offered thanks for his capture of the
town, and then heard Mass.

It is impossible accurately to state the English
losses during the siege of Rouen. They were
certainly not high—indeed when compared with
those which the French suffered they were almost
negligible. But Henry had lost some captains of
sterling worth and tried experience. Among the
dead were Gilbert, Lord Talbot, John Blount,
Richard, Lord Grey of Codnor, and Thomas Butler,
the Prior of Kilmainham. With his customary
concern for the spiritual welfare of his men he made
arrangements for Masses to be said for the repose
of the dead men's souls.

For two months Henry remained in Rouen.
Immediately after the conclusion of the siege he
proceeded to deal with the pacification of the town.
Nine persons had been excluded from his general
pardon : among them were Jean Segneult, Alain
Blanchard, Robert de Livet, Guillaume Houdetot,
and ' that person who spoke the foul words.'
Segneult and Houdetot won their freedom on payment of heavy fines : Robert de Livet was sent
to languish in an English prison ; Alain Blanchard
was summarily executed. Guy le Bouteiller, another leader of the defence, made his submission
and entered Henry's service ; he appears to have
been the first Norman gentleman of consequence to
have done so. Every opportunity was given to
the townsmen to make their peace with the English
king, and there is ample evidence to prove that a
very large number quickly seized the chance of saving
their lives and property. Those who refused lost
their possessions, and were exiled.

Nor did Henry forget the obligations of government. His captains were scattered throughout the
duchy to put down the lawless brigand bands which

preyed upon the countryside ; and he introduced
a uniform standard of weights and measures—a
much needed reform. He saw that the damage
done during the attack on Rouen was made good ;
and he was naturally alive to the importance of
safeguarding his military positions.   Only two
important strongholds held out against him—the
famous Château Gaillard and Mont-St-Michel.
But both were well masked by his troops ; and
there was little likelihood that the garrisons could
do serious damage to his reputation.[16] At last he
was Duke of Normandy by right and by might ;
and whilst he was always ready to ascribe to God
the credit for that achievement, he was human
enough to appreciate the pride which he personally
felt as a result of his martial successes.

CHAPTER EIGHT

' HEIR OF FRANCE '

HARDLY for a moment did the rival parties in France cease their diplomatic intrigues. Envoys came and went between the camp of the English king and the ' courts ' of the dauphin and Burgundy. Henry listened patiently to all that they had to say, without committing himself to either side ; and while smooth-tongued diplomats and learned clerks talked and argued about formalities he quietly continued to consolidate his conquests. He had stated his demands in language which left no doubt as to its meaning : it remained now for the Burgundians and Dauphinists (for such was the name by which that party went after the death of the Count of Armagnac) to show a readiness to accept those demands. Did they not represent the justice of Heaven ? How, then, could the French refuse to regard them as reasonable and just without incurring the charge of impiety ? Nevertheless Henry himself would welcome peace— though he was ever careful not to let his enemies know this. The conquest of Normandy had been costly in men and money ; and the refusal of the Norman gentry to recognise him as their lawful duke might result in a weakening of the allegiance of the poorer sort of people in the duchy. Henry was above all things a realist : he did not have to be told that the submission of these poorer people was chiefly brought about by fear of the English power and not by love for the justice of Henry's cause ;

and he did not want to face the formidable task of dealing with a revolted province.

About seven weeks after the siege of Rouen opened, the master of the dauphin's household came to the Duke of Clarence with the information that his prince was ready to discuss terms with Henry. An English embassy, under the leadership of Archbishop Chichele, was thereupon appointed to meet the representatives of ' the so-called regent of France ' at Alençon. The instructions which they received from Henry were clear and to the point. They were to make it clear to the Dauphinist that their king recognised the Duke of Burgundy as the strongest power in France ; but he was not as strong as the English, and if necessary Henry would crush his power in a day. This was to be a subtle hint to the Dauphinists that without English help they could never hope to overcome their hated Burgundian rivals. The envoys were to ask for the hand of the Princess Catherine and to find out the value of her dowry ; but Normandy was to be excluded from all discussions relating to Henry's territorial rights. Henry held Normandy by right and by conquest : he meant to keep it, but at the same time he meant to have his rights in Aquitaine and elsewhere.

The Dauphinists were not prepared to concede these demands. As usual, the conference developed into talk and argument. The English envoys pressed the French to put their case in writing. They had come to suspect—and rightly too—that the oral promises of the French king would ultimately be twisted to the disadvantage of Henry ; and as long as such an atmosphere of suspicion and mistrust prevailed it was impossible to come to a satisfactory agreement. So the conference at Alençon was added to the list of abortive conferences ; and for the breakdown of the negotiations

the Dauphinists could only blame themselves.
They had made fair promises, but would not commit
them to writing : obviously they never meant to
keep them.

On the selfsame day as Henry gave his instructions to the embassy appointed to treat with the
dauphin he wrote to the Duke of Burgundy to tell
him that he would be willing to listen to any just
and reasonable offers which he might care to make ;
and in due course both sides appointed embassies
to meet at Pont de l'Arche to treat for peace.   The
English representatives were the same as those
who had failed to come to terms with the Dauphinists
at Alençon ; and the case which they presented
was similar to that placed before the dauphin's
envoys.   When the conference at Pont de l'Arche
opened much time was wasted in discussing whether
Latin or French should be the language of the
deliberations ; and as usual the French envoys
could not be persuaded to make a clear statement
of their offers.   They played for time with the
request that they must return to the French court
for further instructions.

When the dauphin learnt that his hated rival
meant to treat with the English he requested Henry
to reopen negotiations.   On January 21, 1419—two
days after the fall of Rouen—English and Dauphinist
envoys met at Louviers, and decided that Henry
and the dauphin should meet on Mid-Lent Sunday
(March 26) at a spot half-way between Evreux and
Dreux.   But the dauphin did not appear, and the
opinion of the English at this insult is clearly seen
in a letter which a certain soldier, signing himself
T.F., sent to friends in England at that time.

> The forsaide Rewle Regent hathe broke the seuretee
> abovesaide, and made the Kynge a *beau nient* (fine fool) :
> so that ther may none hope he hadde as yette of pees. . . .
> Cirtes alle the ambassadors, that we dele wyth, ben

yncongrue, that is to say, in olde maner of speche in Englonde, ' they ben double and fals : ' whyth whiche maner of
men I prey God lete never no trewe mon be coupled with.

The Duke of Burgundy, however, saw that it
was imperative that some sort of a peace must be
patched up with the English. As virtually regent
of France for the mad Charles VI., the duty of
defending the State against its enemies devolved
upon him ; and as a result he found himself in a
quandary. If he allowed the English to advance
unchecked through the realm of France he would
be accused of lack of patriotism and possibly of
being in English pay : if he fought the all-conquering
king of England he would dissipate his own military
strength and thereby become an easy prey for his
Dauphinist enemies. Far better would it be to
come to an arrangement with Henry : the English
king had long desired to ally himself by marriage
with the House of Valois, and the issue of that
marriage might one day bring the kingdoms of
England and France under the rule of one man.
He must not be blamed for taking this view : he
lived in an age which saw nothing unnatural in
such an arrangement. Peace with the king of
England would enable him—possibly with English
help—to turn to destroy the Dauphinists. This
possibility was sufficient in itself to persuade him
that the negotiations, broken off at Pont de l'Arche,
must be continued ; and in the spring of 1419
envoys from both the English and Burgundian sides
were arranging for a continuance of the peace talks.

By the end of March, therefore, an arrangement
was reached at Mantes. The Burgundians, speaking
on behalf of the French king, consented to a marriage
alliance and recognised Henry's territorial demands.
Nothing was said about the conditions by which
these French lands were to be held of the king of
France ; but it was understood by both sides that

as a *quid pro quo* for the concessions which the
French had made Henry would considerably modify
his claim to the throne of France. A further step
was taken early in April at Vernon when it was
arranged that Henry should meet the king and
queen of France, the Princess Catherine, and the
Duke of Burgundy at some place to be decided
upon between the towns of Mantes and Pontoise
on May 15, 1419.

The date of this meeting was changed to May 30,
owing to the illness of the French king. The place
chosen was Le Pré du Chat, a meadow near Meulan,
on the banks of the Seine, about half-way between
Mantes and Pontoise. Great preparations were
made for the interview. The conference ground
was enclosed within a wooden palisade ; and the
approach from the side of the river was barred by
stakes firmly fixed into the bed of the stream.
Each king could bring as escort 1500 armed men ;
and minute arrangements were made to prevent a
clash between the French and English soldiers.
The French were to remain on the Meulan side of
the enclosure : the English on the side opposite
them. There were to be no games of skill, and
the slightest evidence of disorderly conduct was to
be sharply and quickly punished. At the centre
of the conference ground was set up a pavilion,
most gorgeously decorated and adorned with the
arms of the two kingdoms ; and on either side were
two tents, in which the two monarchs and their
advisers could confer in private.

On the day of the meeting the place presented
a splendid spectacle of colour.

> . . . . The Englishmen fixed there tents and pauillions
> maruelouslie imbordered wth signes and semblances of
> Lillies and of Roses, and of other signes of all goulde ;
> and on th'other side of the place the Frenchmen raysed
> there tents, so that the apparaunce of the tents was in
> sight to bee compared to a righte fayre cittie.

About three o'clock in the afternoon the heralds announced that the proceedings were about to begin. At a given signal Henry and Isabella (Charles VI. could not appear owing to an attack of insanity) left their respective tents and advanced to meet each other. Each was accompanied by sixty lords and knights and sixteen counsellors. The Duke of Burgundy walked immediately behind the French queen. Henry saluted Isabella with a kiss on the hand, and the Duke of Burgundy bowed the knee to the English king. Henry thereupon led Isabella into the conference pavilion, and attended her while she took her seat on the throne set up for her : that done, he went to his throne, which was twelve feet away from that of the French queen. The Earl of Warwick was the master of the ceremonies. He told the assembly in French why the meeting had been arranged ; and then the company adjourned for the splendid feast which had been prepared for them. With that the day's proceedings ended ; and Isabella returned to Pontoise, and Henry to Mantes.

The next meeting took place on June 1. On that occasion the Princess Catherine accompanied her mother and the Duke of Burgundy to Le Pré du Chat to meet the man who was so determined to marry her. Every care had been taken to ensure that the princess created a good impression : her gowns had cost the French court 3000 florins. Every one, however, was agreed that Catherine looked charming—a truly desirable bride for the all-conquering king of England. When Henry kissed her it was noted that she showed 'some shamefastnes' or true virginal modesty ; and the English liked her all the better for that. Catherine herself could not know that she had completely conquered the heart of the conqueror of her father's realm : Henry had at last met the woman of his dreams, and was resolved that nothing should now thwart his desire to make her his queen.

The meetings of the monarchs were continued at regular intervals during the month of June. The splendid pageantry which attended the comings and goings of the principals shrouded the difficulties which the diplomats were experiencing in the council chamber. Henry claimed in full sovereignty Normandy and the lands specified in the Treaty of Brétigni. The French were still disposed to reject these claims ; and countered them with a demand that Henry should renounce his over-lordship rights to Anjou, Maine, Touraine, Brittany, and Flanders. This the English refused : they held that his overlordship of these lands was reasonable and just. On the other hand, he was prepared to renounce his claim to the French throne, and to agree not to make peace with the enemies of the king of France provided that the French would give a similar undertaking not to treat with the enemies of England. Once again the value of the princess's dowry was a bone of contention : the French showed little inclination to pay the 800,000 crowns which they had hitherto promised, and advanced counter-claims.

It was not long before Henry realised that another abortive conference was taking place. Moreover, he knew the reason : the Duke of Burgundy was in correspondence with the dauphin ; and there was a likelihood that some sort of a reconciliation would be effected between them. Henry had a private interview with the duke and told him that he was wearied by the perpetual delays : the French must give an answer one way or another to his demands. It was during that interview that high words passed between the two men. Henry hotly told the duke :

> We will hustle the king out of his kingdom and you with him !

17

The duke retorted no less impudently :

> Sire, you will be pretty tired ere you fling us out.　Be
> very sure of that !

These disagreements created suspicions, and when
Henry came to the conference ground on June 13,
his escort were put in battle order as though he
feared treachery from the Frenchmen.　But nothing
happened, and three days later he entertained to
a sumptuous feast the men of both armies.　Peace
was as far away as ever ; and when Henry and his
ministers arrived at the conference ground on
July 3, they soon found that the French did not
intend to put in a further appearance.　The conference of Meulan had broken down completely,
and there was nothing for it but for the struggle
to be continued.

A certain Madame de Giac, who had been one
of Burgundy's mistresses, was responsible for
bringing the duke and dauphin together.　They
had a personal interview at Pouilly early in July,
and on the 11th of the month solemnly swore to
forget the enmities of the past and to co-operate
in the protection of France against her English
enemies.　A week later the reconciliation was
approved by royal edict : the Parisians went mad
with delight at the prospect of domestic peace and
the expulsion of Henry and the English ' midges.'

But duke and dauphin had reckoned without
Henry.　He was well aware of the former's double
dealings, and while he had no intention of severing
diplomatic connections with him he was resolved
to give him a further taste of the English power.
On July 30, therefore, Gaston de Foix and the Earl
of Huntingdon, with a force of 3000 men, were
sent to seize Pontoise.　This place was defended
by the Seigneur of L'isle Adam with 1000 men-at-
arms and 2000 crossbowmen, and was an important

Burgundian stronghold. So well did Henry lay his plans, and so skilfully were they carried out, particularly by the Gascon Gaston de Foix, that on the following morning the place was in English hands. To Henry this was his most important capture in the whole of France : the road to Paris was open ; and in the capital the news of the English success struck dread into the hearts of the citizens.

Burgundian and Dauphinist were irreconcilable. Old wounds were not to be healed by solemn pledges ; and old memories could not be forgotten. On the capture of Pontoise it was whispered by the Dauphinists that the place had been treacherously sold to the English by the Burgundian garrison. It was a baseless charge ; but the success of English arms undoubtedly caused Burgundy himself furiously to think of the wisdom of his recent action. With the French court he had fled from St Denis to Lagny—so hastily, that the party went without dinner ; and he eventually removed to Troyes. His discomfort was increased when news came that the Duke of Clarence had made an armed reconnaisance of Paris. Influences were at work to make the reconciliation between Burgundy and the dauphin a reality ; and in August arrangements were made for the two leaders to have a further interview at Montereau, a small town standing at the junction of the Seine and Yonne. Burgundy, warned that the Dauphinists meant to do away with him, was hesitant about the meeting : in fact he actually did not appear on the day named. The dauphin protested that his fears were groundless : Burgundy was therefore persuaded to meet him on September 10, in the middle of the bridge at Montereau.

Precisely what happened at that fateful meeting is not known. The duke and dauphin took with them to the enclosure in the centre of the bridge ten followers ; and the gates were fast closed behind them. It was said that in kneeling before the dauphin Burgundy's sword became entangled in his legs : he tried to disentangle it, when Robert de Lairé, one of the dauphin's attendants, cried out :

Would you touch your sword in my lord's presence ?

Thereupon Tanneguy du Chastel dealt the duke a terrible blow with his axe ; and pandemonium ensued. The dauphin was lifted out of the enclosure by the faithful Tanneguy du Chastel ; and in a few moments the Burgundians were either killed or taken prisoners.

This account makes the Dauphinists the culprits : they themselves sought to show that the deed had been provoked by the Burgundians. One point seems clear : it was not a premeditated crime. It also seems equally clear that the real blame rested with the dauphin's party, who acted without thought of the terrible consequences of their senseless act. For Duke John of Burgundy was to be infinitely a more relentless enemy dead than alive : his murder was a memory which true Burgundians could never forget, and in their search for revenge they were willing to become the active allies of the English forces. Sixteen years were to pass before the crime at Montereau was forgiven, and it was during those sixteen years that France touched the nadir of her misfortunes. And when Burgundian and Dauphinist sunk their hatreds and behaved as Frenchmen the cause of England in France was doomed to failure.

Shortly after the duke's murder, Queen Isabella wrote to Henry asking him personally to avenge Burgundy's murder and to continue the negotiations broken off at Meulan ; and she did not have long to wait for the active support of the new Duke of Burgundy, Philip le Bon. All the Burgundian leaders urged him to come to terms with Henry : the governors of Paris were of a similar opinion. Envoys passed to and fro between Henry in Mantes and Philip le Bon in Arras ; and on Christmas Eve an alliance between the two parties was formally concluded. It was agreed that Henry should marry the Princess Catherine, and that one of his brothers should be betrothed to one of the duke's sisters. More important was the Burgundian recognition of Henry's demand to be regent of France during the lifetime of Charles VI., and his successor on the French throne on his death. With the Burgundians the main consideration was the promise of English help against the Dauphinists ; and the Duke Philip pledged himself to persuade Charles VI. to accept the Arras terms as the basis of peace between England and France.

These negotiations did not put a stop to Henry's military schemes. They were prosecuted without interruption, for the more Henry held in his hand the better would be his position when the time came to dictate terms of peace. The fall of Gisors and Château Gaillard in September immeasurably strengthened his position in Normandy ; and the capture of Meulan gave him another fortified out-post in the valley of the Seine. Poissy, St Germain, and Montjoie were taken by Humphrey of Gloucester in November ; and Henry himself gave careful consideration to problems connected with the administration of the duchy of Normandy.

Nevertheless, rosy though the English prospects were in 1420, the dauphin still received the support of the larger part of the kingdom. Nearly all the southern half of France stood by him. The Count de Foix, brother of Gaston who had so bravely taken Pontoise, caused considerable inconvenience to the English in Languedoc ; and the Dauphinists had received promises of help from Castile and Scotland. Early in January 1420, a Castilian fleet inflicted a severe defeat on an English fleet outside Harfleur : a large number of ships were sent to the bottom and 700 men were slain or drowned. But the dauphin could not drive home these advantages ; and from the English point of view they were soon to be negatived by the formal treaty of peace which was signed and sealed at Troyes.

The early part of 1420 was spent in drafting the treaty. It was a business which required great care and accuracy : Henry was determined that there should be no loopholes of which the French might take advantage. He had dealt with the diplomats of the French court long enough to know that they were past masters in evading treaty obligations. This time the position was to be accurately defined so as to preclude such an eventuality.

Thus the envoys to whom Henry entrusted the task of making the preliminaries of the peace were men of tried experience—the Earl of Warwick, the Earl Marshall, John, Lord Roos, Sir Gilbert Umfraville, and Sir Lewis Robsart. Before the end of March they were in Troyes near the court of the French king ; and on April 9, the hapless Charles— his mind so enfeebled that it is very doubtful whether he knew what all the fuss and bother were about—placed his seal to the preliminary treaty.

By the terms of this treaty of Troyes, Henry V. achieved his life's ambition. It gave him everything for which he had asked and fought for : it represented not so much the triumph of his arms as the divine recognition of the justice of his cause. The French gave him the hand of the Princess Catherine, to whom he promised to make an allow ance befitting to her queenly station. He was ready to allow Charles and Isabella to retain their titles of king and queen of France during their lifetime ; but he was to be ' heir of France,' and in that capacity was to become the regent of the realm while Charles lived, and king on his death. He promised to rule the kingdom ' with the counsel of the nobles and wise men of the said realm,' and to allow his French subjects to retain their national institutions and laws. Henry was too wise a ruler to contemplate a political union of the two realms : his arrangement was nothing more than a union of two ruling houses, and had he been granted a longer life he might have been able to show the mediæval world that his idea was practical and possible of achievement. Finally, the contracting parties agreed to make war against ' Charles bearing himself for the dauphin of Vienne.'

On May 8, Henry began his triumphal progress to Troyes. As he passed by St Denis he made a pious visit to the famous abbey ; and then marched his men in full fighting order under the walls of the French capital. The Parisians gave him a great welcome. Their representatives had already visited him, and had returned with tales that he was a wondrously just prince. His route then lay through Charenton, Brie, Provins, and Nogent ; and as he drew nigh to Troyes there came to meet him the Duke Philip and a great cavalcade of people. On all sides were shouts of approbation as Henry and the duke rode into the town. Even in the hour of victory Henry could remember a detail concerned with the welfare of his men—a detail perhaps which they themselves found distressingly inconvenient !

> Because the wines of the countrie (Champagne) were so famous and strong . . . this prudent prince, desyringe the health and wellfare of his people, caused to be pro-

claymed throughout his hoast, that no man shoulde pre-
sume vppon paine of his displeasure, as to be punished at
his will, to drinke any wines wthout puttinge to water.

Soon after his arrival in Troyes, Henry called
upon his prospective father-in-law.   They had
placed poor Charles on a throne at one end of the
great hall of the hostel in which he was lodged,
and when Henry appeared at the door he made no
sign that he wished him to approach the royal
presence.   Knowing something of the shortness of
Henry's temper and the exalted view which he
took of his majesty, those in the hall were on
tenterhooks lest Charles' seeming lack of courtesy
should result in disaster ; but Henry appeared not
to notice the affront—or more likely knew the real
reason for it ; and when he bent the knee before
his future father-in-law he whispered some words
of encouragement to him.   At once Charles recognised him, and said he was glad to see him.   Henry
passed on to pay his duty to Isabella ; and when
he came to the Princess Catherine he warmly kissed
her.   Observers in the hall at Troyes were delighted
to be able to record that the kiss gave Henry ' great
joy.'

On the following day, after the articles of the
treaty were formally examined by representatives
of both nations, the party went in great state to
the cathedral Church of St Peter.   The ' accustomed disease ' made it impossible for Charles to
attend, but Isabella was there to act on his behalf ;
and with Henry, the Duke of Burgundy, and the
chief men of England and France she swore solemnly
to observe the treaty which bereft her husband's
house of its sovereignty and the greater part of his
kingdom.   Before the ceremony was ended, Henry
pledged his troth to the Princess Catherine before
the high altar in the church.

No sooner was the ' great peace ' made than

messengers—English and French—hastened out of
Troyes with copies of the treaty. In the French
towns which recognised the Burgundian government of the French king it was duly proclaimed
and sworn to ; and on May 30 the authorities in
Paris made their obedience. Some time passed
before England was aware of the exact conditions
of the peace : the treaty was not proclaimed in
London until June 14. But when it had been
read to the assembled multitudes around Paul's
Cross, the city went wild with excitement : the
Londoners then as now were not sparing in their
enthusiasms, and in 1420, as in 1934, they were
loyally attached to the reigning house.

Twelve days before London heard the terms of
the ' great peace,' Henry had married Catherine in
the Church of St John in Troyes. It was Trinity
Sunday—a day of happy omen for a king who
always carried in his host a banner emblazoned
with the symbol of the Blessed Trinity ; and the
people of Troyes and the visitors were treated to
a splendid spectacle. The princess and her mother
rode to the church in a carriage drawn ' by eight
snow-white English hobbies, the gift of the bridegroom ' ; and Henry himself, and his attendants,
wore the richest raiment. The marriage ceremony
was performed ' after the French custom ' by
Henri de Savoisy, Archbishop of Sens, attended by
a great number of dignitaries and priests. There
was the customary ' breakfast ' ; and in the evening
came the blessing of the marriage bed and the
' bedding ' of the couple.

Not even love—for there is no doubt that Henry
was deeply in love with his young wife—could
make Henry forget his duty to the State. He had
pledged himself to war against his brother-in-law,
the *ci-dévant* dauphin ; and on the day following
the wedding he announced his intention to put

that promise into effect by marching against
one of the more important of the Dauphinist
strongholds in the district, Sens. On June 4,
therefore, with Charles VI. and the Duke of
Burgundy, and accompanied by his wife and her
mother, he led his army out of Troyes. The
invalid king and the ladies were lodged at
Villeneuve-le-roi : Henry and Philip of Burgundy
went on to Sens.

When they had wrested Sens from the Dauphinists without much difficulty, Henry and Duke
Philip pushed on to Montereau, which was strongly
held by Guillaume de Chaumont, Seigneur of
Guitry. A surprise assault put them in possession
of the town on June 24 ; but the garrison in the
castle were determined to fight to a finish. Was it
the memory of the murder of Duke John—a memory
freshened by the solemn removal of his corpse from
the parish church in Montereau for burial in the
Burgundy country—which caused Henry to per-
petrate an act of cruelty so foreign to his nature
and perplexing to his friends in a later age ? He
ordered eleven men of the garrison, whom he had
captured, on pain of death to persuade their
comrades to hand over the castle ; and when they
failed in their mission he kept his promise and
hung them on a common gibbet in sight of the
castle. Contemporaries certainly thought nothing
of the incident. Had he not shown his fine sense
of justice by hanging with the men of Montereau
a groom from his retinue for killing a knight ?
And ought not the blame to be shifted to the
shoulders of the Seigneur of Guitry who knew that
resistance to ' the heir of France ' was as treasonable
as it was hopeless ? So hopeless, indeed, that on
July 1 he decided to surrender the castle to
Henry.

At Melun, however, the victorious advance of

Henry and Duke Philip received a check. It was one of the chief of the Dauphinist strongholds in the Seine country ; and it served as a useful base for attacks on Paris. Henry and Duke Philip believed that they would soon have the place in their hands ; but the magnificent resistance of Arnaud Guillaume, Seigneur of Barbazan, and his garrison of six to seven hundred men, put their calculations completely out ; and the siege lasted from July 13 to November 17.

The siege of Melun is an important landmark in the military career of Henry V. There again, as at Harfleur and Rouen, he showed that patience in attack which exasperated his enemies and saved his men from disaster. He showed, too, that attention to detail which contributed more than anything else to the success of his movements. Nothing was to be left to chance. To keep communications with every division of the besieging force, a bridge was built over the Seine : all kinds of ordnance, firing from well-screened emplacements, were used to batter down the walls : his position was protected by trenches : his men were properly housed and provisioned. His most difficult task was that of keeping good relations between his men and the Burgundian soldiery ; for though allies in name they had little love for each other in fact. Even the Burgundian leaders and their allies seem to have questioned the wisdom of his strategy—more particularly Lewis, the Count Palatine of the Rhine, who chafed at the enforced inactivity of a siege and wanted to make an assault on the town. Eventually Henry let them have their way : he knew that experience must be bought dearly by rash men. They assaulted and were driven helter-skelter back to their lines with great loss. His own captains had no sympathy with the Burgundians : they said so openly

in Henry's presence. But he gently checked
them :

> Supposing their intention had not been accomplished,
> nevertheless the affair had been valiantly done and under-
> taken ; and in matters of war mistakes might be as valu-
> able as successes.

There was no further talk of assaults in the Burgundian division : they were prepared to leave the
conduct of the siege in the capable hands of the
English king.

Henry certainly found the taking of Melun a
tough proposition. His miners drove their mines
underground with their accustomed skill ; but the
garrison countermined so successfully that they
checked the attackers' subterranean progress ; and
terrible fights took place in the underground
galleries. A French chronicler, whose brother was
actually a member of the garrison, tells how on
one occasion Henry and the Seigneur of Barbazan
met and fought it out below the surface. With
his love for a good fighter Henry asked his opponent's
name :

> I am Barbazan.

The Gascon was taken aback when Henry said :

> And you have fought with the king of England.

They called their duel a draw, and retired, each
admiring the other's skill in the use of arms.

Of stout stuff Barbazan and his men were made.
When Henry brought Charles VI. to his camp and
persuaded him to call upon the garrison to surrender,
they contemptuously told him that while they
would render him the obedience which they owed
him as their king, they would never bow the knee
to an English prince. Henry was most anxious to
bring matters to a speedy end. He knew that in
the neighbourhood the dauphin Charles had a

relieving force ; he saw sickness laying low his men ; and one by one Burgundian captains drew off to their own estates. But in Melun he had an ally who would not desert him—famine ; and when Barbazan and his men had come to the end of their resources they asked for terms. And in the end they had to accept the only terms which Henry would offer them—an unconditional surrender.

On November 17, therefore, Barbazan led his men out and placed them at the king's mercy. Although it was known that all who had taken part in the affray on the bridge at Montereau were to be executed, Henry gave Barbazan, who had been present when Duke John was murdered, his life. He could not find it in his power to execute one who had fought so valiantly with him in personal combat. At the same time he could be relentlessly cruel to the twenty Scots who were serving in the Melun garrison, and they were summarily put to death. No doubt he argued that they were traitors taken in arms against their lawful king, for James I. of Scotland was with Henry during the siege ; and he was not concerned to reflect that his cousin of Scotland had no other alternative, being for many years a prisoner in English hands.

Winter was at hand, and Henry felt that time had come for him to pay a visit to Paris. There was a further reason for his presence in the French capital : he had learnt that the Burgundian captains and their companies, holding the strategic points in the city, were none too certain in their loyalty ; and even during the siege of Melun he had taken the precaution to supersede them by English captains, and to replace the count of St Pol by his own brother Clarence as the captain of the town. On December 1, riding on the left of his father-in-law, Charles VI., Henry made his triumphal entry into Paris. Behind rode, on the left of the

street, the Duke of Burgundy, and on his right
the Dukes of Bedford and Clarence ; and then on
his flanks followed a cavalcade of English and
French barons and knights. The two kings and
their entourage received a typical Parisian welcome :
the populace shouted themselves hoarse—*Noel!
Noel!* ; and the principal citizens—the clergy, masters
of the great university, and rich merchants—escorted
the kings through the streets. Choristers and clergy
chanted a solemn *Te Deum* and *Benedictus qui venit*
as the two kings drew near to the mother church
of Paris—Notre Dame ; and together they prayed
at the high altar. At nightfall they separated :
Charles took up his residence in the Hôtel St Pol,
Henry and his brothers in the Louvre, and Duke
Philip in the Hôtel d'Artois.

On the following day all Paris was again *en fête* :
it was known that the two queens—Isabella and
Catherine—were to make their entry into the city.
From the Porte St Antoine they were escorted
through the streets by a magnificent cavalcade
headed by the dukes Philip, Clarence, and Bedford ;
and the reception which they received was not less
enthusiastic than that given to their husbands.
The authorities had made the fountains to flow with
wine and rose water : on all sides there was merry-
making and rejoicings.

The enthusiasm of the Parisians is understandable : for years their city had been the pawn in
the game of the factious rivalries of Armagnac and
Burgundy, and not once but many times the streets
had run deep with blood of murdered men and
women. Under such conditions industry and commerce could not hope to prosper, and the poor
suffered as a result of the depressed state of
the economic life of the city. Patriotism is not
infrequently a secondary loyalty with men of business—unless by chance it coincides with their own

enrichment ; and all that the merchants of Paris
wanted was peace to pursue their industrial and
commercial aspirations. They believed that the
coming of Henry of England would bring them that
peace : they were prepared to forget that he was
both a conqueror and an alien.

On December 6 Charles and Henry attended the
opening of the States General. It was the duty of
the chancellor, Jean le Clerc, to outline the royal
intentions ; and this he did in the customary
sermon, at the same time formally asking the Three
Estates for their advice and counsel. The Treaty
of Troyes was next read, after which Charles rose
in his place and told the members that he was
pledged to abide by it ; he was certain that it was
for the good of the realm, and consequently he
enjoined them loyally to accept it. After the
Three Estates had deliberated, they came together
again to tell Charles and Henry that they heartily
endorsed the treaty ; and they urged that all who
refused to accept it should be pronounced traitors.·
It was only natural that on the matter of taxation
they should express the hope that it would be
lightened and equally distributed : they were
complacently prepared to agree to any measures
which their king devised for the peace and safety
of the realm.

Henry lost no time in dealing with the problem
of reorganising the government of his father-in-
law's kingdom. Orders were given for a recoinage
—a much-needed reform in a country where the
coinage had been consistently debased ; and the cost
was to be shared by all sections of the community
—the very poor only being accorded exemption.
Henry would not grant even the University of Paris
exemption from this impost : in fact he read them
a sharp lecture on their public duty when they
dared to plead with him for favoured treatment.

Steps were promptly taken for the protection of the realm against Dauphinist attacks ; and a beginning was made on the more difficult business of an equitable assessment of taxation. Two days before Christmas Charles VI. held a *lit du justice* at which the dauphin and his party were charged with the wilful murder of Duke John of Burgundy. They were naturally not present to answer the charge ; but in their absence they were duly found guilty, and sentenced to perform penances and build churches in which prayers were to be offered for the repose of the murdered man's soul. Thereupon the *parlement of Paris*, the supreme court of justice in France, registered the verdict ; and at the same time endorsed the decision of Charles VI. that his son was no longer capable of inheriting the crown of France.

Christmas was celebrated by Henry and his English subjects in great style and ceremony. His court at the Louvre quickly became famous not only for the magnificence of the hospitality which was dispensed there, but also for the rich splendour of the costumes of the English lords and their ladies. The Parisians were quick to notice that their own king lived in more humble style in the Hôtel St Pol—a pathetic shadow of the monarchy which he represented ; and attended by none of the great men of his kingdom. The splendour of the English court might arouse their keennest interest ; but it also served to emphasise the unpleasant fact that Henry was a conqueror in their midst ; and to many of the nobly born this thought ate like a canker into the recently-expressed loyalty to 'the heir of France.' Moreover, on all sides they saw Englishmen in control of departments of government ; and the marching feet of English soldiery through the Paris streets drummed into their heads the knowledge of their servitude to the English king. Evidence on the

subject appears to be scanty, but it is now believed
that Henry met with irritating signs of disapproval
of his rule soon after his arrival in Paris, and nothing
remained for him but to proceed further with the
policy of anglicisation and to treat the people to
more frequent displays of his military power.

But there was other work to do.   Henry felt
that it was imperative for him to pay another visit
to Normandy ; and in response to petitions from
his native land he had decided to return for a little
time to England.   He had been away for three and
a half years—and much had happened in that period.
It was only natural that his English subjects should
want to see their king again—their king who had
humbled the proud kingdom of France, and by the
force of his arms and the wisdom of his statecraft,
had compelled the Frenchmen to accept him as
the heir to the throne of the Valois dynasty.   For
Henry's part he welcomed the prospect of a return
home ; he could show his English subjects the queen
whom he had chosen out of love ; and doubtless he
felt himself in need of a rest.

Henry took his leave of Paris at the end of
December 1420, but before he left he appointed his
brother Clarence to act as his deputy and the Duke
of Exeter to guard the person of Charles VI.   With
his customary meticulous care for detail he saw to
it that they had their orders, and were given an
adequate force to maintain the English position ;
and he made a final disposition of captains and
troops in that part of France which acknowledged
his sway.   He did not know as he rode out from
Paris that he was never again to see his brother
Clarence alive : he cannot have been unmoved at the
childishly pathetic farewell which Charles took of
his daughter.   Actually Catherine left Paris some
days before Henry ; but they met on the road to
Rouen, and on New Year's Eve entered the capital

18

of 'the ancient heritage' of England's kings in
royal state. Henry spent a busy three weeks in
Rouen, reviewing the arrangements which he had
made for the government of the duchy and seeing
that everything was in order before he sailed from
the shores of France. Two years to the day on
which Rouen capitulated to the English he set forth
with his queen for Calais and England. (January
19, 1421.)

Henry had no cause for complaint at the reception which he and Catherine received in the French
towns through which they passed on their way to
Calais. On all sides the king received professions
of loyalty and the queen rich presents. The
splendour of the royal entourage gave the common
people a subject for gossip : with the royal couple
rode the king of the Scots, the Duke of Bedford,
and the earls of March and Warwick ; and the escort
which marched with them consisted of picked men-
at-arms and archers—finely proportioned and well-
disciplined fellows whose skill in war made them
feared throughout the length and breadth of France.
Outside Calais Henry and his queen were met by the
merchants of the Staple and the local clergy, who
brought them with a great show of loyalty to their
town. The queen's comeliness at once aroused the
admiration of the people ; and that pleased Henry
mightily.

Dover was reached on February 1 after a pleasant
crossing ; and as the king's ship was run aground
for the landing some of the barons of the Cinque
Ports rushed into the water and carried Henry and
Catherine to land on their shoulders. All along the
road to Canterbury were cheering crowds, come to
welcome a victorious king and queen of England ;
and in the mother church of the kingdom Henry
and his wife knelt side by side at the high altar to
receive the blessing of Archbishop Chichele and to

give thanks for the joy which had come to them.
Catherine remained in Canterbury for some days :
Henry hastened on to London to make certain that
everything was ready in the capital city of his
kingdom for the official reception of the queen. On
February 21 he joined her at Eltham, and together
they set off for London. At Blackheath the mayor
(Will Cambryge) and the sheriffs (John Butlere and
John Wellys) with the aldermen and representatives
of the various city gilds met them, and escorted them
to the city. The occasion gave the Londoners an
opportunity to indulge their passion for pageantry ;
and the spectacles which they offered their sovereign
and his queen were as magnificent as those which
they had staged so successfully to welcome Henry
on his return from the victory of Agincourt. Everywhere Catherine met with manifestations of the
friendliness of her husband's people ; they forgot
that she was a princess of France, and welcomed
her as the woman whom their beloved king had
chosen to be his wife and queen.

Catherine spent her first night in London in the
famous fortress palace of the Tower. From there
on February 22 she was escorted by noblemen, the
mayor, sheriffs, aldermen, and gildsmen to the
abbey church of Westminster, She wore a snow-
white gown, which became her figure, and her
girlish nervousness was charmingly human. After
her coronation by Archbishop Chichele

> she was brought fulle worthely towards the palys into the
> grete halle

of Westminster. It was to be Catherine's day.
Henry was present during the coronation ceremony ;
but he was to take no part in the feasting and merry-
making which had been arranged to follow. It
would never do if his majesty overshadowed that
of his queen on the greatest day in her young life.

So it fell to Catherine's lot to preside over the wonderful feast which was laid in the great hall of the palace at Westminster.   The following is an account by one who was almost certainly present among the guests from the city of London :

> Fyrste the quene sette in hyr astate, and the Arche-byschope of Cantyrbury and the Byschoppe of Wynchester sate on the ryght syde of the quene . . . ; and on the lyfte syde was the Kyng of Schottys sette in hys astate ... ; the Duchyes of Yorke and the Countas of Huntyngdone sette in the same syde, and the Duke of Glowcester was ovyr seer, the Erle of Marche knelyng on the hye dyes on the ryght syde of the quene and held a cepture in hys hond of the quenys, and the Erle Marchelle knelyng on the lyfte syde at the dyes helde anothyr cepture of the quenys ; and the Countasse of Kentt was syttyng at hyr ryght fote of the quene undyr the tabylle, and the Counteys Marchalle sate on the lyfte syde of the quene undyr the tabylle.

The guests were accommodated at three great tables.   At the head of one were the barons of the Cinque Ports ; at another ' the mayre of London and hys aldermen ' ; and at the third the bishops and the abbot of Waltham.   The high officers of the king's household were in attendance ; and so praiseworthy were the efforts of the royal cooks that more than one guest preserved his copy of the menu.   As it was the season of Lent flesh foods were prohibited ; but before the diners was placed fish in every form ; and in the preparation of the *subtleties* great artistic genius was displayed.[17]

Henry had never intended to remain long in England.   He was painfully aware that the French had accepted the terms of the Treaty of Troyes under duress, and that the greater part of his father-in-law's kingdom acknowledged the dauphin, Until the dauphin's power was broken Henry's position in France would always be precarious ; and the task which he must set himself to perform on his return to France was to break that power.

That meant money and men ; and the purpose of the royal progress through England, undertaken immediately after Catherine's coronation, was to collect these essential sinews of war. He went westwards to Bristol—a wealthy city even in those days ; and then turned northwards and passed along the Welsh border until he came to Shrewsbury. From there he went to Kenilworth, where Catherine joined him ; and together they visited Coventry and Leicester. On April 2, the royal couple were in York, lodged in the quarters of the dean ; and while Catherine rested in the northern city and saw its sights and treasures Henry made pilgrimages to famous shrines in Bridlington and Beverley. Wherever he travelled Henry negotiated loans, and discussed the raising of reinforcements ; and while he experienced little difficulty in replenishing his depleted exchequer he found it by no means easy to collect suitable fighting material. Time and again he was told that the men had little inclination for service in foreign parts ; and he must have seen with his own eyes the hurt which husbandry had suffered owing to the lack of men in the country districts. The drain on the man power of England in Henry's reign was much greater than people imagine.

It was as he rode back to York from Beverley that the news of the disaster of Beaugé reached Henry. He never turned a hair when he read the fateful dispatch which told him of the death of Clarence, Lord Roos, and Sir Gilbert Umfraville, and of the capture of the earls of Huntingdon and Somerset, Lord fitzWalter, and Edmund Beaufort. The loss of so many brave captains must have hurt him grievously : none knew better than he their courage in battle and wisdom in counsel. Those who rode with him were ignorant of the contents of the dispatch which was handed to the king : it was

not until the following day that Henry revealed
the terrible news to them. Then they marvelled
at the strength of his self-control and his splendid
fortitude in adversity—lessons which he had learnt
in those harrying operations against Glyn Dŵr.

Henry knew as soon as he read that dispatch
that his presence was urgently needed in France ;
but he also knew that an indecent haste to return
would have disastrous results not only in France
but also in England. It would be rumoured in
Dauphinist France that at last the victor of
Agincourt had learnt to respect the military
power of Frenchmen : that would spur them on to
greater efforts. To show his own subjects in
England that he took a grave view of the disaster
at Beaugé would immediately produce a wave of
national despondency throughout the kingdom ;
and a despondent people lend money reluctantly
and have little stomach for fighting.

So Henry appeared not to hasten his departure.
On May 2 he met for the last time an English
parliament. Cardinal Langley, as chancellor,
preached the opening sermon, in which he praised
Henry's modesty in victory and patience in adversity. He was as modest as Julius Cæsar, as
patient as Job. The cardinal spoke in high appreciation of the services which Clarence had rendered
the State ; and then proceeded to tell the lords
and commons that they had been summoned by
their king

> to remedy any wrongs that had been committed since the
> last passage of the king.

Nothing was said in the chancellor's oration of the
other reason for the meeting of parliament—the
ratification of the Treaty of Troyes. But, after the
commons had chosen Thomas Chaucer again as
their speaker, the treaty was approved without

criticism; and parliament then turned to deal with routine parliamentary business. Actually it was a most uneventful session : at this distance of time it would seem that the parliament-men were quite indifferent to the magnitude of the task which confronted Henry in France.

During April and May of 1421, Henry was busily at work supervising the preparations necessary for the shipment of an army overseas. He had collected a force of between 800 and 900 knights, and more than 3000 archers. New guns were cast, and siege engines made; and the bowyers and fletchers of the kingdom were ordered to send in vast supplies of bow staves, arrows, and goose feathers. Early in June, Henry took his reinforcements across the Channel to Calais.

The news that Henry was back again in the country must have put heart into the captains who in his absence had fought manfully to protect English interests. Matters had gone badly with them since the king had returned to England : everywhere the Dauphinists had attacked the English and Burgundian outposts and strongholds; and their efforts were meeting with a large measure of success. The victory which they had won at Beaugé had broken that long spell of failures for French arms : the engagement was nothing more than a skirmish, but in the overwhelming defeat of the English it had been clearly demonstrated to the world in general and to France in particular that the king of England was not invincible. For long enough he had boasted that the invincibility of his arms was the proof that God had chosen him and his people as the instrument for the punishment of the people of France. It was only natural, therefore, that after Beaugé the divine character of the English attack on France should be called in question.

Beaugé was the ghastly error of judgment of a reckless captain. On leaving for England Henry had ordered Clarence to carry punitive raids through Anjou and Maine, where there were a number of Dauphinist strongholds ; and Clarence had scrupulously obeyed his brother's orders. He was a dashing leader of men, brave as a lion ; and at first his movements were singularly successful. Success probably went to his head : he conjured up visions of a spectacular victory over the French— a victory as notable as that which his eldest brother had won at Agincourt. He himself would win renown, and at the same time he would give the world proof of the great love which he had for his royal brother. What passed through Clarence's head during the few hours prior to the fight at Beaugé no man will ever know : it is certain that a blind recklessness had taken hold of him, and that he had lost for the moment whatever resourcefulness he had.

On March 21, which chanced to be Good Friday, Clarence found himself at Beaufort - en - Vallée. Near at hand, in the neighbourhood of Beaugé, was a Dauphinist force under the command of the Earls of Wigtown and Buchan. This news reached Clarence on Easter Eve while he was dining with his captains. He left the table with these words :

Let us go against them, they are ours.

The Earl of Huntingdon, who was with him, urged caution ; but Clarence would not hear of it ; and with a thousand men went out to make contact with the enemy. As they drew near to Beaugé that splendid knight, Sir Gilbert Umfraville, again advised Clarence not to risk a battle until they had discovered the disposition of the enemy : it would be better, so Sir Gilbert said, to postpone the engage-

ment until after the sacred festival of Easter,
Clarence mistook the advice for fear :

> If thou art afeard, go home and keep the church.[18]

Those words must have stung Sir Gilbert to the
quick ; he gravely replied :

> Nay, my lord, you have no company to fight.   See my
> cousin Grey and I have only ten men with us and no
> more ; yet you shall never say that we thus left you.

The afternoon was well advanced when Clarence's
men won the bridge which spanned the river near
the castle of Beaugé. That had been a stern
encounter : a party of Scottish archers holding
the bridge had put up a terrific fight, and inflicted
heavy losses in the attacking force. Their withdrawal in disorder undoubtedly led Clarence to
think that the enemy resistance had been broken.
He dashed off in pursuit ; but a little beyond the
town he was met by the main body of Wigtown's
and Buchan's force ; and a hand-to-hand struggle
took place. Clarence was early struck down, and
in a little time his force was cut to pieces.

It was Thomas Montacute, fourth Earl of Salisbury, who saved the English fortunes in France
immediately after the disaster of Beaugé. By a
masterly manœuvre he was able to extricate his
force, composed chiefly of archers, from a seemingly
hopeless position at Beaufort-en-Vallée and retire
in good order into Normandy. Once in the duchy
he called for reinforcements, and on the principle
that the best form of defence is attack he immediately set out against the Dauphinist contingents
operating along the southern border of the duchy.
He kept so close a watch on the army which the
dauphin had at Le Mans that the French daily
expected to have to fight a pitched battle ; and
he forced another Dauphinist force to abandon

the siege of Alençon. More than that : with consummate skill and daring he conducted a raid through the heart of Maine and into Anjou ; and in doing so had carried through successfully the plan which Henry had made for Clarence.

Salisbury had checked the Dauphinists' attack on Normandy : that caused them to change their plans. The dauphin then turned his eyes to Paris. If he could seize the capital he would have succeeded in undoing the greater part of Henry's work. His army took Montmirail before the end of May, and at once laid siege to Chartres. Many of the castles in the neighbouring country passed quickly into his hands : more important was the fact that men were willing to abandon the Burgundian cause and join his party. He had useful friends in Paris, where the English position had been seriously weakened since Henry's departure for England. The merchants quickly found that the cost of the recoinage was to fall upon their shoulders, since they received no compensation for coins of underweight ; and the poor found that their daily supplies of food from outside the city were often seized by Dauphinist raiding parties. Only just in time did the Duke of Exeter discover a plot to seize the person of Charles VI., and remove him to his son's camp ; and there is evidence that Dauphinist sympathisers were ready secretly to admit armed men into the city.

Henry has sometimes been blamed for landing his army at Calais in June 1421. It was in his interests to advance from Harfleur : by doing so he would have given a demonstration of his power to districts whose loyalty hung in the balances between himself and the dauphin ; and he would have chosen the shorter route to the capital. On the other hand, the Dauphinists were particularly active in Picardy, thanks to the able leadership of Jacques d'Harcourt, Count of Tancarville, Guy de Nesle, Seigneur of Offémont, and Pothon de Xaintrailles ; and Henry knew that Duke Philip was being hotly pressed. He knew that it was essential to the success of his plans to retain the friendship and support of Burgundy ; and in the summer of 1421 the best way of doing that was to use his reinforcements to relieve the Dauphinist danger in northern France where Burgundian influence was strongest.

The dauphin's threatening movements in the neighbourhood of Paris caused Henry to abandon whatever plans he had made for ridding Picardy and northern France of Dauphinist bands. In a conference with Duke Philip and the chief of his supporters it was agreed that the newly arrived English reinforcements should march to the relief of Chartres, while Henry himself should go with all speed to Paris, where the situation was far from satisfactory. Henry was in Paris for only four days (July 4–8) : then, collecting as many men as were available for service outside the capital, he went to join his brother, Humphrey, who had been put in command of the force sent to relieve Chartres ; but before the English king came to Mantes he learnt that the dauphin had called off the siege and retreated on Touraine.

It is impossible not to have the profoundest contempt for the dauphin's handling of the situation after Beaugé. At no time did he display an energetic appreciation of the advantages which his followers had gained. He boasted as soon as he learnt that Henry was back again in France that he would give him battle : yet those were empty words, and as soon as the English began to march to the relief of Chartres he turned tail and ran away. The dauphin's excuses that his followers were drifting back to their homes and that he was short of supplies are the proof of his weak leadership and inefficient administration ; and such a petulant conception had he of his princely dignity that he was unwilling to allow the more capable of his captains to take charge of the defence of France.

Thus at Mantes, Henry was joined by his 'trusty, lovyng, and faithful brother,' Philip of Burgundy. Together they worked out a new plan of campaign : Burgundy was to return northwards to deal with Jacques d'Harcourt ; and Henry meant to move against Dreux, an important Dauphinist stronghold on the west side of Paris. He must have known that Dreux was strongly fortified and competently held ; but he was now a past-master in the art of conducting sieges ; and he was resolved to take the place. On July 18 his men were in position around the town : Gloucester and the King of the Scots were detailed off to conduct the actual siege operations. Henry himself remained near at hand at St Denis de Moronval. The garrison and townsmen put up a stern resistance ; and when it became evident that there was no hope of relief from the side of the dauphin they capitulated (August 20).

Henry had learnt from spies that the dauphin was mustering a great army to give him battle near Beaugency on the Loire. As soon as Dreux surrendered, therefore, he made ready to march against his brother-in-law ; and passing by Chateaudun, La Ferté Villeneuil, and Messas he was in the neighbourhood of Beaugency by September 8. A day or so later the town was taken ; and the Earl of Suffolk and a detachment actually made their way across the Loire and successfully raided territory which had always accepted the Dauphinist position. Nor were the raiders attacked by the large enemy force under Tanneguy du Chastel who was near at hand : it appeared as though once again the reckless daring of Henry's strategy had paralysed the Dauphinist resistance.

It was clear that the dauphin would not give his adversary battle. Henry thereupon marched up the Loire. His men took and burnt the suburbs of Orléans—and more important found there provisions which helped to keep them going. For the country in which they had been operating was a wilderness, and his army suffered terribly on the march. Dysentery laid many of the men low, and stragglers who fell out to rest by the wayside received little pity from the French peasantry. Henry quickly realised that his force was not sufficiently strong to undertake the siege of the great Dauphinist town of Orléans ; and he marched reluctantly in a north-easterly direction to the district of the Yonne. His movements were watched by enemy patrols, but they did not seriously hinder the advance. Many of Henry's men made the journey in farm carts, so enfeebled were they by disease ; but the fit were able to gain some notable successes—the capture of Rougemont and Villeneuve-en-Yonne. He had failed to bring the Dauphinists to battle : he had, however, robbed them of the two important centres from which they had hitherto threatened Paris from the south.

In the meantime Philip of Burgundy had met with less success in Picardy and Northern France. There the Dauphinist captains, Jacques d'Harcourt, Pothon de Xaintrailles, and Guy de Nesle, were far away from the lethargic influence of the dauphin ; and they fought as they themselves wanted to fight. All along the line they held the Burgundians in check, and in a desperate fight at Mons-en-Vimeu were able to leave the field with honours easy.

There was near Paris one Dauphinist centre which continued to threaten the capital. This was Meaux, a large and well-fortified town, which com-

manded the valley of the Marne. Within its walls
was a band of desperate fellows—the most daring
and unscrupulous adventurers in the dauphin's
service. They had made themselves feared and
hated in the neighbourhood by the ruthlessness of
their behaviour ; and the most famous among them
was the Bastard of Vaurus. At the head of the
townsmen was Louis Gast : the military operations of
the garrison were directed by Guichard de Chissay.

The object of Henry's march from Orléans had
been to deliver an attack on Meaux. It was a most
carefully planned movement : he meant completely
to isolate the town by removing all chance of help
from such Dauphinist strongholds as Rougemont
and Villeneuve-en-Yonne. On October 6, therefore,
he took up his position around the town, and began
what has been called his ' masterpiece ' in the art
of scientific siege warfare.

The Marne ran through the town and therefore
divided the attacking divisions, but this disadvantage
was quickly overcome by the bridging of the river.
His divisional commanders were the Duke of
Exeter, and the Earls of March and Warwick ; and
since the siege was destined to be a winter operation
Henry saw to it that his men were well provided
with shelters and well protected by trenches. All
the available artillery and siege engines were
hastened to Meaux ; and from the moment that
the siege began it was prosecuted with furious
energy. The guns hurled their stone shots against
the walls ; the great engines were gradually worked
closer and closer to the defences ; and miners
laboured tirelessly underground. Ever watchful
for an advantage to hurl his men over the battered
walls, Henry was constantly present during the
operations ; and once again his men learnt to know
the magic of his sympathy and understanding.

Day after day the siege continued. Meaux was

defended by men who knew that they would get no quarter from a king so famous for justice as Henry of England ; and they fought with all the courage of desperate men, resolved to sell their lives dearly when there was no hope of saving them. Even the weather fought against the English. It happened to be a very wet December : the rain fell in torrents, and the country around the town was quickly flooded. Vast areas of water divided the attacking divisions ; and the sodden dug-outs and shelters afforded poor comfort for the men. There is evidence to show that these discomforts caused considerable murmuring among the English troops : some of the captains were even disposed to favour a calling off of the siege, and many of the men deserted. Henry kept a firm hand on the situation : he would have no grousing in his army, and he would sanction no relaxation of discipline. His own example of patience in adversity and constant attention to duty did more than anything else to keep up the spirits of his men. They saw at Meaux, as the veterans among them had seen at Harfleur, Agincourt, Rouen, Melun, and a score of other places, that he was asking of them nothing which he was not ready himself to perform. Nevertheless, it has been estimated that by Christmas 1421 Henry had lost nearly 20 per cent. of his men : this in itself reveals the seriousness of the siege, which he had begun with not more than 2500 fighting men.

Christmas brought Henry the greatest joy of his life. Not many days before the festival he had learnt that his beloved Catherine had been safely delivered of a man child on December 6. He learnt with pleasure from the messengers that

> throughout the kingdom there was perfect joy displayed, more than there had been seen a long time before about any other royal child.

With his exalted conception of his obligations he must have experienced in greater measure that satisfaction which comes to a man when he knows that his line will be continued into the realm of future things—that when his poor body is brought again to dust his name in another will be imperishable. Henry had worked and fought and schemed ; and his achievements had been notably great : now there existed some one for whom all the labour had been worth while—his son, the future ruler of England and France. These thoughts cannot have escaped him ; and they doubtless encouraged him at a time when despondency loomed near at hand in the English camp and his own body was beginning to feel the ravages of the disease which was soon to lay him low.

There was little time at Meaux for pleasant ruminations on the joys of fatherhood. Never had a garrison shown such contempt of Henry's power : they mocked him from their walls, and repulsed all his attacks. Some time before the end came those desperadoes in Meaux had brought a donkey on to their walls and

> made it bray by the force of the blows which they gave it, mocking the English, and saying that this was their king, and that they ought to come and help him.

Early in March, Guy de Nesle, Seigneur of Offémont, and a party of forty men made a gallant effort to get into the town under cover of darkness ; but Guy accidentally fell into a ditch full of water, and the noise which his men made in effecting his rescue aroused the Englishmen and resulted in the capture of the whole party.

Easter came and went, and Meaux still held out, though Henry had by this time captured a part of the town. Terms were offered, but were contemptuously rejected. Henry was thereupon driven to devise all manner of siege engines in order to win his way into that part of the town called 'The Market' where the defenders were strongly posted. One of Henry's inventions was a lofty wooden tower—higher than any tower in the town —from which a bridge could be let down on to the fortifications; but before it was completed the defenders asked for terms.

On May 10 the great siege of Meaux came to an end. Henry's terms were not heavy. The defenders generally were given their liberty, but twelve of the leaders, and some of the soldiery, were to be in the mercy of Henry and Charles VI. Louis Gast and

the man who blew the trumpet on the walls

were tried and executed in Paris. The Bastard of Vaurus and a kinsman suffered summarily at Meaux. They were drawn through the captured town on a hurdle and hung on an elm tree outside the town, where they had previously hung many of their victims and already called 'the Vaurus Tree.' Few men had pity for these two desperadoes: they had shown none in their lives, and could expect none at their death.

In the northern districts Burgundy had registered some successes while Henry was engaged in taking Meaux. Little by little the Dauphinist resistance was worn down; and by the end of the summer it was Henry's proud boast that to the north of the French capital only Le Crotoy, Guise, and St Valery-sur-Somme continued to hold out in the dauphin's name.

19

CHAPTER NINE

' INTO THY HAND, O LORD '

HAD Henry in the closing stages of the siege of
Meaux some strange prescience of his approaching
end ?   Some time before the garrison made terms
he sent messengers to England to ask Catherine to
join him in France as soon as she was able to do so ;
and it is inconceivable that he should have asked
her to leave their infant son so soon after birth unless
he felt that he needed her presence.   Catherine
crossed to Calais on May 12, escorted by the faithful
Bedford :   the baby prince, Henry, remained in
England in the care of his other uncle, Gloucester,
who had taken Bedford's place as regent.   Catherine
and Henry met at Bois de Vincennes on May 26 ;
and four days later they rode together into Paris to
keep the festival of Whitsun.

As during their former visit the Louvre was
placed at their disposal, and they kept court with
traditional splendour.   Thither came crowds of
nobles and their ladies, wearing costly robes and
gowns and enjoying to the full the amusements
which had been provided for their entertainment ;
and once again there were murmurs that the presence of the ' heir of France ' in the capital resulted
in the complete and indecent overshadowing of the
majesty of poor Charles VI., whose poverty compelled him to live in simple style.   Nevertheless Paris
gave Henry and Catherine a magnificent welcome
as they rode through her streets on the eve of Whit
Sunday.   The Parisians knew the English king to
be a hard man, but a just ; and the poorer people

especially welcomed him because he would not allow the rapacious Burgundian nobles and wealthy city merchants to oppress them—as they had been so cruelly oppressed in times past. On the Tuesday and Wednesday in Whit week the city authorities staged a *mystery* dealing with *The Life of St George*. It was a delightful compliment to Henry and his fellow-countrymen ; and the king himself is said to have been highly appreciative of the citizens' thoughtfulness.

Henry could never afford much time for rest or amusement. All his life had been given over to the business of State ; and at no time in his career was his burden more grievous than in the years immediately following the Treaty of Troyes. South of the Loire that treaty was regarded as nothing better than a scrap of paper, to be repudiated at the earliest possible moment : north, in the district of Vimeu, a handful of Dauphinists were causing considerable inconvenience to the English and Burgundian captains. Henry was determined at all costs to have Vimeu under his control : he would show Jacques d'Harcourt and the other Dauphinist captains that they could not defy him so impudently ; and then, when that task was done, he would direct his thoughts to their master, the dauphin, and drive him out of southern France.

Such were Henry's plans when he left Paris with Catherine on June 11. They must first journey to Compiègne to witness the capitulation of that town on June 18. It would be a grand opportunity for Catherine to see the awe in which her own people held her husband's power. They travelled leisurely, and spent the first night with Charles and Isabella at Senlis. It was here that Henry learnt that a number of Dauphinists in Paris had laid a plot to admit his enemies into the city. He dashed back to the capital, nipped the plot in the bud, and

meted out condign punishment to the conspirators.
Assuring himself that Paris was quiet and that
his own position was no longer threatened, Henry
returned to Senlis, and then escorted his queen
to Compiègne.

But Henry was already a very sick man. Long
before the siege of Meaux was completed he was
ailing. His indomitable courage and tremendous
strength of will kept him going : he knew only too
well that weakness on his part would have a de-
pressing effect upon his troops who had suffered
such hardships during the siege. What the king's
sickness was it is difficult to say. Waurin, the
Burgundian chronicler, writing some time after
Henry's death, said :

> I have since been truly informed concerning the princi-
> pal disease by which the said king was brought to his
> death, that it was an inflammation which seized him in
> the fundament, which is called the disease of St Anthony.

To attempt to diagnose the trouble at this distance
of time would be futilely dangerous ; but it is interesting to record that nearly all the contemporary
evidence suggests some kind of internal trouble.
It is known that the English troops lying around
Meaux suffered severely from dysentery—many of
the men had been on the sick list long before they
came to the town and had been carried in carts
during the march from Orléans ; and it is not
unlikely that Henry himself was a victim of dysentery. On the other hand, the king's health had not
been good for some time : months before a physician
had been brought from England to attend to him.
A later chronicler recorded that Henry was unable
to keep any food on his stomach ; and this statement
has led many to believe that the king suffered from
a duodenal ulcer. Life on active service in the
Middle Ages must have been hard, and the hardships

which men were called upon to endure would tax
the strength of the strongest constitution. There
is no evidence that Henry had inherited any of the
physical defects of his father : indeed, he appears to
have been a very strong man.

The news of Henry's indisposition must have
gladdened the hearts of the dauphin and his supporters. They resolved to strike while the English
king lay sick at Senlis, and their blow was to be
directed against Burgundy. A great Dauphinist
army was thereupon mustered and marched against
the Burgundian fortress of Cosne, which stood on
the upper reaches of the Loire ; and so hotly pressed
were the garrison that they had undertaken to
surrender the place to the Dauphinists unless relief
came on or before August 16.

Little did the Dauphinists know the character
of the man of whose illness they were hoping to
take advantage. As soon as Henry heard of the
arrangements which had been made for the
surrender of Cosne he prepared to go to the
garrison's relief,

> forgetful of his illness, but mindful of his compact with
> the Duke of Burgundy.

He meant to show those insolent Dauphinists
that he was not too ill to bring about their downfall.

Henry was too weak to ride at the head of his
men : it was consequently arranged that he should
travel by horse litter. Weakened by lack of
nourishment, his body racked with excruciating
pains, he was in spirit the same Henry who had led
his men from Harfleur to Calais in 1415. He
discussed the plan of the campaign with his captains
with his customary clarity of vision : he encouraged his men as they marched. But by the
time the army reached Corbeil the disease had got

the better of him : his physicians told him that
he must go no farther, and reluctantly he handed
over the command of the relief force to Bedford and
Exeter. Soon they were to send him news that
the Dauphinists had abandoned the siege : to a
sick man of Henry's temperament such news was
infinitely better than the attentive ministrations
of the royal physicians ; and it is significant that
after a short rest at Corbeil he announced that he
felt well enough to make the journey to Paris.
Acting on the advice of his physicians he went by
river barge as far as Charenton : they urged that
he should use that form of transport into the
capital itself. But Henry would not hear of such
a thing, and at Charenton he left the barge and
mounted his horse. The ' heir of France ' must
not enter Paris as a sick man : he must ride at the
head of his entourage, as he had always done in the
past. For the first time since he came to France
Henry found that he was fighting a losing battle.
The jolting motion of riding brought on a fearful
spasm of pain which so weakened him that he could
not even protest when his attendants sadly lifted
him into his horse litter and bore him slowly to
the castle of Bois de Vincennes, where, so a contemporary noted,

> alas ! he entered his bed of pain.

It was a bed of sickness from which he was to be
lifted as a dead man.

But if disease could break his body it could not
kill the fine courage of his spirit. It is certain
that as soon as he came to Bois de Vincennes he
realised that he was to be gathered to his fathers.
He displayed no trace of impatience that he was to
be cut off in the prime of his manhood : it was
God's will ; and he concerned himself with making

arrangements for the care of his baby son, whom he had never been privileged to see, and the protection of the lands which he had won with so much blood and suffering. Strangely enough, in the last hours of his life he appears to have given little thought to the queen whom he so obviously loved : she was only at Senlis, but he never sent for her to come to his side. Did he feel shy that she might pity his enfeebled body ? He had taken her as a man of strength who had lived and dared on the field of battle : now he was a miserable invalid doomed to die like the weakest of men. Or, was he to the very end a martyr to his duty ? Love was a personal thing : it must wait until he had arranged for the government of the distracted land of France and the safeguarding of the English interests there. In all probability both sentiments weighed heavily with Henry in his last days at Bois de Vincennes.

Before the end came, Bedford, Exeter, and Warwick hastened to the bedside of the dying king. Burgundy himself was unable to come to Bois de Vincennes : as his deputy he sent one of the trustiest men in his household, Hue de Lannoy. Throughout those painful days Henry's mind constantly turned to spiritual matters : he was surrounded by his chaplains, and he prepared himself serenely and quietly for death.

On August 30, Henry felt that he was sinking, and called to his side those faithful counsellors upon whom he had relied so much in his lifetime—his brother, John of Bedford, his uncle, Thomas of Exeter, the Earl of Warwick, Sir Lewis Robsart, and seven or eight others who were at hand. In 'a firm voice' he told them that he was dying ; and in their presence humbly asked pardon of God for any wrong or injustice which he had done in his lifetime. Not even the imminence of death could make him forget the splendid fellows who had fought with him in the French wars.

> For the good services rendered to me especially in these wars I give thanks to you and to your other fellow-soldiers. . . . If death had not prevented me I had intended to have awarded to each worthy rewards.

Then, as if meaning to meet the charges which were to be levelled against him by posterity, he passed on to justify his attack on France.

> It was not ambitious lust for dominion, nor for empty glory, nor for worldly honour, nor any other cause, that drew me to these wars, but only that by suing of my right, I might at once gain peace and my own rights. . . . And before the wars were begun I was fully instructed by men of the holiest life and the wisest counsel that I ought and could with this intention begin the wars, prosecute them, and justly finish them without danger to my soul.

Who dares to say that these were the words of a hypocrite ?

Quietly Henry passed on to review the arrangements which he had made for the continuance of his great work. It was to John, wisest of all his brothers, that he entrusted his most precious possession—his baby son—beseeching him ' by all the loyalty ' which he had given him always to

> be kind and faithful to the fair child Henry, your nephew.

To John he gave the custody of the Duchy of Normandy until the child king should come of age, and he counselled him not to make any peace with the dauphin which would alienate ' the ancient heritage ' of England's kings. With the object of binding closer to the English side the Duke of Burgundy, Henry told them that he wished him to be the regent in France ; if he would not accept that dignity then Bedford was to take it. He was most concerned that nothing should endanger the Burgundian friendship. He saw that ruin would result if Burgundy was estranged ; and he seems to have feared that the real danger would come from the side of the impetuous Humphrey of Gloucester. It was a shrewd piece of advice, for in the end the rashness of Gloucester did much to alienate the sympathies of Burgundy. Henry undoubtedly hoped that by making Humphrey responsible for the government in England during the minority of Henry VI. he would prevent him intermeddling in the affairs of France. None knew better than he did Humphrey's great potentialities— for good or evil.

Bravely the little party around the dying king's bed clung to hope. Physicians were sometimes wrong : they had not yet despaired of saving their royal master—at least not openly. So the group of friends in the sick man's room tried to cheer him. He would recover : then he himself could carry out his plans. A realist to the end, Henry was not to be buoyed up by false hopes. He called his physicians to his side, and asked them how long they expected him to live. Faced by the question from which every doctor shrinks, they tried to beg it with the reminder that it was in God's power still to restore him to good health. Henry would not be put off in that way : he commanded them to tell him the truth. One of the physicians at last came forward, and tearfully told him the dread information.

> Sire, think you on your soul. For saving the mercy of God we judge not that you can live more than two hours.

Henry heard the words unmoved. Then asking his counsellors to withdraw a little from his bed he summoned his confessor and the royal chaplains. With them

> he saide the vij psalmes of pennance and the Letanie wth the suffrages accustomed.

When they came to the eighteenth verse of the fifty-first Psalm—*O be favourable and gracious unto Sion : build thou the walls of Jerusalem*—Henry stopped them, and prayed :

> O Good Lord, thou knowest that if thie pleasure had bin to haue suffered me to liue my naturall age my firme purpose and intent was, after I had established this realme of Fraunce in sure peace, to haue gone and visited Iherusalem, and to haue re-edified the walls thereof, and to haue expulsed from it the Miscreants thine aduersaries.

Then the recital of the Penitential Psalms was continued, after which he received the Viaticum and Extreme Unction. Just before he died he must have suffered some strange torment, for he cried out :

> Thou liest ! thou liest ! my portion is with the Lord Jesus.

Clasping firmly in his hands the crucifix, he drove the evil spirit back, and his face bathed in a wonderful serenity he opened his eyes and quietly said :

> In manus tuas, Domine, ipsum terminum redemisti.

And with those words hardly passed his lips ' Henry Fifte of England ' entered his rest, a little after two o'clock in the morning of August 31, 1422, in the thirty-sixth year of his age.

> For whose death the Duke of Bedford, his brother, and the Duke of Excester, his vncle, and generally all the other Princes, Lords, Estats, and Commons of Englande made greate lamentacions and bewaylings in right great anguish and heauines.

To John of Bedford then fell the task of carrying the dead king's body back for burial among his own people. The embalmers were put to work to prepare the body for its last great march. The entrails were buried in the church of St Maur-des-Fosses,

> and his corps wel embalmed and seled . . . was inclosed in a circle of lead.

It took some days to complete the arrangements for the removal of Henry's body to England. A lifelike image, fashioned out of boiled hides, was laid upon the coffin, there was a crown upon the head, a sceptre in the right hand and an orb in the left. Coffin and image were then placed upon a magnificent funeral car, to which were harnessed 'foure grete horsses : their trappings were emblazoned with the arms which the dead king used to bear in his lifetime—England, England and France quarterly, France, and King Arthur. Torch-bearers walked on either side of the funeral car. Then came a company of 500 men-at-arms, riding black horses and carrying their lances at the reverse ; and behind them rode the chief mourners—the dukes of Bedford, Burgundy and Exeter, and the king of the Scots. Wherever the cortège halted for the night the coffin was borne reverently into a church, to be prayed and watched over by clergy and friends ; and when it passed through some of the larger French towns it invariably happened that a party of townsmen bore over the car

> a cannopie of maruelous great value, such as is vsed to be borne over the blessed Sacrament on Corpus Christy day.

At Rouen, John of Bedford took his leave of, and Catherine joined, the sad procession. John must remain behind in the 'ancient heritage' to continue the work of his dead brother ; and it should require no great effort of imagination to realise the grief which he must have experienced as he watched the funeral car move off along the road to Calais. John had always been his brother's favourite : Henry had always been John's hero. They understood each other perfectly : they served each other loyally. The niceties of mediæval convention would not allow Catherine to travel with the cortège : she followed discreetly behind with the women of her household, stricken with grief.

The saddest part of the whole journey came when Henry's body was landed at Dover early in a stormy November : there crowds of his fellow-countrymen, weeping quietly, watched the grim funeral car pass down the very streets in which but a little time before the living Henry had ridden to continue his work of conquest in France and to win further renown for his people. Slowly the procession made its way to London, pausing at Canterbury so that a solemn requiem might be said in the mother church of the kingdom—the church in which Henry himself had joined with Sigismund to praise God for the victory which Bedford had won in the battle of the Seine, the church in which he had prayed with Catherine when he brought her to England as his queen. Outside the city of London waited the mayor, sheriffs, aldermen, and gildsmen, dressed in black robes : it was to be their privilege to escort the body to their city. Hushed was the excitement which had accompanied their previous welcomes, absent were the splendid spectacles of pageantry which they had staged in his honour when he last came to their city : London's city fathers had come to take into their keeping the last earthly remains of one whom they had loved as a Londoner, and to lay gently those remains in the fairest church in their city. It was November 5, 1422, when Henry's corpse was borne into ' Paul's church.' That night it rested there, guarded by the greatest and the humblest in the land ; and next morning Archbishop Chichele, assisted by the majority of the bishops, said a solemn requiem for the quiet repose of the dead king's soul. As the cortège left the cathedral for the abbey church of Westminster it passed along streets lined with citizens—a man from every house along the route bearing in his hand a lighted torch ; and before went the grave-faced priests and choristers chanting the *De Profundis*. Finally they laid his body to rest in the most honoured spot in the abbey church—between the shrine of St Edward Confessor and the chapel of Our Lady.   His people had honoured him greatly during his short life : they were equally generous in their tribute to him dead.   Wrote one chronicler :

all things generally were done more honnorablie and solemnly than had bin seene in Englande at the buryinge of anie Kinge or Prince of longe time before.

And from a thousand lips went up that final prayer : *Requiescat in pace.*

A BIBLIOGRAPHICAL NOTE

A STUDENT of history who decides to write a *life* of Henry V. has a great pleasure in store for him : he must at once turn to a work which is in every way a model of what a history ought to be—I refer to the late Dr Wylie's *The Reign of Henry V.*, the last of the three volumes being completed for publication by Mr W. T. Waugh. Here is a work which presents its readers with a splendid picture of the history of Henry V.'s reign, being encyclopædic in its presentation of detail and meticulously accurate in the sources from which facts were secured. It is not too much to say that without these three volumes no one will get a proper understanding of the history of Henry's times.

Of the biographies, mention must first be made of *Henry of Monmouth*, by the reverend Mr J. Endell Tyler. This work was first published in 1838, and has the defects of that period — propensity to indulge in verbose moralising and a blind hero-worship ; but it was a task lovingly undertaken by one who, like the present writer, came from the country in which Henry was born ; and its value ought not to be underestimated. Some of Mr Tyler's remarks about the Owen Glyn Dŵr rebellion are unreliable ; and his treatment of Henry's campaigns in France is meagre and unsatisfying.

Mr C. L. Kingsford's *Henry V.*, published in 1901 in the Heroes of the Nations Series, is another book worthy of the highest praise ; and not less inferior is Professor R. B. Mowat's *Henry V.* Both biographies should be read : they cannot fail to interest the reader.

Sir J. E. Lloyd's *Owen Glendower* is a scholarly work by Wales's leading historian, and as is to be expected it presents the best picture yet produced of the great rebellion in which Henry learnt his first lessons in warfare. The present writer's *Owen Glyn Dŵr* presents the same story in a way which it is hoped the ' general ' reader, as opposed to the serious student of history, can appreciate.

The works of the chroniclers who wrote about Henry are many. *Gesta Henrici Quinti* was written by Thomas Elmham, who was one of Henry's chaplains ; and his account of the battle of Agincourt is that of an eye-witness. This work must not be confused with *Vita et Gesta Henrici Quinti*, which at one time was thought to have been written by Thomas

Elmham : it was probably composed about 1445 by a foreigner, who may have been attached to the household of the Duke of Gloucester.

The Memorials of Henry the Fifth in the Rolls Series contains three records : (1) *Vita Henrici Quinti*, by R. Redmayne, who lived in the sixteenth century ; (2) *Versus Rhythmici in laudem Henrici Quinti*, by a monk of Westminster ; and *Liber Metricus de Henrici Quinti*, by Thomas Elmham.

Vita Henrici Quinti, by Titus Livius or Titus Livius Forojuliensis, is a valuable source book, although the author wrote at least fifteen years after Henry's death. He was apparently an Italian who belonged to the Duke of Gloucester's entourage, and much of his information may have been derived from his ducal master.

A highly interesting piece of contemporary evidence is John Page's *The Siege of Rouen*, a rhyming narrative by a soldier who was present at the siege of that Norman town. It has been published by the Camden Society in *The Historical Collections of a Citizen of London in the Fifteenth Century*, which also contains William Gregory's *Chronicles of London*—another valuable source book. Similarly *The Chronicle of John Hardyng, Liber de Illustribus Henricis, Chronicon Adae de Usk*, and *Original Letters Illustrative of English History* (collected and edited by the late Sir Henry Ellis) present various aspects of the story of Henry's life.

The First English Life of King Henry the Fifth is a book to be carefully consulted, although it was not written until the beginning of the sixteenth century : it is obviously based upon a certain amount of reliable evidence, and serves to corroborate the evidence of some of the other chroniclers. The edition edited by Mr C. L. Kingsford contains a scholarly introduction. Then there is that stand-by of the Elizabethan history student —*Chronicles of England, Scotland, and Ireland*, by Raphael Holinshed.

Waurin's *Receuil des croniques et anchiennes istories de la Grant Bretaigne à present nommé Engleterre, 1399-1422*—a Rolls Series publication—is useful in that it gives a French point of view. The author was present at the battle of Agincourt in the French army. *Histoire de Charles VI.*, by J. J. des Ursins, is another source book to be consulted ; and mention must also be made of *La Chronique*, by Enguerrand de Monstrelet.

For the battle of Agincourt one is compelled to turn to *The History of the Battle of Agincourt* (Sir N. H. Nicholas), a work published in 1827, but so thoroughly done that it has never been bettered. Its only defect is perhaps a certain harshness of outlook on Henry's character—a typical example of the judgment of fifteenth-century human behaviour by nineteenth-century standards.

To the *Dictionary of National Biography* one has constantly to turn for information about the characters who play their part in the stirring drama of Henry's reign. A good political history—such as Dr Kenneth Vickers' *England in the later Middle Ages*—is invaluable ; and the reverend Mr W. W. Capes' *A History of the English Church in the Fourteenth and Fifteenth Centuries* will provide a reliable text-book for consultation in matters of ecclesiastical history.

I have not attempted to make this bibliographical note exhaustive : there are so many excellent publications nowadays dealing with the sources of evidence for specific periods of history, and to these the serious student will naturally turn for help and guidance. What I have done is merely to give a record of some of the works which I myself consulted in the making of this *life* of Henry V., and if it proves to be of help to my readers then I am amply repaid for whatever work was entailed in preparing this bibliography.

J. D. G. D.

20

APPENDIX A

Indenture made between Henry the Fifth and Thomas Tunstall [19]

THIS Indenture, made between the King our Sovereign Lord of the one part, and Monsieur Thomas Tunstall of the other part : Witnesseth that the said Thomas is bound to our said Lord the King, to serve him for a whole year in a voyage which the same our Lord the King in his person will make, if it pleaseth God, in his Duchy of Guienne, or in his kingdom of France : commencing the said year, the day of the muster of his people of his retinue, at the place which shall be appointed by our said Lord the King, within the month of May next coming, if he shall then be ready to make the said muster. And the said Thomas, shall have with him in the said voyage for the whole year six men-at-arms, himself counted, and eighteen horse archers ; the said Thomas shall go to the said Duchy of Guienne, he shall take for the wages of each of the said men at arms forty marks, and for each of the said archers twenty marks, for the said whole year. And in case that in company of our said Lord the King, the aforesaid Thomas goes to the aforesaid kingdom of France, he shall take for the wages of each of the said men-at-arms twelve pence a day, and for each of the said archers six pence a day, during the year above-said. And in case of the said voyage to France, the said Thomas shall take reward usual for him and his said men-at-arms, at the rate of one hundred marks for thirty men-at-arms the quarter. Of the which rewards for the said parts of Guienne shall be paid to the said Thomas, for the performance of this Indenture, for half the first quarter ; and for the other half, when he shall have made the said muster ready to go to the said parts of Guienne, if our said Lord the King shall go there, or shall send him there. And in case it happens that after the said muster our said Lord the King shall not go to his said Duchy of Guienne but shall go to the parts of France, then the said Thomas shall be paid so much as shall be owing to him for the said first quarter, besides the sum received by him as above, for the wages and reward, as well as for himself as for the above-said men-at-arms and archers ; so passing to the said parts of France. And for surety of payment for the second quarter, our said Lord the King will cause to be delivered to the said Thomas, in pledge, the first day of June next coming, Jewels which by agreement with the said Thomas, shall be fully worth the sum to which the said wages, or wages with reward, for that quarter shall amount. The which Jewels shall be the same that the said Thomas is bound to return to our said Lord the King, the hour that he can redeem them within a year and half and one month next after the receipt of the same Jewels. And also that it shall be lawful for the said Thomas and for all others whatsoever, to whom the said Jewels shall be delivered to the said Thomas, after the end of the said month, to dispose of the said Jewels at their pleasure, without impeachment of the king or of his heirs, according to the contents of the Letters Patent, under the Great Seal of the King granted to the aforesaid Thomas in this case. And for the third quarter the said Thomas shall be paid for him and his said retinue, within six months after the commencement of the same third quarter, according to the quantity of wages, or wages with reward, for the country to which they have gone, or shall be, during the said quarter. And respecting the payment of the wages, or wages with reward, as the case shall be for the last quarter of the year above said, if for the moiety of the said third quarter, the King, our said Lord, shall not give such security for the payment to the said Thomas as he shall reasonably demand, then at the expiration of the third quarter, the said Thomas shall be acquitted and discharged towards our said Lord the King of the covenants specified in this present Indenture. And the said Thomas shall be bound to be ready at the sea, with his said people well mounted, armed and equipped, suitably to their condition, for his muster on the first day of July next coming : and from the time of their arrival at the place above said, the said Thomas shall make muster of his people before such person or persons as it may please our said Lord the King to assign, as often as he shall reasonably require. And the said Thomas shall have as usual from the said King, shipping for him, and his retinue, their horses, harness, and provisions, and also re-shipping, as others of his condition shall have in the said voyage. And if it shall happen that, on the part of our said Lord the King, the said Thomas before his passage of the sea be countermanded, he shall be bound for the said sum to serve the same our Lord the King, in such parts as shall please him with the aforesaid men-at-arms and archers, according to the rate of wages accustomed in the parts where they shall be ordered by the command of our said Lord the King, except those that may die, if any shall die in the mean time. And if it shall happen that the ' Adversary of France,' or any of his sons, nephews, uncles, cousin-germans, that may be, or any King of that kingdom, or Lieutenant, or other chieftains having command from the said

' Adversary of France,' shall be taken in the said voyage by the said Thomas, or any of his retinue, our said Lord the King shall have the said ' Adversary,' or other person of the rank above said, who shall be so taken, and shall make reasonable agreement with the said Thomas, or to those whom he may be taken.   And respecting other profits of ' Gaignes de Guerres,' our said Lord the King shall have as well the third part of the ' Gaignes ' of the said Thomas as the third of the third part of the profit of the people of his retinue in the said voyage taken, as the ' Gaignes ' of the prisoners, booty, money, all gold, silver, and jewels, exceeding the value of ten marks.

In witness of which things on the part of this Indenture relating to our said Lord the King, the aforesaid Thomas has put his Seal.   Done at Westminster, the xxix day of April, the year of our said Lord the King, the third.

Sigillo Avulso
Eodem modo mutatis mutantis
fiunt Indenturæ cum
GILBERTO UMFREVILL.   ROBERTO DE STANLEY.
THOMA STRIKLAND.

APPENDIX B

Here bigynneth the servyce at the First Course :

Brawne with mustarde. Dedel in Borneux. Furmente with baleyne. Pike. Laumprey powdred. Great Elis poudred. Trought. Codlyng. Plaies and merlyne fried. Crabbes great. Lech lumbarde florisshed wth colars of esses and brome coddes of gold in a Target with the armes of the kyng and the quene departid. Tarves. A Sotelte, callid a pellican on hire nest with briddis and an ymage of Seint Katerine with a whele in hire hande disputyng with the Hethen clerks, having this Reason in hir hande, MADAME LA ROIGNE ; the Pellican answeryng CEST ENSEIGNE ; the briddes answeryng EST DU ROY PUR TENIR JOIE. A TOUT GENT IL MET SENTENT.

The ii^d Course is this folewyng :

Gely florisshed with columbyne floures of white potages. Blaundesore. Breme. Congre. Soles with mulet. Cheveyne. Barbel with Roch. Samon fressh. Halibut. Gurnarde rostid. Roches boilet. Smelt fried. Losters. Lech damaske with the kyngs worde UNE SANZ PLUZ writon of white lettres. Lamprey in paste suyng. Flampan florisshed with a scochyn roial, theryn three crownes of golde and plantid with floure de lice of golde and floures of camomil wrought of confections. A Sotelte, a panter with an ymage of Seint Katerine in the same tariage and a whele in hire hand, and a Reason in hire other hand. The Reason was this : LA ROIGNE MA FILE. The panter answeryng IN CEST ILE : another best answeryng with this Reason, DF ALBION : another best answeryng, AVES RENOWNE.

This is the iii^d Course folowynge :

Dates in compost. Creme motley. Carpe. Dorrey. Turbut. Tench. Peerch with gogyns. Sturgeon fresshe. Welkes. Porpes rostid. Memise fried. Creves de ewe douce. Shrympes grosse. Elis with laumprons rostid. A Lessh callid the White Lessh, with hauthorne leves grene and redd hawes.

A mete in paste with iiij aungels in forme of Sent Katerine whele in the myddes with a Reason—

IL EST ESCRITE   PAR MARIAGE PURE
PUR VOIR ET DIT   CE GUERRE NE DURE

A Sotelte, a Tigre lokyng in a mirour and a man ridyng on horseback armed with a tigre whelp in his barme, and throwyng mirours for his defence ; and a Reason writon, PAR FORCE SAUNZ DROIT JAY PRIS CE BEST. Another Reason for thanswere of the tigre—

CILE DE MIRROUR
MA FAIT DISCOUR.

TEXTUAL NOTES

NOTE 1 (p. 5).

The 'consideration' which was placed on the priest's service book was usually 6s. 8d. If this was the case, then Henry of Bolingbroke's gift from his father amounted to £160—or about £4000 by modern values.

NOTE 2 (p. 18).

His rooms are said to have faced the gateway of St Edmund Hall.

NOTE 3 (p. 29).

Henry of Bolingbroke was not the legal heir to the vacant throne. Lionel, duke of Clarence, the third son of Edward III., left a daughter, Philippe, who married Edmund Mortimer, Earl of March. Their son, Roger, held the earldom of March, and on his death in 1398 his rights passed to his six-year-old son, Edmund Mortimer. Bolingbroke, therefore, tried to claim that the House of Lancaster was descended from Edmund called Crouchback, who was the eldest of Henry III.'s sons, but had not succeeded to the throne because of bodily and mental infirmities. This plausible theory was carefully examined by experts, but they could find no documentary evidence to support it. See *Chronicon Adæ Usk*, pp. 30–31.

NOTE 4 (p. 44).

Lord Grey had announced that he would punish Gruffydd ap Dafydd ap Gruffydd in no uncertain manner as soon as he could get him into his clutches. This threat called forth a spirited letter from 'the strengest thiefe of Wales,' part of which is here quoted :

> And hit was told me that ye ben in purpose for to mak your men bran (burn) and sle (slay) in whade soever cuntre that I be and am sesened in. With owten doute as mony men that ye sleu, and as mony howsin that ye bran for my sake, as mony wol I bran and sle for your sake ; and doute not I wolle have both bredde and ale of the best that is in your lordschip.

Grey rose to the occasion, using verse to give his answer.

> But we hoope we shall do the a pryve thyng ; a roop, a ladder, and a ryng, heigh on gallows for to henge. And thus shalle be your endyng ; and he that made the be ther to helpyng ; and we on our behalfe shalle be welle willyng.

For an account of this incident, see *Owen Glyn Dŵr*, J. D. Griffith Davies, pp. 33–34.

NOTE 5 (p. 50).

Hotspur agreed to Gwilym's terms, but stipulated that nine of the garrison must be handed over to him for punishment by death. Gwilym had nine of his comrades seized in their sleep, and sent them out to Hotspur shackled like common felons.

NOTE 6 (p. 55).

Negotiations between Grey's friends and Owen were not completed until October 1402 ; and when Grey was eventually given his liberty he was forced to swear never to appear again in arms against Owen. The payment of the ransom literally beggared Grey, as Hardyng, the chronicler, noted :

> Ten thousands marke, and fully paide were dear
> For which he was so poor than alle his lyfe
> That no power he hadde to werr ne stryfe.

NOTE 7 (p. 59).

Obviously Sycharth, which was the name of the mansion on the Cynllaith Owen lordship.

NOTE 8 (p. 106).

Anne of Burgundy, a woman of great charm and sagacity, eventually married John, Duke of Bedford.

NOTE 9 (p. 123).

Henry IV. had died so hopelessly in debt that his executors refused point-blank to administer his estate. It was in those days considered a sacred duty to carry out the testamentary wishes of a dead man—unless, of course, you were not afraid of bad luck pursuing you.

NOTE 10 (p. 141).

The hostility of French and English in ecclesiastical matters is more fully discussed in Chapter VII. See pp. 202–3.

NOTE 11 (p. 146).

By the Treaty of Brétigni, 1360, the French ceded to Edward III. in full sovereignty Calais, Ponthieu, Guisnes, Guienne, Gascony, Poitou, and Santogne, and agreed to pay 3,000,000 crowns for the ransom of King John, who had been captured at Poitiers in 1356.

NOTE 12 (p. 153).

See Appendix A.

NOTE 13 (p. 201).

King of the Romans was the title used by an emperor-elect prior to his consecration as emperor by the Pope.

NOTE 14 (p. 203).

It is said that Baldassare Cossa was in the habit of boasting that he had raped two hundred women, among whom were his brother's wife and a number of nuns ; and until he decided to 'seize' the papal throne he seldom darkened the door of a church.

NOTE 15 (p. 213).

At one time, during the Council of Constance, it looked as though Henry Beaufort, Bishop of Winchester, might be elevated to the papal dignity. His English connections (and particularly his known support of the war against the French) at once ruled him out of the list of possible candidates.

NOTE 16 (p. 238).

Château Gaillard surrendered on September 23 1419.   Mont-St-Michel never surrendered to the English.

NOTE 17 (p. 264).

See Appendix B.

NOTE 18 (p. 269).

'To keep the church' was a reference to the *treuga Dei*, by which fighting was prohibited on certain holy days ; and Good Friday, Easter Eve, and Easter Day were such holy days.

NOTE 19 (p. 295).

This indenture was printed in *The History of the Battle of Agincourt* (N. H. Nicholas) which was published in 1827, and was a translation made from an indenture deed printed in Rymer's *Fœdera*.

NOTE 20 (p. 298).

Taken from *A Chronicle of London, 1089 to 1483*.   Edited by Sir N. H. Nicholas and Mr E. Tyrrell, 1827, pp. 164–5.

INDEX

Abbéville, 179.
Abergavenny, 72, 74, 137.
Abergavenny, Lord of. See
　Beauchamp, William.
Aberystwyth, 61, 73, 79, 81.
Agincourt, x, 2, 12, 42, 86, 176,
　184, 185, 186, 187, 188, 189,
　190, 191, 193, 199, 200, 206,
　212, 213, 226, 263, 266, 268,
　275.
Albany, Duke of. See Stewart,
　Robert.
Albret, Charles d', 144, 178, 180,
　191, 206.
Alcobasse, Pietro di, 83.
Alençon, 223, 225, 240, 269.
Alençon, John of [duke], 188.
Allemagne, 220.
Anctoville, Raoul d', 105.
Anglesey, 42, 47, 78, 81.
Anjou, 146, 147, 223, 245, 268,
　270.
Anne [queen of England], 14,
　134.
Aquitaine, 146, 150, 158, 240.
Archenfield, 71.
Arlette, 224.
Armagnac, Bernard VII. of
　[count], 106, 207, 227.
Armagnac, Bonne of, 106.
Arques, 177.
Arras, 107, 249.
Artas, Janico d', 231.
Arundel, Earl of. See either
　fitzAlan, Richard or fitz-
　Alan, Thomas.
Arundel, Thomas [archbishop of
　Canterbury], 23, 27, 29, 32,
　33, 37, 98, 99, 100, 101, 102,
　109, 113, 119, 122, 127, 128,
　129, 130, 132, 133, 135, 136,
　140, 170.
Ashton, John, 225.

Avignon, 141, 202, 203.
Azores, 86.

Bacqueville, 150.
Bailleul-en-Vimeu, 179.
Bangor, 73.
Bannockburn, 42.
Bar, Edouard of [duke], 191.
Barbazan, 255, 256, 257.
Bardolph, Thomas, Lord, 90.
Bardolph, William, 90, 107.
Bari, 203.
Barlow, Thomas, 17.
Beauchamp, Richard, 57, 72, 79,
　117, 137, 144, 192, 221, 222,
　228, 244, 250, 262, 274, 283.
Beauchamp, Thomas, 9.
Beauchamp, William, 15, 69.
Beaufort, 146, 147.
Beaufort-en-Vallée, 268, 269.
Beaufort, Duke of. See Somer-
　set, Henry.
Beaufort, Edmund, 265.
Beaufort, Henry, 17, 97, 100,
　101, 110, 122, 130, 148, 152,
　157, 159, 200, 215, 264, 302.
Beaufort, John, 16, 47, 70, 95, 99.
Beaufort, Thomas, 98, 149, 154,
　171, 172, 207, 210, 215, 231,
　236, 261, 270, 274, 282, 283,
　286, 287.
Beaugé, 265, 267, 268, 269, 271.
Beaugency, 272.
Beaumaris, 26, 46, 48, 78.
Beauvais, 167.
Bec, 228.
Bedford, John of [duke]. See
　Lancaster John of.
Benedict XIII. [pope], 203, 204,
　205.
Benet, John, 155.
Berkeley, 25.
Berkeley, Thomas, Lord, 79.

303